T0330036

Economic Learning, Experiments and the Limits to Information

To Dinah, Matti and Nuala

Economic Learning, Experiments and the Limits to Information

Atanasios Mitropoulos

Senior Credit Risk Analyst, WestLB AG, Düsseldorf, Germany

Edward Elgar
Cheltenham, UK • Northampton, MA, USA

Published by
Edward Elgar Publishing Limited
Glensanda House
Montpellier Parade
Cheltenham
Glos GL50 1UA
UK

Edward Elgar Publishing, Inc.
136 West Street
Suite 202
Northampton
Massachusetts 01060
USA

A catalogue record for this book
is available from the British Library

Library of Congress Cataloguing in Publication Data

Mitropoulos, Atanasios, 1971–
    Economic learning, experiments and the limits to information/
Atanasios Mitropoulos.
        p. cm.
    Includes bibliographical references and index.
    1. Economics—Study and teaching. I. Title.
HB74.5.M58   2004
330'.072'4—dc22

                                                        2004040437

ISBN 1 84376 720 1

Printed and bound in Great Britain by MPG Books Ltd, Bodmin, Cornwall

Contents

Contents

Preface

For over a century the analysis of learning constitutes a major research area in psychology. Economists, to the contrary, for a long time dealt with issues of learning only occasionally. Whatever the reasons, things have changed during the past 15 years. There are now several branches within economics that intensively discuss the impact of learning on social outcomes.

A prerequisite for learning is the need for information. The precise consideration of information, thus, is a crucial element in any model of learning. While psychologists once started off with the analysis of situations that involve little information and extremely simple learning models, and they then gradually extended their scope to complicated social environments, economists have proceeded the other way round. Their starting points were (i) full information and (ii) highly sophisticated adaptive models, respectively. They then went on to add less information and simpler models of learning behaviour to their analysis. This process developed very quickly and has now reached the stage at which basic psychological concepts are reconsidered and incorporated into economic thought.

The present work stands at the very end of this process. It reanalyses models of learning that have been developed within a time span of over half a century by both psychologists and economists, and applies them to a setting involving extremely little information. The setting does not even allow for the application of the sophisticated models which economists initially have proposed. We are, thus, bound to resort to basic psychological concepts in order to model behaviour.

In our study, psychology and economics are also mingled together in another way. The situation we study is very close to what psychologists have termed the minimal social situation. They studied it as early as in the 1950s, though their interest quickly faded. We take up this setting because it seems to serve our purpose of elicitation of adaptive strategies particularly well. At the same time we reinterpret the setting in the form of a global game, a fairly new concept that is now being intensively discussed in economic theory.

Despite the influence of both disciplines, that is, economics and psychology, the focus of this study clearly rests on the economics part. The prime motivation for the following analyses is to work out determinants for inefficiencies within social interactions. The model of the mind, which is the main concern of psychology, will only serve as a means of gaining insight into the reasons for inefficient behaviour.

The methods of analysis used in this work mainly consist of simulations and experiments. We are reviewing some theoretical results. However, the global-game setting, as yet, impedes any rigorous analytical derivation of results. Furthermore, experimental evidence in the past has shown that the behaviour of subjects is very sensitive to information. We, thus, feel obliged to, first, gather sound experimental data and to compare them with predictions from existing models, before turning to examine asymptotic properties, especially since experimental evidence on environments involving little information is scarce.

Another important concern of this study is to further the experimental methodology. In particular, we propose a method of how to deal with the provision of little information. We also discuss alternative implementations of similar experimental settings. A special chapter is devoted to point at problems of data analysis when dealing with serially correlated data.

In any case, as with most scientific research, this book poses more questions than it is able to answer. It should be read as an exploratory study that tries to throw light on a topic that scrapes the boundary of economic ratio in its current form. Nevertheless, we believe that the study of learning under little information is of greatest importance to economics, if this discipline wants to keep pace with a world in which information, once gathered, depreciates faster and faster.

The book is organised as follows. The first four chapters are meant to thoroughly introduce the topic of the study. Chapter 1 introduces the notion of learning as we use it in the following analyses. We review several trials to define learning and show that none is entirely convincing. We further review various arguments in favour of studying learning in economics and finally present a synthesising view. The main point is that the study of learning currently promises large benefits for the understanding of human behaviour. It should be considered on the grounds that it throws light on diverse aspects of behaviour and seems able to contribute significantly to the development of theory.

Chapter 2 introduces aspects of information that are dealt with in the later chapters. We first review the assumptions of classical game theory and continue by discussing the impact of lack of information on theory and on the experimental design. It is argued that even attaining common knowledge of the payoff structure is not easily accomplished. As soon as lack of information is introduced, correspondence between theory and experimental design becomes much more difficult. Several discussions within the literature point to a number of pitfalls that have to be circumvented by careful design. We further give a brief introduction into the notion of 'little information' and present some parts of our experimental methodology, especially the use of a global game. We conclude this chapter with a section on the motivation for studying situations characterised by little information.

Chapter 3 introduces the models of learning behaviour that are used in subsequent chapters. Many are well known, such as Bush and Mosteller (1955) and Roth and Erev (1995); others are less known, such as Karandikar et al. (1998). We give an insight into their conceptional differences and contrast them with extremely simple benchmark learning rules (such as win–stay lose–change) as well as extremely complicated rules, such as Gilboa and Schmeidler's (1995) case-based learning.

Chapter 4 reviews previous experimental evidence on learning under little information. We only give a brief overview of early psychologists' experiments and mainly focus on recent experimental studies by economists.

The next three chapters report on three experiments. Chapter 5 deals with a preliminary experiment on the game 'mutual fate control'. Here, a game environment very similar to earlier psychologists' studies was used to discriminate between two learning rules that make different predictions for long-run play. After showing the methodological difference to the earlier studies it is shown that, while aggregate results conform to predictions of the one learning rule, individual play can better be fitted econometrically by the other learning rule. The conclusion is that neither rule performs satisfactorily.

Chapter 6 reports on the extensive global-game experiment which incorporates the experiment of Chapter 5. In this experiment we investigate the impact of two parameters: the underlying game (which is unknown to the players and may be any of three coordination games or a competitive game) and the experience with the learning task. It is shown that under little information even in the extremely simple pure coordination game coordination may not be achieved within 40 repetitions. Furthermore, it is shown that experience does not improve the frequency of coordination, but does improve the speed of coordination, conditional on coordination being achieved. We discuss the predictions derived from all of the learning rules that were introduced in Chapter 3 by way of simulations as well as extensive regressions. However, none of the learning rules yields satisfactory results. It is argued that extensive use of multi-round patterns impedes proper fit of simple round-by-round adaptive rules.

Chapter 7 contains a short study about the impact of structural information that is provided prior to the start of play. It is shown that, while subjects in the experiment we reported on in Chapter 5 had little information and showed considerable difficulties to coordinate, provision of a small piece of information in a new experiment completely alters the results. Now, subjects almost always coordinate and do so very quickly. By inspection of individual play we show that round-by-round behaviour significantly differs between the two treatments and explain the difference by the implicit change of the global-game environment, namely, the four payoff schemes that have previously been contained by the global game can now be reduced to only one payoff scheme. We conclude that initial information – though rarely explicitly modelled in theory – can be crucial for learning behaviour.

Chapter 8 deals with the potential pitfalls one faces when trying to compare learning rules according to their predictive success, as has been done rather often in the literature during the past years. We characterise measures of predictive success by three components and devise a set of measures which we subsequently use to compare the learning rules we introduced in Chapter 3. Several well-known measures (such as the mean squared deviation and the proportion of inaccuracy) are among them. We use the data from the experiment we reported on in Chapter 6. Our results show that each of the three components that make up a measure (the definition of distance, the interpretation of probabilities and the way observations are defined) may all affect the resulting order among learning rules according to predictive success.

Finally, in Chapter 9 our results are compared with the open questions that remain within the learning literature. Our conclusion is that the theory of learning in economics is still in its infancy, but first steps towards comprehensive modelling have been taken.

Acknowledgements

First, I would like to thank my wife for her constant support while I was working on this thesis, and my children for showing to me the very principles of learning. I would also like to thank my supervisor Professor Dr. Joachim Weimann, as well as Jeannette Brosig, Axel Ockenfels, Bodo Sturm, Carsten Vogt, Chun-Lei Yang and all my other colleagues at MaxLab and the University of Magdeburg for valuable discussions and recommendations. I received further valuable comments from Thomas Brenner, Henrik Brinkmann, Ido Erev, Werner Güth, Oliver Kirchkamp, Bertrand Koebel, Wieland Müller, Frank Silber, Gerhard von Weizsäcker and several anonymous referees. Financial support by the Deutsche Forschungsgemeinschaft is gratefully acknowledged.

Also we are grateful for the kind permission by Elsevier to reproduce material previously published in the *Journal of Economic Psychology* and *Economics Letters* that forms the basis of Chapters 5 and 7, and for the kind permission by Anthony Courakis to reproduce material previously published in the *Greek Economic Review*, that forms the basis of Chapter 6.

1.   Introduction to Learning

1.1   LEARNING AND EVERYDAY LIFE

Today, the term learning enjoys extreme popularity. It is mentioned explicitly as often as it is implicitly. Educational institutions are growing rapidly, for example universities, private training courses or educational computer software. Newspapers and magazines are selling more copies than ever. Advertisements for job vacancies urge interested applicants to prepare for continuous learning. Travel agencies report that the ordinary way of spending one's holidays at the beach is becoming out of fashion and that active exploration of foreign culture is booming. The saying that learning will remain one's prime occupation for a whole lifetime is becoming more and more popular.

One may object that learning has always been popular. After all, learning promises an improved performance in job activities. Well-informed people are readily regarded as an authority and therefore have some influence on the fate of their community. For the same reason they are often in demand and act as opinion leaders. But the recent trend goes beyond what was formerly known as the teachers' suggestion to the pupil, that accumulated knowledge is the base for a successful career.

On an individualistic level, learning is now associated with an active life, keeping pace with technological, political and societal developments. It is regarded as a goal in itself, a status symbol. However, the new aspect this view is promoting is only that the means 'learning' is being treated as the end to which action is directed. Otherwise, the role of learning is not much different from earlier paternalistic suggestions.

1.2   LEARNING IN ECONOMICS

A different notion arises when learning is used in connection with the performance of *groups* of people, such as businesses or economies. Accumulation of knowledge among a group of people promises improved joint performance, wealth and living standards. Politicians have rarely been so keen to promote human capital. They sometimes even resort to flowery images similar to those of More's (1518/1901/1993) *Utopia* that meant to describe the result of achieved societal sophistication. While being a resource in itself, knowledge promises not only to give an economy a comparative advantage in global competition, but also internally to improve the use of scarce resources.

The efficient use of resources is what economics is all about. In this respect, that economists worry about 'learning procedures' and the result of 'learning' is overdue. Indeed, for roughly a decade, economists devoted increasing amounts of effort to the exploration of various notions of learning.

The study of processes that are commonly termed 'learning' have long been the realm of psychology. It is thus unavoidable that we refer to many sources from psychology throughout this book. In many instances, however, we see that psychology has more to offer than just a lot of earlier experience on that matter. It sometimes gives hints at how to model and implement tests of learning theories which would not immediately come to the mind of a trained economist. Of course, this is changing as economics adopts and modifies more and more concepts originally proposed in psychology. The result is a fruitful blend of various theories and thoughts that together clarify notions of learning and help to explain and predict dynamic choice.

1.3   DEFINITIONS OF LEARNING

An Intuitive Approach

A notable difference between economics and psychology is that psychologists have long been trying to devise a definition for learning, while economists, as yet, have rarely done so. My questioning of people unrelated to both psychology and economics most often resulted in the intuitive answer that learning can easily be defined as the acquisition of knowledge or information. As Walker (1996, p. 2), a psychologist, notes, there is a central problem with this definition. It is relatively easy to judge for oneself whether one has acquired knowledge or information – recall, for example, the famous exclamation 'Eureka!' by Archimedes (287–212 BC) after acquiring knowledge about weights that are dived into water. But it is not at all easy to judge other people. Any lecturer marking written examinations or undertaking an oral examination has had this experience. In order to assess whether a person has acquired knowledge, one either has to observe the process of acquisition or one has to infer the change in knowledge from the difference of the stock variable 'knowledge'. Unfortunately, knowledge has no physical representation. So, the first alternative is obsolete, since the growth or depreciation of knowledge cannot directly be observed.[1] The second alternative is impeded by the same immaterial nature of knowledge and information. We are not able effectively to quantify the amount of knowledge that a person possesses, either before or after the acquisition of new entities.

Still, change in behaviour between the time before and the time after the person received a piece of news tells us that this person may have learned something. But changes in behaviour per se are not sufficient for a definition of learning since other processes, which may not be subsumed under learning, may also be the cause for this change. Walker mentions several such examples: fatigue (that is, a temporary unconscious depression of response due to a strong stimulus, such as a loud sound), habituation (a temporary unconscious depression of response after a change of the environment) and sensitisation (that is, an unconscious increase in level of response after repeated stimulation).

Early Psychologists' View

One definition of learning, which is popular in psychology, is that of Kimble (1961, p. 6): learning is to be understood 'as a relatively permanent change in behavioral potentiality that occurs as a result of reinforced practice'. This definition excludes all the above mentioned phenomena; they are all either short-lived or do not affect the potential in a person's behaviour. Indeed, this definition also satisfies most concerns expressed by economists. Learning should affect behaviour in a permanent way. Learning is purely defined on a phenomenological level, that is, if a change in behaviour cannot be observed, then it should not be considered as learning. Learning affects future behaviour, as long as in the future the requirements for the exhibition of changed behaviour are fulfilled. A person is also assumed only to learn via practice, which means that only the interaction with the environment can be the cause for learning.

Economists' Reply

The phenomenological basis of Kimble's definition might surprise many economists. There is no reference to some unobservable process in the brain. Kimble refrains from resorting to models of the mind, such as, for example, cognitive maps, and focuses solely on the observable actions of the learning subject. What economists are likely to object to, however, is that learning must be a consequence of reinforcement. By now, economists have discussed a multitude of possible causes for learning, among which reinforcement is only one alternative. Apart from reinforcement, discussions of learning also involve imitation, selection and gained insight.

The reason why economists are particularly reluctant to accept the requirement of reinforcement of actions, may be that, implicitly, intentional optimisation is excluded from learning processes. The observation of a move by an opponent may cause the subject to revise beliefs about the likely actions of his or her opponents. Such a change in knowledge about the environment may cause the subject to revise his or her decision in order to choose the optimal response to the new set of beliefs. Under Kimble's definition such behavioural change is not regarded as learning.

In fact, there is a more fundamental problem as Kimble's definition suggests that reinforcement causes a change in the decision function of the subject. Consider, for example, the decision function f_t at time t mapping the power set of environments E (that is, the set of all potential environments) into the set of actions A. According to Kimble, feedback now causes one action $a \in A$ to be reinforced. The result is some change in the decision function. We do not need to specify this function at this stage. The new decision function is, say, $f_{t+1} \neq f_t$. What is implicitly assumed, here, is that the environment $e \in E$ as perceived by the decision-maker remains unchanged. Economists, however, would never accept this. Feedback automatically changes the amount of knowledge held by the subject and thus changes the input into the decision function, that is, the subjective environment e. Therefore, latent change of behaviour may not only be modelled as a change in decision function (the behavioural potentiality) but may be conceived of as consistent with a unique decision function and a critical change in knowledge.

Recent Refinements

Brenner (1999, p. 3), a trained economist, makes a similar point. He devises a broader definition that says: 'by *learning* I understand any cognitive or non-cognitive processing of experience that leads to a direct or latent change in economic behaviour, or to a change of cognitive pattern that influences future learning processes' (ibid., italics in the original). Mind you, Brenner not only includes optimisation (subsumed under cognitive processing of experience), but also tries to formulate the inclusion of meta-learning, that is, the change of the way one learns.[2] Furthermore, Brenner is prone to include anything that manifests itself as a change in behaviour, including even the notions of behavioural change that Walker deliberately tried to avoid (see above).

Walker's (1996, p. 3 ff) own trial to improve on Kimble's definition is more cautious. Basically, he substitutes 'information processing' for 'reinforced practice' and deletes the requirement of 'relative permanence', so that the definition now reads: 'learning is a change in behavioural potentiality that occurs as a result of information processing.' However, one has the impression that he, too, now includes fatigue, habituation and sensitisation in his definition, unless unconscious reflexes to stimuli do not constitute a way of processing information.

1.4 ECONOMISTS' VIEW OF DEFINITIONS

The extensive discussion of definitions of learning mainly served to illustrate the difficulties that arise from the trial to assess what learning actually is. Why, then, did economists rarely deal with that matter? Why did they not clarify the term learning before starting to write dozens of papers on it? I can only speculate about the answer. My reading of economic literature led me to believe that economists are more pragmatic than psychologists. Authors of learning models view their models to represent crucial parts of a commonly accepted notion of learning. The point in their analyses is independent of how the set of learning theories is defined, as long as their learning model is an element of this set. A philosophical dispute about what *exactly* may be termed 'learning' seems cumbersome and adds little to the understanding of behaviour.

We basically follow the economists' point of view and refrain from further developing ideas about the definition of learning. We are content with the intuitive approach, namely, to say that learning is the acquisition of knowledge, and add the assumption that it is observable within the environment currently under investigation. So, when specific information is provided, and subjects do change behaviour in a permanent manner, then this change may be assumed to be the result of the processing of the information just received. In this respect, experiments are the natural environment in which to study learning, since the acquisition of knowledge and information can carefully be controlled, so that analysts have good reason to believe that changes in behaviour are indeed the result of the processing of the received information, and not merely the result of an unspecific mess of joint stimuli.

1.5 WHY STUDY LEARNING?

Independent of the questions of how and whether to define learning, anybody who is dedicating extensive efforts to the analysis of learning behaviour has to ask *why* one should study learning. Again psychologists and economists differ in their answers. Psychologists tend to view themselves as serving basic scientific goals, such as those summarised by Bachrach (1981) as *description, prediction, control* and *understanding* (see also Walker 1996, p. 11). It is, therefore, the duty of scientists to analyse any changes in behaviour from any of the four aforementioned points of view.

Economists are much more demanding. They stipulate that advances in science have to be *significant* in order to be accepted as contributions to the field of research. The consequence of this requirement is that one has to assess how much novelty a new thought or a new observation contains compared with the existing body of scientific knowledge. The emergence of literature on learning, especially on adaptive learning, in economics during the past decade has provoked some critical assessments by economists. In the following we review some of them and discuss their similarities and differences in argument. Our conclusion is that, even though there are conflicting views on the details, there is broad agreement that learning theories promise to make significant contributions to economics in general.

The Early View

For a long time, economists' view of the significance of learning theories in economic thought was limited to the justification of normative concepts of decision making. For example, Simon (1956) states:

> Learning theory and game theory (together with the closely related statistical decision theory) purport to provide theories of *rational* behavior. Implicit in any theory of learning is a motivational assumption that learning consists in the acquisition of a pattern of behavior appropriate to *goal achievement, need reduction*, or the like. (Simon 1956, p. 267, italics in the original)

From the point of view of current economic methodology, Simon's postulation on the scope of learning theory sounds archaic, at best. At that time, when making inferences on social interaction, economists insisted on the rationality assumption. By and large, economics was viewed as a normative theory that made prescriptions for, rather than descriptions of, behaviour. Economists naturally extended the relevancy of their goal to theories of learning.

An early trial to break through this long-standing convention was made by Arthur (1991). He argued that 'calibrating theoretical behavior to match human behavior would allow us to ask questions that are not answerable at present under the assumption of either perfect rationality or idealized learning' (Arthur 1991, p. 353). For this reason he calls for the study of parameterised adaptive algorithms that may be fit to imitate actual human behaviour sufficiently closely, so that predictions of actual play based on these calibrated models may perform better than alternative concepts.

Based on this methodology a large body of experimental studies has grown. Even though research on these grounds is still in progress we dare to draw negative conclusions from this line of investigations. As we show in Chapters 5 to 8, estimation results are not robust as to the differences in the environment the subjects are playing in. Furthermore, a multitude of possible goals can be formulated according to which alternative predictions can be compared with each other, whereby each goal may favour different types of theories. Overall, earlier findings together with our own observations lead us to believe that the trial to imitate actual human behaviour by the use of calibrated adaptive rules can only be sustained, if calibration is restricted to very special settings. However, this is not the only way learning theories may be of value to economic thought.

The Classic View

Probably, one of the keenest advocates of the study of learning in economics is Vincent P. Crawford. In his survey, Crawford (1997) provides further arguments in favour of studying learning. We consider his line of argument as the classical way to defend learning against the alternative approaches to economic behaviour, since it follows the historical path of economists' interests. The starting point is the view that the study of games is a useful simplification of real situations that are characterised by *strategic uncertainty*, that is, by individuals who face uncertainty about the likely action of others while, at the same time, their action is crucial to the payoff accruing to themselves as well as to one or more opponents. Now, what economics tries to capture is the interaction between these individuals (whom we call *players* in the context of a game) concerning the allocation of a set of goods (which is represented by the *payoffs* that accrue to the players when consuming the good). Games formalise this environment in a systematic way. First, they specify the players, that is, players are given a set of potential actions and a certain amount of information. Second, the rules of how players may interact with each other are described by a directed tree. Finally, payoffs for all players are determined via an exhaustive payoff function that maps all possible combinations of actions into payoff consequences. Players are assumed to act in predetermined ways, thereby generating actions and information that may be used (or may be relevant in other ways) for actions and information at later stages of the game. Different theories of decision-making may predict different outcomes of the games. These predictions may then be compared with results observed in laboratory experiments or field studies, and we (as consumers of scientific research) are finally left with a set of conclusions that draws a more or less complete picture of what explanatory power the actual theories are endowed with.

The analysis of games has developed (and has partly incorporated from other fields) techniques with which to gain insight into the incentives of the situation described by the game. These techniques give a first guess as to what might be observed when actual players face that game. Apart from *non-cooperative game theory, cooperative game theory* and *evolutionary game theory*, Crawford also mentions *adaptive learning models*. He continues to argue that all these concepts have led to considerable insight. However, experimental evidence suggests that actual behaviour among human subjects seems not to accord with any single approach. He, thus, draws the conclusion that one has to identify the particular circumstances that determine the applicability of one or the other technique to predict behaviour.

Crawford goes on to describe different settings, that is, games, in which different concepts contribute to the understanding of actual behaviour to a different degree. The most striking example of the failure of several traditional techniques to predict actual behaviour of human subjects are the studies on the coordination game that were conducted by Van Huyck et al. (1990; 1991). These studies comprise several treatments of coordination games, all characterised by a number of pure-strategy Nash-equilibria that are Pareto-ordered. The coordination problem arises from the Pareto-dominated equilibria being risk-dominant (in the sense of Harsanyi and Selten 1988). Refinements are not able to single out a particular equilibrium, since equilibrium selection depends on the way the refinement is being modelled.[3] As it turns out, cooperative game theory is wrong simply because the assumption of efficient allocation of resources is not being matched by experimental subjects. Instead, under various payoff schemes, groups of subjects quickly coordinate to inefficient equilibria. Similar to static equilibrium refinements, evolutionary theory cannot make a unique prediction; depending on the details of the evolutionary process either equilibrium may be selected in the long run (Kandori et al. 1993; Robson and Vega-Redondo 1996). While all other techniques more or less fail to account for behaviour, adaptive learning models are able to give hints at possible explanations. Since deviation from equilibrium always incurs immediate costs, most adaptive learning models predict that subjects cannot reach efficiency once they coordinated on an inefficient equilibrium (Crawford 1991; 1995).[4]

Similar difficulties with explaining subject behaviour in experiments accompanies the literature on sequential bargaining games. Ever since the seminal investigation by Güth et al. (1982) the Ultimatum Game has been the centre of research on off-equilibrium behaviour. At the beginning, the observation that aroused most interest was the substantial and persistent deviation from the single subgame-perfect equilibrium (SPE) by experimental subjects. Since then, there have been multiple trials to account for the observations. Several static approaches developed explanations for initial deviation from the SPE, among which the most prominent are (i) the theory of reciprocity (Rabin 1993; Dufwenberg and Kirchsteiger 1998; Falk and Fischbacher 2000) that assumes intentions of players are to be taken into account by opponents and which predicts that unfair offers by proposers will be answered with costly breakdown of negotiations by receivers, (ii) the theory of inequality aversion (Fehr and Schmidt 1999; Bolton and Ockenfels 2000) that assumes all payoffs of an allocation to enter into players' utilities and hence fair outcomes to be a direct concern, and (iii) the theory of errors in decision-making (Selten 1975; McKelvey and Palfrey 1995; 1998). The observation, however, that subjects in the laboratory adjust their decisions after receiving feedback from previous rounds and that they remain far from equilibrium play after many repetitions calls for the additional consideration of dynamic theories of choice. The pioneering work, here, is Prasnikar and Roth (1992) which triggered a large body of literature on adaptive learning. Crawford thus concludes that theories of learning contribute a significant amount to economists' ability to predict the likely behaviour of human beings. At least, they complement alternative approaches.

A Synthesising View

Compared to Crawford, Börgers (1996) follows a more economic reasoning on the advancement of science. He stipulates a cost–benefit analysis to any scientific progress. To him, it is, thus, not sufficient to contribute only to the amelioration of scientific knowledge. Rather, it is required that scientists do their research in the most efficient way (from an *ex ante* point of view, of course). Again, the starting point is the traditional way of analysing decision processes. Until recently, the rationality hypothesis, in the sense that decision-makers optimise something which is usually called *utility*, has often been assumed without further questioning. Analysis then focused on how the utility functions of the decision-makers must look like in order to account for observations made either in the field or in the laboratory. Tests of theories thus always constituted a combined test of the validity of all assumptions, including the rationality assumption. In case such tests fail, there is a need for further developments of the theories, in order to find a plausible explanation for the observed facts. In the past, such improvements have been carried out mainly in a way whereby the assumption of rationality has not been questioned. Instead, theories were rendered more elaborate and more complex until data could be fitted into the models.[5] Börgers now argues that there is a threshold of complexity so that, if that threshold is exceeded, models no longer appear to be useful and one is bound to believe that the basic assumption of rationality is not appropriate. He believes that the current state of theoretical research has reached this threshold. To him it looks salient to put more effort into the development of models that make do without optimisation.[6]

Saying that we need theories of decision-making that do not rely on perfect optimisation does not necessarily mean that the study of learning leads to fruitful results. Indeed, although offering a similar view to Börgers, Conlisk (1996) calls for more investigation on the bounds of rationality and proposes explicitly to take into account the previously rarely modelled deliberation cost of decision-making. Without doubt, this is one approach that might take us further into the understanding of behaviour which is otherwise difficult to rationalise. Still, it remains an approach very close to perfect optimisation: instead of assuming unrestricted optimisation, optimisation is now subject to certain ad hoc restrictions such as cognitive capacity.

However, there is substantial evidence that subjects adapt their decisions to the feedback they receive from repeatedly playing the same situation.

Since Thorndike's (1932) seminal book, many studies on individual decision-making report such processes. Similar evidence on the level of strategic interaction started with Schelling's (1960, pp. 53–67) informal experiments. Models of rationality as well as models of bounded rationality, as proposed by Conlisk, have difficulties in incorporating change in decisions over repetitions of the task. Within this framework, the adaptation of choice from one repetition to the next can only be accounted for by a change of the optimal strategy owing to the change in the set of information available to the individual. The evidence from experiments, however, suggests that subjects' choices are too variable to be justified by the increments in acquired information, which are often very small.

A different view arises, if feedback is interpreted as a stimulus for change in behaviour. As illustrated above, this is what the term learning is often identified with, especially in psychological literature. If this kind of learning is not conceived of as a dull application of a rule that simply maps stimuli to changes in decisions but as a method of acquiring skill in decision-making, then it may contribute to our understanding of the principles of decision processes. Such an understanding can then serve as a basis for successful predictions even in situations that have previously been viewed as difficult to explain. Explicit models of learning thus provide the prospect of finding a single theory that correctly predicts behaviour close to rationality in some situations and correctly predicts seemingly irrational behaviour in other situations. Such theories thereby avoid the amount of complexity needed by theories that are based on the rationality assumption, be it bounded or unbounded. Börgers's view is that, at present, improvements in the understanding of behaviour are much easier to attain via the consideration of simple adaptive learning than via an extension of traditional models.

1.6   OUR APPROACH TO LEARNING

There is still the question of how to advance learning theories most efficiently. In the past decade two strands of learning theories have been particularly popular: evolutionary theory and adaptive learning models. Evolutionary theory heavily relies on the analogy to the biological principles of mutation and selection. Critics point out that this analogy is far-fetched (for example, Börgers 1996), since replicator dynamics, which is by far the most common modelling tool in evolutionary theory, can easily be derived from biological principles but can hardly be supported by social interaction among human beings. Some attempts have been made to justify the use of the replicator dynamics with learning models that seem to be closer to economic modelling of human behaviour (Börgers and Sarin 1997; Brenner 1998; Schlag 1998; Hopkins 1999a; 1999b; 1999c). However, each one succeeds in finding parallels only between replicator dynamics and very special models of learning or very special modelling techniques. The results cannot be generalised to large classes of learning behaviour.

Many different adaptive learning models have been proposed to account for many different situations. Chapter 3 is devoted to an overview of these (at least for situations with little information). One is forced to ask how to select between the large number of proposed adaptive learning rules. Börgers (1996) has dealt with this question and made a statement which we take as our working hypothesis for the research we report in the present work:

> There is a plethora of conceivable learning models, and one may wonder how theoretical researchers should choose their focus. The obvious answer appears to be that attention should be restricted to those models that have been empirically successful. I want to argue in favour of an approach which is more open minded than this answer suggests. The empirical evidence regarding rationality in decision problems and games is still very incomplete. Further evidence needs to be collected. It would be dangerous to commit prematurely to a narrow class of learning models. A more fruitful approach for theoreticians is to identify different categories of learning rules, and to try to find properties which learning rules in the same category share. (Börgers 1996, p. 1381)

Even though the present work does not deal with comparisons between learning theories on the level of formal modelling, our contribution to the theory of learning is very similar in spirit. It (i) considers a large number of adaptive rules (Chapter 3), (ii) compares qualitative predictions of learning rules for a number of different games (Chapters 5 and 6), (iii) reports new experimental evidence on decision-making in repeated games (Chapters 5 to 7), and (iv) critically reviews various methods of quantitative comparisons between rules (Chapter 8). But before turning to the analyses, we have to consider the informational assumptions that underlie our studies.

NOTES

1. Do not confuse 'knowledge' or 'information' with 'news', which has a physical representation.
2. Note, that Brenner's mentioning of learning processes within his definition of learning does not constitute a true circular reference, as one might suspect at first glance. Learning is meant to include the change of future learning processes which themselves are defined by the first half of the definition, that is, by a 'cognitive or non-cognitive processing of experience that leads to a direct or latent change in economic behaviour'.
3. See, for example, Kajii and Morris (1997).

4. Crawford (1997) acknowledges, however, the open question of why subjects do not coordinate on the efficient cell right from the start.
5. A nice example of how traditional economists tried to defend the rationality hypothesis against alternative explanations in the face of seemingly irrational behaviour is Simon's (1956) response to Estes (1954). Estes reported on the probability matching phenomenon and explained it by way of an adaptive learning model. Simon accounts for the same phenomenon by keeping the rationality assumption and adds the assumption of misguided beliefs. He shows that by matching the probabilities of rewards the subjects then respond optimally to their subjective perception of the environment. He then argues that this subjective environment – although not being the true one – belongs to the class of possible environments consistent with the instructions given to the subjects. Indeed, probability matching, by now, has largely been disconfirmed (see, for example, Vulkan 2000). One may still doubt, however, whether Simon's argument was the correct one.
6. Conlisk (1996, p. 684) even accuses traditional economists of having pampered the rationality assumption by comparing the predictions on comparative statics that were drawn from their models with the null hypothesis of predicting no effect. He calls for a fair comparison between rational models and alternative models.

2. Introduction to Little Information

2.1 INDIVIDUAL DECISION-MAKING

The rise of game theory has largely been attributed to its explicit treatment of information and decisions. Before game theory started to spread, economic studies were based mainly on the analysis of optimal decision-making in a stationary environment. Strategic considerations were ignored while focus remained on situations with full competition (that is, competitive markets) or no competition (such as a monopoly). Aggregated data – in particular demand and supply – were treated as the sole determinants of allocation within markets. The virtue of such an approach is that optimal decisions of agents can easily be derived simply by maximising the objective function.[1] However, many economically relevant situations had thus been ignored. A particularly illustrative example is the treatment of principal–agent problems which have often been modelled as optimisation problems. The principal was assumed to try to optimise welfare while having instruments to induce welfare-improving actions by the agent. Usually, control over the agent was not full, for example, the principle's observation of actions involved noise, so that sanctioning could only partly occur. The agent, on the other hand, was assumed to optimise profit and to have no influence on the principals' achievement of welfare.[2]

The corresponding line of experimental research investigated subjects' choices in situations involving risk and uncertainty. Even though experimenters often tried to suggest a correspondence to real-life situations and subjects were urged to act as if their choice was payoff-relevant for another person, the setting could conveniently be modelled by a player who had to choose between two or more risky prospects. The early experiments were conducted by psychologists who were interested mainly in a coherent model of the mind. Later, economists intruded into this field of research and compared subjects' behaviour with normative models of optimal decision-making.[3] The basic contribution of all these investigations is to elicit a large number of heuristics and biases that have to be considered when predicting individual decisions on risky options. However, the modelled environment does not involve other persons about whom one has to form beliefs or whose payoff the decision-maker might affect.

2.2   GAMES AND COMMON KNOWLEDGE

Returning to our previous model of the conflict between the principal and the agent, a natural extension would be to allow the agent to influence the information base on which the principal makes his or her decisions. This translates to a game involving two players, each provided with a set of actions, whereby each pair of actions yields specific outcomes to both players. Such simultaneous interactions necessitated the modelling of the action space as well as the space spanned by beliefs. These models required special concepts of analysis.

Even though solution concepts for such models of strategic situations were discussed as early as in Cournot (1838/1991), it was not until von Neumann and Morgenstern's (1944) seminal axiomatisation of games that interactive considerations of economic behaviour were opened to a wider public. In the early phase, game theory was fully involved in deriving and applying useful equilibria under full (or *complete*) information. It is illuminating to notice that as early as the first comprehensive equilibrium concept was introduced (Nash 1950) the author already indicated that this assumption is very demanding: 'we need to assume the players know the full structure of the game in order to be able to deduce the [equilibrium] prediction for themselves. It is quite strongly a rationalistic and idealising interpretation' (Nash 1950, p. 23; insertion by the author).

Later, the assumption needed to support the prediction of Nash-equilibrium play was specified to be that of *common knowledge* of the best response structure. The concept of a payoff structure being common knowledge involves not only that all players know the payoff structure, but also that all players know that all players know the payoff structure, and that all players know that all players know that all players know the payoff structure, and that all players know . . . ad infinitum. From this definition it becomes immediately obvious that this assumption can never be expected to hold in real situations. Firms and households are hardly ever provided with the necessary information to transform their environment into a deterministic game which they subsequently can analyse. It is often argued that professionals in the real world have gathered enough experience to confidently set up a payoff matrix. We doubt this, since the speed of organisational changes and the currently rapid emergence of new technologies cause relations between businesses to change almost on a daily basis. Furthermore, the adoption of new technologies causes a change in production functions, which are usually kept secret since its disclosure is a prerequisite for the competitor to effectively calculate payoffs.

As early as Rosenthal (1981), theorists pointed at the potential pitfalls of the assumption of complete information about the payoff structure. Conclusions about the likely play of subjects may heavily depend on the knowledge assigned to the players. More recently, experimenters also started to investigate the dependence of subjects' behaviour on the informational assumptions. The experimental evidence suggests that subjects are likely to react even more sensitively to changes in information than do Nash-equilibria.[4] And not only static choice, but also the way people adapt their choice to feedback in repeated games is significantly altered, if the quality of feedback information is changed.[5] Sometimes, however, subjects appear to be less sensitive to changes in the informational base than is predicted by theory (for example Huck and Müller 2000). As important as investigations into relaxed informational conditions seem to be, the modelling and analysis of incomplete information is accompanied by a sharp rise in complexity. In the next section we briefly review theoretical concerns of games involving incomplete information.

2.3   MODELLING INCOMPLETE INFORMATION

Models involving players that are endowed with complete information have been criticised on the grounds that they cannot possibly be implemented. In order to verify predictions drawn from such game-theoretic models that use the assumption of common knowledge of the payoff matrix, modern experimental practice tries to meet the requirement of common knowledge by public announcement of the instructions, whereby experimenters are careful to use simple games, introducing them with a terminology that is easy to understand, and sometimes even letting subjects play practice rounds before starting the payoff-relevant phase of the experiment. Still, subjects can never be sure of the game being common knowledge, since one can never exclude the possibility that any of the other subjects might have been distracted for a moment and missed an important aspect of the game, or alternatively, due to a different cultural background or due to lack of language skills may have misunderstood parts of the instructions.

In game theory, it was not until 1967 that the assumption of common knowledge of the payoff matrix was relaxed. In a series of papers Harsanyi (1967–68) laid out how games under incomplete information could be transformed into games with complete information, with the only difference lying in Nature choosing one game from a set of possible games. In another seminal paper Harsanyi (1973) used this insight in order to prove that mixed-strategy equilibria are stable provided that the underlying game is being modelled as a dominance-solvable game involving perturbed payoff information. In particular, if players, who are involved in playing a game with unique mixed-strategy equilibrium, do observe their own payoff matrix but can observe the payoff matrices of their opponents only with random noise, then players are driven into exhibiting mixed-strategy equilibrium behaviour, even though in the corresponding unperturbed game they had no incentive to do so, ceteris paribus.

At this stage, however, the modelling of incomplete information was not very much advanced. On the one hand, it was assumed that players could only observe realisations of random variables concerning their own payoffs but, on the other hand, the parameters guiding the random processes were assumed to be common knowledge. Intriguingly, it was not until Aumann (1976) that the consequences from relaxing the assumption of common knowledge were analysed. Aumann showed the impossibility of an agreement among players to disagree when rationality is imposed. Using an illustrative example Rubinstein (1989) extended this point. Rubinstein's famous electronic mail game showed that a small deviation from common knowledge of the game might well be crucial and may lead away from behaviour determined by the Nash-equilibrium under complete information. The game runs as follows: first, Nature chooses between two payoff-bimatrices assigning equal probability to each. Then, player 1 is informed of Nature's choice and sends a message to player 2 indicating which bimatrix had been chosen. Subsequently, messages are exchanged between the two players, each message containing the confirmation of the reception of the previous message. With some small probability τ each message may fail to reach the other player. Eventually, the transfer of a message will fail, and in case it does, the whole process stops. The situation at the end of this process is that neither player now knows whether it was their message or the message of the other player that did not arrive. The result is that, even though the players have gained some higher order knowledge about the structure of the game, they are not able to consistently play the Nash-equilibrium of the chosen game. This holds even when one assumes that players are only ε-optimisers, that is, when they are satisfied with payoffs close to optimality.

Subsequently a vivid exchange of arguments developed that led to diverse results. The first counter-argument to Rubinstein was formulated by Monderer and Samet (1989) who show that when common knowledge is approximated by common beliefs, then players approximate Nash-equilibrium behaviour. All that is needed is that, first, players share common p-beliefs about the true game, which means that all players believe the true game to occur with probability at least p, that, second, such beliefs are formed for a set of states of measure $1 - \delta$, with δ lying below a small threshold, and that, third, players are ε-optimisers. Monderer and Samet argue that these conditions are rather easily met in reality; if not in the field, then at least in the laboratory.[6] Kajii and Morris (1997) extended their argument to fairly general models of incomplete information and showed that Nash-equilibria in 2×2 games can be expected to be robust to slight deviations from common knowledge of the payoff matrix.

From this literature one may firmly conclude that Nash-equilibria constitute a sensible concept for modelling likely play, provided that players try to optimise payoffs and provided that knowledge of the payoff functions is close to common knowledge. Experimental designs using public announcements of instructions seem to fulfil the informational requirements that are needed for this result to hold. Thus, experiments based on games that assume full information stand on a firm ground. However, the complexity of argument that is needed to come to this conclusion is much more demanding than fresh students of game theory typically expect.

The implementation of games under incomplete information is an altogether different case. For such environments, theoretical literature is much less advanced. So far, there are hardly any results on the stability of equilibria. We may expect large enough deviations from common knowledge to cause a significant change in behaviour. And behaviour in this less-than-complete informational setting may be much more sensitive to small variations than behaviour under complete information. For example, Friedman and Shenker (1998) put great effort into the derivation of a solution concept for network games. Network games are games in which an unspecified number of players (possibly even varying over time) tries to gain access to a resource that's capacity is limited (for example a server).[7] In such a setting players are not provided with full information about the environment. In particular, they do not know the exact payoff function, and they do not even know how actions affect one's own and other players' payoffs. A first theoretical result, that Friedman and Shenker are able to prove is that, if players may choose asynchronously, then 'reasonable' learners[8] converge to the serially unoverwhelmed set of strategies.[9] For synchronous play the solution set can be reduced to the serially undominated set. Still, these solution sets are rather broad, and one wishes to specify solutions with more accuracy. But, for the moment, researchers have not been able to formulate tighter results.

Despite the lack of theoretical results, we believe that the study of games under incomplete information is an important research task, theoretically as well as experimentally. We will lay out our argument in more detail below. Our conclusion from these considerations is that information, or to be more precise, the state of beliefs among the subjects after information has been processed, is a rather brittle characteristic and must be considered with a great degree of caution. When dealing with incomplete information, experimentalists are forced carefully to devise the experimental design, and to make as sure as possible that the informational state of the subjects at each stage of the experiment is as required for the analysis of the underlying problem. Otherwise, as outlined above, behaviour of the subjects might show substantially different behaviour than predicted, even when the model predictions were correct. For this reason we devote a large amount of space to describing and analysing the informational settings. The results from behaviour in our experiments are re-examined in the light of possible misunderstandings or cognitive constraints. In Chapter 5, we will critically review some earlier experiments that do not conform to our standards of precaution and will show that our results differ distinctly from the ones obtained from these earlier studies. In fact, the experiment we report in Chapter 6 was partly motivated by ambiguities resulting from the design of the experiment we report in Chapter 5.

2.4   GLOBAL GAMES

Investigations into equilibrium selection point out that lack of information may lead to counter-intuitive results. In order to show this, Carlsson and van Damme (1993) devised a different notion of incomplete information which they termed *global games* and which we use for our experimental design in Chapter 6. Global games are games of incomplete information in which the actual game is drawn from a distribution of a given set of games. Carlsson and van Damme are able to show for 2×2 games that, as the probability distribution over games converges to a singleton, placing all probability on one game, and if this game is a stag-hunt game with one pure-strategy equilibrium being risk-dominant (as defined by Harsanyi and Selten 1988) and one pure-strategy equilibrium being payoff-dominant, then iterated elimination of dominated strategies leads to the selection of the risk-dominant equilibrium. To the contrary, intuition tells us that subjects in the laboratory are likely to coordinate on the payoff-dominant rather than the risk-dominant equilibrium. Indeed, experiments show that there is a bias towards the payoff-dominant action in initial behaviour.[10] However, after repetition, subjects usually follow the basin of attraction as predicted by evolutionary dynamics. Whether subjects finally end up playing the payoff-dominant or the risk-dominant equilibrium, thus, depends on the incentives of the particular game. The selection result by Carlsson and van Damme also runs counter to the previously outlined argument by Harsanyi that any Nash-equilibrium can be justified by appropriately perturbing payoff information. The authors point out that the difference between the two results stems from the difference in modelling payoff-perturbations: Harsanyi allows perturbations only to affect payoffs of the other players in an independent way. Belief formation, hence, is unaffected by one's private information. To the contrary, Carlsson and van Damme model incomplete information by way of perturbation of the whole payoff matrix; so player's observations are correlated and belief formation depends on one's own information. Morris et al. (1995) extend Carlsson and van Damme's result by providing sufficient conditions for games with larger strategy spaces.

Even though we will not deal with stag-hunt games throughout this book, this literature makes a suggestion for a lesson to be learnt that concerns the games we analyse. This lesson can be summarised by the following: the way incomplete information is modelled may be crucial for observed behaviour. In other words, it does make a difference whether payoff perturbations are correlated among subjects or are drawn independently. We decided to use the global-game approach (particularly in Chapter 6) since our prime interest is in behaviour under uncertainty about the strategic situation through which players are linked with each other. The random choice among whole games makes explicit with which probabilities players are involved in a particular form of strategic interaction.

One alternative way of modelling the same is to use – possibly correlated – perturbations of single payoff entries or a subset of payoff entries within one basic matrix. For two reasons we did not follow this latter approach. First, the basic matrix would naturally be considered as a benchmark, even though the random draw of games might render a strategically different game equally likely. Scholars of game theory, through training may free themselves from such cognitive fallacies, but instructions describing such a random draw are very likely to lead inexperienced subjects into confusion.[11] Second, as outlined in Chapters 5 and 6, the global game approach allows us to start from a diverse set of games and to combine these games in a rather lean manner to an uncertain environment.

2.5 LITTLE INFORMATION

The global game approach serves our purpose to implement a situation that is characterised by particularly little information. The set of games among which the true game is randomly chosen will be equivalent to the set of all 2×2 games that involve only payoffs 0 or 1. We also exclude any weakly dominated strategy. This environment will, hence, substitute the earlier experimental practice in psychology and economics to foreclose the game setting and thereby to avoid any limitation on the set of possible games. The use of a global game serves to transform the state of uncertainty, in which subjects are not told anything about the payoff matrix, into a probabilistic assessment of the game.

Such a transformation process has been applied before. When trying to replicate the Ellsberg (1961) paradox in individual decision-making, uncertainty was often modelled by way of a probability distribution over distributions of differently coloured balls in an urn. The results turned out to be similar to the situation under uncertainty, that is, to the situation in which any information on the distribution of balls in the urn had been foreclosed (see, for example, Hey 1997). As we lay out in more detail in Chapters 5 and 6, in the realm of games the probabilistic informational design of an uncertain situation looks superior to the design using uncertainty.

2.6   WHY STUDY LITTLE INFORMATION?

The study of games in which players are provided with little information about the underlying payoff functions is of interest not only from a theoretical point of view. It also promises to give insights into aspects of actual behaviour in the real world that have previously been ignored. Examples for industries in which lack of information is an important characteristic can readily be found among the new markets that have emerged either due to newly developed technologies, or because former state monopolies have been opened to competition. In such market environments one may expect that the ongoing technological vicissitude and the lack of experience leaves firms with an incomplete description of the underlying game. We believe that lack of information is even more widespread than this. In many well-established markets a lot of change occurs on the level of management. Mergers, changes of ownership, cross-capitalisations and substitutions of top-level managers occur very frequently and may significantly change rules within a market. Such processes rearrange the links between market participants and may create strategic environments for which the value of previous experience depreciates to a large extend. Those who seek cooperation may quickly turn out to compete against each other, while former competitors may suddenly be involved in the trial to coordinate.

Examples for such processes can easily be found in the computer industry. Computers and mobile phones, for example, have gone through various developments. Until recently, private households tended to weigh the high costs that accrue to both types of goods and decided to use only one of the two technologies; those with computers were commonly stamped as 'writers' and those using mobile phones were classified as oral communicators. Now that the improved production technologies allow for lower prices, the products are most often used complementarily. Computers already use mobile phones for the transfer of data. The opposite development can be observed between software products, such as, for example, browsers and office packages. While, earlier, each programme was limited to fulfil a single task, each programme was added functionality so that browsers could substitute office packages and office packages could substitute browsers.

In order to get an idea of which games we are going to consider in later chapters, imagine yourself in the position of running a business that is set in a quickly evolving market. You may have the choice between several management options, say A and B, and you may neither know whether you compete against another business nor whether option A is an aggressive option as compared with action B, or not.

On the level of social relationships one may also think of a multitude of situations in which the modelling of the interaction between individuals requires the consideration of uncertainty. For example, a worker changing his or her employer also changes the work environment. In particular, a new worker will typically be unaware of the personal characteristics of colleagues, nor will he or she know about all norms that are specific to the new company or section. In such an environment, due to lack of knowledge of colleagues' aims and interests, a worker's strategic relation to those colleagues is not immediately clear. There may be some colleagues who share the same interests while others view the new person as competitor. So this situation is similar to not knowing whether oneself is involved in a competitive game or a coordination game. One may, however, have a rough idea of how likely the respective situations are. This environment corresponds to knowing the probabilities of the matrices within the global game.

Situations in which uncertainty about the strategic situation plays an important role are also reported in biology. As an example, consider the flies studied in Otronen (1993). These flies organise themselves around oviposition sites (usually carcasses). While females are attracted to these sites for ingestion, males are more interested in an opportunity to mate. With this in mind, males are distributed around the carcass waiting for arriving females. For these flies the size of the male flies plays an important role for competition and reproductive success. Large males attack other males more often and regularly win over small males. A complex competitive setting ensures that small males, though weaker than large ones, can regularly be observed around the most promising and most competitive sites. Intense investigations by the author have revealed that the distribution of large and small males remains stable over long periods of time, while – from a disaggregated point of view – a lot of change is occurring. Since each oviposition site generates a different distribution of male flies, each fly newly arriving at a site faces some uncertainty about its probability of reproductive success.

The study of individual behaviour of the flies leads the author to conclude that 'males may gain information on patch quality and male density quite quickly after arrival but it will take longer for them to assess their competitive weight. This could occur only during encounters with other males' (Otronen 1993, p. 738). In this example, male flies obviously need the repeated competitive interaction with other males in order to gain information about their payoff matrix. The only difference to our game setting is that flies can be sure of a competitive environment, while our setting will allow for competition as well as coordination.

A final and more general argument in favour of the study of models involving uncertainty has been uttered by Börgers and Sarin (1997, p. 3). They motivate payoff uncertainty by costs that might be necessary for the acquisition of information. They argue that wherever an individual is involved in a situation that requires rather habitual behaviour, information costs will appear to be high as compared with the potential gains in payoffs. Our experiments will be concerned with such situations in which decisions have to be made repeatedly; each decision concerning a rather small amount of payoff. Still, long-run average payoffs will be highly dependent on short-run behaviour. For such environments several models have been proposed to account for subject behaviour in the laboratory. The next chapter introduces a large number of such learning rules that are applicable to situations with little a priori knowledge and little informational feedback from repeated play.

NOTES

1.   This is not to say that optimisation of a function is a trivial task. Rather, the concept of a single relevant objective function is a simple one as compared with the derivation of an equilibrium between multiple objective functions.
2.   Mitropoulos (1996) provides an overview of the principal–agent and the team-incentives literature.
3.   Camerer (1995) provides an extensive overview of this literature. Alternative overviews are provided by Conlisk (1996) and Hey (1997).
4.   An illustrative example is provided by Kagel et al. (1996).
5.   See for example Mookherjee and Sopher (1994). We review more literature on learning under little information in Chapter 4.
6.   A more elaborate review of related literature provide Dekel and Gul (1997).
7.   Shenker (1995) provides a detailed account of network games.
8.   Reasonableness involves the trial to optimise payoffs, monotonicity and a certain amount of experimentation.
9.   A player's strategy is overwhelmed by another strategy when the maximum possible payoff from this strategy is below the minimum possible payoff of the other strategy. See, for example, Friedman and Shenker (1996).
10.   A survey of this literature is provided by Van Huyck (1997).
11.   For an experimental study that investigates the impact of the way tasks are presented on subjects' behaviour see Ho and Weigelt (1996).

3.   Models of Adaptive Learning

3.1   INTRODUCTORY REMARKS

The adaptive learning models we are going to present in this section have been selected to fulfil some requirements that will turn out necessary for the subsequent analysis of our experimental data. Because the study will mainly involve games with little information, rules may not refer to information that is not available. In particular, the payoff matrix is not provided. So, any learning rules referring to complete matrices are excluded here.

Many of those learning rules that have been discussed in the past do not require knowledge about the whole payoff matrix. However, they assume knowledge about the structure of the game which under little information is not provided, either. For example, the widely studied *fictitious play* rule does not require players to know the full payoff matrix of their opponents. Instead, the rule postulates that players choose the action that maximises expected payoffs as calculated from the empirical distribution of opponents' choices. In order to perform this optimisation task, however, two kinds of information are essential. First, players have to know which is their best response to any of the opponents' possible actions and, second, they must be able to observe the actions chosen by their opponents. In our experiments such information is not provided to the subjects.

Since we are dealing only with repeated 2 × 2 games, we further restrict learning rules to map onto choices between two actions. Many of the following learning rules have explicitly been developed to fit this case. Some rules, however, had been developed for larger strategy spaces. Thus, a simplification as compared to the original version was needed. The two-action case is a common abstraction of real-life decision tasks. In game theory it is usually applied for reasons of mathematical simplicity. There is also experimental evidence showing that the number of alternative actions, often called *task complexity*, affects play even if the strategic implications of the game remain the same (see, for example, Rapoport and Boebel 1992; Ho and Weigelt 1996).

3.2   BRIEF HISTORICAL OVERVIEW

For a long time learning has been the realm of psychologists. Starting from the early twentieth century many psychologists have contributed to the elicitation of basic aspects of learning within animals and humans. Also, psychologists were the first to propose mathematical models for learning behaviour which could subsequently be tested using statistical methods.

Despite its importance, the following list of learning models contains only few that have originally been proposed by psychologists. The reason for this is that a more detailed analysis of specific features of these models and their econometric evaluation using modern statistical methods set in only recently, while the early psychological literature brought about few formal models that kept on being discussed. However, as we will see from the models themselves, they all share basic features that go back to the seminal prototypes developed by psychologists.

Early Psychological Studies on Learning

The advent of the study of learning has been marked by the animal experiments conducted by Thorndike (1898) and Pavlov (1954) at the end of the nineteenth and the beginning of the twentieth centuries. Then, the aim of the experiments differed greatly from what is investigated in laboratory experiments today. Despite ample knowledge about probabilistic modelling that had already been introduced by mathematicians, the Zeitgeist postulated a deterministic picture of the world. Most empirical research was, thus, devoted to elicit the deterministic properties of nature. For psychologists, this view led to intense investigation of actions of either animals or humans that can be brought about independently of the subject's consciousness. The trial to condition actions of subjects on signals by way of repeated exposure to some situation that is connected to the signal then led to the study of learning. Today those experiments are subsumed under the name of *classical conditioning*. The most prominent example is probably Pavlov's dog whose flow of saliva was successfully conditioned to the ringing of a bell.

Soon, researchers went on trying to condition actions that are performed consciously. Thorndike (1932) gives an extensive account of such experiments. The basic difference from the former tasks lies in the fact that the stimulus was no longer subconsciously or unconsciously connected to the response. Instead, the stimulus was a punishment or a reward. Typically, punishments were implemented by electric shocks. Rewards could either be food, in the case of animals, or, in the case of humans, verbal confirmations of the correctness of the decision. Since these stimuli were seen as operands that helped to establish a desired action (as opposed to the stimuli in classical conditioning that resulted from innate connections between some signal and some response), this type of task was named *operant conditioning*.[1]

At that time some typical features of learning had already been established. Some of them continued to have significant impact on the modelling of the way learning proceeds. Nowadays the most prominent is probably the *law of effect* previously formulated verbally by Thorndike (1898). In its original formulation it stated that a stimulus–response connection is strengthened, if the response resulted in satisfaction. Later this law was interpreted probabilistically, to say that actions chosen in some situation that result in success are chosen with higher probability at the next occurrence of the same situation. All the learning rules discussed below more or less conform to this law.

Another widely accepted feature of learning is the *power law of practice* (Blackburn 1936, cited in Crossman 1959). It states that, if a subject faces the same task repeatedly, he or she will learn more quickly at the beginning and converge to some action profile as the series of repetitions proceeds. Many of the mathematical models presented below comply with this law as long as the learning rule is applied to a stationary decision problem. However, if the learning rules are applied to two or more participants within a repeated game, this law may no longer be effective. Instead, the result may be recycling behaviour.

Closely related to the above is the *recency phenomenon* which refers to the observation that more recent feedback has a stronger impact on current choice than feedback received further in the past (see, for example, Shimp 1966). Usually, this is mathematically implemented via a discounting factor multiplied by previous choice probabilities or related contingencies such as cumulated propensities. In its statistical implementation the discounting factor is usually allowed to take on values larger than 1, thereby including the possibility that the initial experience carries more and more weight as the game progresses. However, recent trials to fit such parameters to experimental data have always led to discounting factors below 1 (see, for example, Erev and Roth 1998; Camerer and Ho 1999).

Methodological Aspects

The imperative of cognitive processes led psychologists to focus on adaptive behaviour. In order to clarify the specifics of the adaptation process, the experimental tasks were chosen such that gradual adjustment of behaviour could be observed. As a consequence, models, which in the early stages were formulated in verbal terms, described round-by-round adjustments of behaviour. The resulting set of proposed learning rules, hence, consisted entirely of adaptive rules. No, or little, attention was devoted to aspects of optimal dynamic choice.

Also, until the early 1950s, learning was solely investigated within single-person decision tasks. The emergence of game theory in mathematics and economics, however, quickly influenced psychology and sociology. Thibaut and Kelley (1959) give an overview of the early experiments on social interaction. One might suspect that, as a consequence of the late consideration of multi-person environments, the adaptive rules derived from the earlier single-person decision tasks were readily adapted to the strategic context. This dominance of individualistic modelling of learning even within interactive decision tasks has prevailed until today.

For mainly two reasons we will follow this line. First, a comprehensive study of all individualistic approaches to learning has, as yet, not been undertaken. While the number of mathematical models of learning has increased considerably during recent years, the number of rules that are directly compared with each other within any one study rarely exceeds two. Notable exceptions are Erev and Roth (1998), Tang (1998) and Erev and Haruvy (2000). Our study is, thus, meant to give an overview of the performance of the most important adaptive rules. The second reason is that, within this study, the environment in which learning behaviour is investigated is deliberately chosen such that the information provided to subjects hardly allows for other than adaptive behaviour. We, hence, try to investigate an environment which – from an *ex ante* point of view – is most favourable for observing adaptive-like motion.

3.3   THE LEARNING RULES

We now introduce the learning rules which we are going to use for our investigations in the next chapters. The rules are ordered according to kinship; so neither alphabetical nor chronological orders have been used. We start with the early psychologists' reinforcement learning rule and proceed with economists' modifications, including those introducing aspiration levels and propensities. An approach most typical for economists, a maximisation approach involving decision errors, marks the end of the list. After that, some additional rules are introduced that involve less sophistication and are not parameterised. They are meant to serve as benchmarks in later chapters. We conclude this chapter with two models which are not dealt with further in the present work.

In order to keep our presentation as simple as possible, we decided to use a unified notational framework. In our setting with two persons, two actions, and two payoff values we denote players by $i \in \{1,2\}$ and actions by $j \in \{A,B\}$. In case the model is based on probabilistic decision processes, we denote the probability of player i to play action j at time t by $p_i^j(t)$. Some models are based on evaluations of approximates to expected payoffs associated with actions. Such approximates for player i and action j at time t are then denoted by $u_i^j(t)$. In some models these approximates are somehow processed to $\tilde{u}_i^j(t)$ which then form the basis for the subsequent decision. The actual choice of player *i* at time *t* is given by $a_i(t)$ and the actual payoff to player *i* at the end of period *t* is given by $\pi_i(t)$. Some models further consider aspiration levels that develop over time. They are addressed by $b_i(t)$.

Most of the models involve parameters that may be fitted to the data. We restricted models to have up to two parameters, which we call α and β. In each model α and β have different meanings and therefore a suffix is added that indicates the model they are related to. The reason for restricting the parameterised models in such a way is to keep degrees of freedom constant. We thereby circumvent the usage of information criteria for the comparison of different theories. We are aware of the fact that the strength of certain adaptation rules is their simplicity while others are better at nesting different aspects of cognition via a number of parameters. Still, we believe that the restriction of the number of parameters to two is a good compromise between reducing theories to their cores and allowing for calibration of our data.

Bush and Mosteller (BM)

The mathematical connection between early stimulus–response models by psychologists and probabilistic modelling as known from mathematics is due to Estes (1950). He showed via a set theoretic approach that the conditioning of responses to stimuli may easily be modelled using linear adjustments of probabilities of responses. Bush and Mosteller took up this idea in a series of papers and developed a comprehensive adaptive choice model which they laid out in great detail in Bush and Mosteller (1955).

The basic characteristic of this model is that each potential action is chosen with some probability, and these probabilities are adjusted via linear operators that depend on the outcome of the directly preceding choice. As they explain (ibid., ch. 9), the probabilistic nature of their model creates a bridge between two then separate strands of psychological research on learning. On the one hand, there was the *reinforcement theory* which was based on Thorndike's law of effect and was further developed by Hull (1943) and Spence (1951) to so-called *behaviour systems*. On the other hand, there was the *association theory* by Guthrie (1935) that described changes in behaviour by changes in the degree of connection between stimuli and responses. From a methodological point of view, Bush and Mosteller's main contribution was to avoid the discussion about unobservable cognitive processes and to base learning theory solely on observable variables. The distinction between reinforcements and connections thus vanished.

Bush and Mosteller's general model allows for various values of probabilities to which the adjustment process may converge. For our purpose, it is, however, sufficient to consider only the case in which the long-run limit probability of a continuously reinforced action is 1. An important feature of this rule is that reinforcement of an action, after having resulted in success (or reward), and reinforcement of this action after the alternative action has resulted in failure (or non-reward), is larger the less likely the choice of this action has been.

Bush and Mosteller deliberately leave open the question as to what constitutes an *event* to which the operator (that is, the process of updating probabilities) is applied.[2] In our two-person two-action environment there are two reasonable ways to implement events. We ascribe one of these models to Bush and Mosteller, but it is essentially the interpretation of their model by Staddon and Horner (1989). Their reading states that there is a linear relation between current choice probability and the subsequent choice probability, whereby the reinforcement parameter may be different between situations in which the action chosen resulted in success (α^{BM}) and situations in which the action chosen resulted in failure (β^{BM}). Mookherjee and Sopher (1994) extracted a slightly different model, which we outline in the succeeding subsection.

The model according to Staddon and Horner translates to

$$
\begin{aligned}
p_i^B(t+1) = p_i^B(t) \\
+ \alpha^{BM} \cdot \left[\left(1 - p_i^B(t)\right) \cdot 1\begin{bmatrix} a_i(t) = B \\ \wedge \pi_i(t) = 1 \end{bmatrix} + \left(-p_i^B(t)\right) \cdot 1\begin{bmatrix} a_i(t) = A \\ \wedge \pi_i(t) = 1 \end{bmatrix} \right] \quad (3.1) \\
+ \beta^{BM} \cdot \left[\left(1 - p_i^B(t)\right) \cdot 1\begin{bmatrix} a_i(t) = A \\ \wedge \pi_i(t) = 0 \end{bmatrix} + \left(-p_i^B(t)\right) \cdot 1\begin{bmatrix} a_i(t) = B \\ \wedge \pi_i(t) = 0 \end{bmatrix} \right]
\end{aligned}
$$

whereby $1[.]$ denotes the indicator function. This scheme takes care of the probabilities not to fall below 0 or to exceed 1. We state the model in terms of the dynamics of probabilities for action B. Similarly, we could have expressed the learning process in terms of probabilities for action A, whereby the only difference would lie in the interchanged position of the parameters α^{BM} and β^{BM}. It is easy to extend this model to more than two actions.[3]

Lakshmivarahan and Narendra (1981; 1982) show convergence results for a slightly modified version of the Bush–Mosteller rule. In two-person zero-sum stochastic games with incomplete information they manage to show that, as long as the probabilistic payoff matrix has a saddle-point, and if positive reinforcement is performed as above but no change of probabilities occurs after unfavourable feedback, the scheme converges to the pure strategy equilibrium. If the learning rule is allowed for negative reinforcement by way of reducing probabilities by a constant probability mass after unfavourable feedback, the process converges to one undominated Nash-equilibrium independent of the shape of the stochastic payoff matrix. Parameter adjustments may, however, be necessary to achieve this.

Mookherjee and Sopher (MS)

A model which is very similar but not quite the same as the one above is the one formulated by Mookherjee and Sopher (1994). They also take a linear difference equation but assign different reinforcement parameters to the vindication or refutation of a specific action rather than the confirmation of either action. Mathematically this means

$$
\begin{aligned}
p_i^B(t+1) = p_i^B(t) \; &+ \alpha^{MS}\left(1 - p_i^B(t)\right) \cdot 1\!\!\left[\begin{bmatrix} a_i(t) = B \\ \wedge \; \pi_i(t) = 1 \end{bmatrix} \vee \begin{bmatrix} a_i(t) = A \\ \wedge \; \pi_i(t) = 0 \end{bmatrix}\right] \\
&+ \beta^{MS} p_i^B(t) \cdot 1\!\!\left[\begin{bmatrix} a_i(t) = B \\ \wedge \; \pi_i(t) = 0 \end{bmatrix} \vee \begin{bmatrix} a_i(t) = A \\ \wedge \; \pi_i(t) = 1 \end{bmatrix}\right]
\end{aligned}
\tag{3.2}
$$

In case $\alpha^{BM} = \beta^{BM}$ and $\alpha^{MS} = \beta^{MS}$ we get identical special cases of the two models. We will see, however, that, depending on the game, the two rules may show different dynamics, if parameters differ.

Cross (CR)

Drawing from the same stimulus–response concept, Cross (1973) formulated another similar model. He objected that, up to then, psychologists did not take into consideration the degree of reinforcement caused by the varying feedback of the environment.[4] Thus, the difference from the two models above lies in the different interpretation of payoffs.

$$
\begin{aligned}
p_i^B(t+1) = p_i^B(t) \; &+ \alpha\big(\pi_i(t)\big)\big(1 - p_i^B(t)\big) \cdot 1[a_i(t) = B] \\
&- \alpha\big(\pi_i(t)\big) p_i^B(t) \cdot 1[a_i(t) = A]
\end{aligned}
\tag{3.3}
$$

To Cross the reinforcement parameter for the linear difference equation is a monotonic function $a(.)$ of the payoff resulting from the respective action. A payoff of 0, hence, does not necessarily mean that the probability of repeating the same action will be reduced. Cross even considers $a(.)$ to be the identity, so that $a(.) = 0$, which for two-valued payoffs coincides with the model by Lakschmivarahan and Narendra we briefly described above. We follow Cross's general approach and use $a(\pi) = \alpha^{CR} \cdot \pi + \beta^{CR}$.

At that time, Cross was already able to prove that his learning rule led to expected utility maximisation in a bandit problem and to the Cournot–Nash-equilibrium outcome in a duopoly with quantitative competition. These results have been expanded by Schmalensee (1975). More recently, Börgers and Sarin (1997) show that, if the Cross rule is applied by all members of a population and time is made continuous by making time gaps arbitrarily small while preserving the number of updates per time interval, then behaviour proceeds according to the replicator dynamics which are known from biology.[5]

Börgers and Sarin (BS)

Early on, psychologists noted the importance of an individual's relative status for the evaluation of respective states he or she is in, and, hence, for decisions among alternative actions. The outcome of an encounter may thus be judged in different ways by the same individual depending on which point of reference is being referred to.[6] A model that is still in the tradition of psychologists' reinforcement rules but introduces aspiration is that by Börgers and Sarin (2000). They let the agent's aspiration evolve according to a simple linear process, while choice probabilities are reinforced by an amount proportional to the distance between the aspiration level and last period's payoff.

$$p_i^B(t+1) = p_i^B(t) \quad -|\pi_i(t) - b_i(t)| p_i^B(t)$$
$$+|\pi_i(t) - b_i(t)| \cdot 1 \left[\begin{array}{c} a_i(t) = B \\ \wedge \pi_i(t) > b_i(t) \end{array} \right] \vee \left[\begin{array}{c} a_i(t) = A \\ \wedge \pi_i(t) \le b_i(t) \end{array} \right] \quad (3.4)$$

Since the Bush Mosteller scheme has been developed for only two possible payoff levels, it can be conceived of as special case of the Börgers–Sarin scheme with the modification that the aspiration level remains fixed at the average of the two possible payoffs. Likewise, the Cross scheme can be considered as a special case of the Börgers–Sarin scheme with the proviso that the aspiration level is kept below any potential payoff level. Note, however, that all the above reinforcement learning rules are restricted to process only current choice probabilities and last period's payoffs. In this respect they all share the feature of complete loss of memory, that is, they can be visualised as infinite-set Markov chains. The Börgers–Sarin scheme departs from this.

The crucial difference from the above schemes results from allowing the aspiration level to form endogenously. Following Börgers and Sarin (2000) the aspiration level of individual i evolves according to

$$b_i(t+1) = \beta^{BS} b_i(t) + (1 - \beta^{BS}) \pi_i(t) \quad (3.5)$$

that is, the aspiration level at the beginning of the next period is a weighted average of this period's aspiration level and the payoff that resulted from last period's play. The second parameter of the model is given by the initial aspiration level, that is, $\alpha^{BS} = b_i(1)$.

Börgers and Sarin (2000) succeed in showing that, for a continuous time approximation of the learning rule, two distinct forces drive behaviour: the first is the replicator dynamics and the second is probability matching. The accordance with replicator dynamics stems directly from the analogy to the Cross scheme without endogenous aspirations. As long as the aspiration level remains lower than any experienced payoff level, the linear adjustment of probabilities on payoffs shares the same properties as the replicator dynamics (Börgers and Sarin 1997). However, if on some occasions a payoff below the current aspiration level is experienced, then the process drives towards probability matching, meaning that an action is chosen with the same probability with which it receives a payoff equal to or above the current aspiration level. In individual choice under risk (that is, in a stationary environment in which the two actions result in rewards or failures with fixed probabilities), this latter behaviour usually leads to a non-optimal expected payoff. Instead, optimal choice would comprise always of choosing the one action that has a higher probability of success. Experimental evidence on the importance of probability matching has been mixed. In a survey, Winter (1982) roughly concludes that probability matching is relevant for choice behaviour only if payoffs are small and/or non-monetary. A similar conclusion is drawn in Vulkan (2000).

Roth and Erev's Reinforcement Learning (RE)

A model still confined to the reinforcement idea but with a different consideration of memory is that by Roth and Erev (1995).[7] The idea of this process is that probabilities are indirectly determined by cumulated propensities.

In order to show how the Roth–Erev scheme can be extended to incorporate endogenously evolving aspirations, we first present the more general ADR scheme as proposed by Erev et al. (1999). The ADR model contains many more variables than the Roth–Erev scheme. Despite this, Erev et al. show that its performance on experimental data is rather poor. We decided to include its description because it illustrates the larger learning context into which the Roth–Erev scheme may be embedded. We will make use of this larger model only briefly, in Chapter 5.

The propensity of an individual i for choosing action j is determined in the following way:

$$u_i^j(t+1) = \begin{cases} \varphi^{|\Delta_i(t)|} \cdot u_i^j(t) + R(t,\pi) & \text{if} > v \wedge a_i(t) = j \\ \varphi^{|\Delta_i(t)|} \cdot u_i^j(t) & \text{if} > v \wedge a_i(t) \neq j \\ v & \text{if} \leq v \end{cases} \quad (3.6)$$

with $\varphi > 0$ being the forgetting parameter,[8] and the small cut-off parameter v (usually assumed to be 0.001) being a positive constant insuring positive propensities. The reinforcement R is calculated as the difference between payoff π and some aspiration level ρ: $R(t, p) = \pi_i(t) - \rho_i(t)$.[9] The original Roth and Erev (1995) scheme now simply assumes $\rho_i(t) = 0$ and $\Delta_i(t) = 1$ for all i and t, so that v becomes redundant. The probability of strategy j being chosen by player i at time t is then given by the size of the propensity divided by the sum of all propensities:

$$p_i^j(t) = \frac{u_i^j(t)}{\sum_{j \in \{A,B\}} u_i^j(t)}$$

(3.7)

The denominator can be interpreted as the total amount of experience.

Denote player i's probability distribution over his or her set of strategies by $p_i(t) = (p_i^A(t), p_i^B(t))$. Then the action chosen by player i at period t is determined by

$$a_i(t) = Z(p_i(t))$$

(3.8)

where $Z(p)$ is a random variable with distribution p.

Erev et al. present an extended version by assuming $\rho_i(1) = 0$ and

$$\rho_i(t+1) = w^{|\Delta(t)-\alpha|} \cdot \rho_i(t) + \left(1 - w^{|\Delta(t)-\alpha|}\right) \cdot \pi_i(t)$$

(3.9)

and $\Delta(t) = AR(t)/RV(t)$ whereby the two components evolve via

$$AR(t) = w' \cdot AR(t-1) + (1-w') \cdot R(t, \pi)$$

(3.10)

and

$$RV(t) = w'' \cdot RV(t-1) + (1-w'') \cdot \left| AR(t-1) - R(t-1, \pi) \right|$$

(3.11)

with $AR(1) = R(1, \pi)$, $RV(1) = |R(1, \pi)|$, and $w = w' = w''$ for simplicity, thereby introducing the two weighing parameters w and α.

Using the simple version by Roth and Erev (1995) and, for notational consistency, substituting φ with the parameter name β^{RE} the updating rule reduces to

$$u_i^j(t+1) = \beta^{RE} \cdot u_i^j(t) + \pi_i(t) \cdot 1[a_i(t) = j]$$

(3.12)

that is, the propensity of an alternative is first discounted by the forgetting parameter β^{RE} and, if this alternative has been chosen in the last round, then its propensity is added to the actual payoff that resulted from that decision, otherwise the propensity stays at the discounted level. The second parameter of the model determines the strength of initial experience, which is defined as the sum of initial propensities, that is,

$$\alpha^{RE} = u_i^A(1) + u_i^B(1) \qquad (3.13)$$

The choice probabilities within a round are then simply proportional to the sum of propensities:

$$p_i^j(t) = \frac{u_i^j(t)}{\sum_{k \in \{A,B\}} u_i^k(t)} \qquad (3.14)$$

For decision problems in stationary probabilistic environments Rustichini (1999) has shown that the Roth–Erev scheme leads to expected payoff maximisation, if after each repetition of the decision task payoff information is provided only for the actually chosen task. In the case of social learning, however (that is, if after each repetition payoff information on all available actions is given), this process is suboptimal.

There are also some results for the application of the Roth–Erev rule within repeated games. Just as Börgers and Sarin (1997) did for the Cross model, Posch (1997) showed that the continuous time approximate of the basic variant of the Roth–Erev model also leads to the replicator dynamics. In a series of papers Hopkins (1999a; 1999b; 1999c) works out the similarities between replicator dynamics and a stochastic version of fictitious play, that is, a model requiring much more information and assuming the ability to optimise. In particular Hopkins (1999c) manages to show that a stochastic approximate of the Roth–Erev model with a certain noise structure shares the same asymptotic properties as stochastic fictitious play. An interesting corollary to this finding is that for 2 × 2 games with unique mixed-strategy equilibrium, different ways to approximate the learning models lead to different asymptotic results: if approximation results to the replicator dynamics, then it is known from Schuster and Sigmund (1981) that the process orbits around the Nash-equilibrium. If, however, approximation leads to stochastic fictitious play, then the process converges to the Nash-equilibrium (Fudenberg and Kreps 1993, Benaïm and Hirsch 1996).

Variant to Roth and Erev (REL)

Erev et al. (1999) propose a variant to the Roth–Erev rule that uses adjustments via approximates of average payoffs and payoff variance and uses a logit form for the assessment of choice probabilities. The propensities, thus, evolve according to

$$u_i^j(t+1) = \begin{cases} \dfrac{u_i^j(t) \cdot \left(c_i^j(t) + 0.5 \cdot \alpha^{REL}\right) + \pi_i(t)}{c_i^j(t) + 0.5 \cdot \alpha^{REL} + 1} & \text{if } a_i(t) = a \\ u_i^j(t) & \text{otherwise} \end{cases} \qquad (3.15)$$

whereby $c_i^j(t)$ denotes the number of times action j had been played by player i until period t. The assessment of probabilities then follows

$$p_i^j(t) = \frac{\exp\left(\beta^{REL} \cdot u_i^j(t) / PV(t)\right)}{\displaystyle\sum_{k \in \{A,B\}} \exp\left(\beta^{REL} \cdot u_i^k(t) / PV(t)\right)} \qquad (3.16)$$

whereby the payoff variability PV is determined via

$$PV(t+1) = \frac{PV(t) \cdot \left(t + \alpha^{REL}\right) + \left|\pi_i(t) - PA(t)\right|}{t + \alpha^{REL} + 1} \qquad (3.17)$$

and the approximate for the average payoff PA is given by

$$PA(t+1) = \frac{PA(t) \cdot \left(t + \alpha^{REL}\right) + \pi_i(t)}{t + \alpha^{REL} + 1} \qquad (3.18)$$

and the initial $PA(1)$ is the expected payoff from random choice and $PV(1)$ is the expected absolute difference between the obtained payoff from random choice and the average payoff from random choice.

Even though this scheme contains only two adjustable parameters, the complexity of the updating process impedes a formal analysis of its properties. In this case we are forced to simulate in order to investigate the characteristics of the learning rule. Erev et al., however, report a particularly good fit of this model on a large set of experimental data.

Karandikar et al. (KA)

Karandikar et al. (1998) also consider evolving aspirations but give up the idea of reinforced choice probabilities. Rather, they vary the idea of win–stay lose–randomise by specifying the randomisation process. The scheme win–stay lose–randomise can be approximated by special cases of the Karandikar et al. scheme. Their approach is not constructive; they only state necessary conditions for the process in order to lead to the theoretical result they report on, but do not explicate the randomisation rule. The model they present looks as follows.

$$
p_i^B(t+1) = \begin{cases} 1 & \textit{if } a_i(t) = B \wedge \pi_i(t) \geq b_i(t) \\ h(b_i(t) - \pi_i(t)) & \textit{if } a_i(t) = B \wedge \pi_i(t) < b_i(t) \\ (1 - h(b_i(t) - \pi_i(t))) & \textit{if } a_i(t) = A \wedge \pi_i(t) < b_i(t) \\ 0 & \textit{otherwise} \end{cases} \tag{3.19}
$$

whereby $h(.)$ fulfils (i) $h(0) = 1$, (ii) $-\infty < \breve{g} < h'(x) < 0$ for all x and some $\breve{g}$, and (iii) $h(x) \geq p' > 0$ for all x and some p', so that the probability of change is bounded away from 0. They also assume that the aspiration levels evolve probabilistically with

$$
\begin{aligned}
P[b_i(t+1) = (1 - \beta^{KA})b_i(t) + \beta^{KA}\pi_i(t)] &= 1 - \eta^{KA} \text{ and} \\
P[b_i(t+1) = (1 - \beta^{KA})b_i(t) + \beta^{KA}\pi_i(t) + G(b_i(t))] &= \eta^{KA}
\end{aligned} \tag{3.20}
$$

whereby $G(b(.))$ is a random variable with density $g(.|b)$.

Since the perturbation of the aspiration level is important only for games involving Pareto-ordered Nash-equilibria (such as in the stag-hunt game or the prisoner's dilemma), we assume deterministically evolving aspiration levels, that is, $\eta^{KA} = 0$, that is, the aspiration level follows the same scheme as in the Börgers–Sarin rule. For further analysis we specify

$$
h(x) = \arctan\left(\frac{\gamma^{KA}}{x^2} + \tan\left(\frac{\pi}{2} \cdot \delta^{KA}\right)\right) \cdot \frac{2}{\pi} \tag{3.21}
$$

whereby γ^{KA} indicates the speed of decline as the gap between aspiration level and actual payoff rises and δ^{KA} denotes the asymptotic bound from below. For convenience and in order to reduce the number of parameters to our standard of two, we specify $\gamma^{KA} = 0.2$ and $\delta^{KA} = 0.1$. As we will argue later in the analysis, these restrictions do not have a great impact on the results. Apart from the adjustment speed of the aspiration level β^{KA}, its initial value $\alpha^{KA} = b_i(1)$ is left adjustable.

As with the win–stay lose–randomise rule, but contrary to all other schemes, the Karandikar et al. scheme suggests a probability assessment that is solely based on the previous action and payoff, and ignores previous choice inclinations. Karandikar et al. show for a fairly general class of repeated 2 × 2 games that players will eventually coordinate on the possibly dominated Pareto-efficient outcome most of the time. Recently, Napel (2000) has shown that, with a slight modification of the Karandikar et al. scheme, players who repeatedly play the sequential ultimatum mini-game will result in playing either the fair outcome or the unfair efficient cell (that is, the proposer gets the whole pie). The exact asymptotic distributions depend on the amount of disturbance of the updating process.

Experimentation Learning (EX)

We next present a learning rule that is based purely on experimentation behaviour and captures the crucial features of the ADR model in a much simpler way. This rule bares resemblance to the search-and-select adaptation rule proposed by Conlisk (1993) and is contained in the set of monotonic learning rules with bounded memory studied by Sarin (2000). It may also be interpreted as a variant of the win–stay lose–change learning scheme, whereby the win–stay part is slightly generalised and the lose–change part is transformed into a lose–randomise rule.

The idea of this rule is to let individuals, first, gather information about payoff and then decide which action to take, based on a fixed number of previous payoff experiences with each strategy. In more detail, we assume each player to record the feedback returned after playing a strategy and keep only the last β^{EX} pieces of feedback information for each strategy. The value of the record of an action thus evolves according to

$$
\begin{aligned}
u_i^j(t+1) = u_i^j(t) \cdot \left(1[a_i(t) \neq j] + 1[a_i(t) = j] \cdot 1[\pi_i(t) = 1] \cdot 1[u_i^j(t) = \beta^{EX}] \right) \\
+ \left(u_i^j(t) + 1 \right) \cdot 1[a_i(t) = j] \cdot 1[\pi_i(t) = 1] \cdot 1[u_i^j(t) < \beta^{EX}]
\end{aligned}
\tag{3.22}
$$

Since, at the beginning of play, players have not yet gathered any information about the efficacy of actions, we initialise the record of each strategy to zero. The discrete parameter β^{EX} denotes the size of the memory of a player. Our notion of the size of the memory is used differently to usual definitions of bounded history, as for example in Milgrom and Roberts (1990; 1991) and Hon-Snir et al. (1998). While bounded history is defined as capturing all payoff feedback dating back β^{EX} periods before the current period, bounded memory considers players that trace all β^{EX} last actions *of each strategy* separately. Particularly, if a strategy has not been chosen for a long period of time, then even experience gathered in the distant past is relevant for the current choice. This model is related to the view that memory is not simply forgotten but, rather, selectively overwritten by new experience.

Since we want to apply our learning rule to a set of particularly simple games we do not bother to formulate a complicated evaluation scheme. In the games to be described, the only payoffs that possibly arise from choosing an action are either 0 or 1 (and people are informed of this prior to playing the game). This simplicity allows us to formulate a rudimentary evaluation scheme based on a fixed aspiration level of 1. Hence, if the payoff of the action is 0 we record dissatisfaction (or failure), and if the payoff of an action turns out to be 1 we record satisfaction (or success).

We will use two different ways of transforming the records of the actions into probabilities. In Chapter 5 we will confine ourselves to use only three levels of probabilities. This will be sufficient, since that chapter is mainly concerned about qualitative features of this rule. There, in case the record for one strategy is unambiguously favourable, this strategy will be chosen with a fixed probability $0.5 < \alpha^{EX} < 1$. In case no action or both actions have a perfect record, the action chosen in the next period is determined according to a random process giving equal probability to each possible strategy. Formally, this translates to

$$p_i^j(t) = \begin{cases} \alpha^{EX} & \text{if } u_i^j(t) = \beta^{EX} \wedge u_i^k(t) < \beta^{EX} \\ 1 - \alpha^{EX} & \text{if } u_i^j(t) < \beta^{EX} \wedge u_i^k(t) = \beta^{EX} \\ 0.5 & \text{otherwise} \end{cases} \quad (3.23)$$

In Chapter 6 we will use the more sensitive transformation

$$p_i^j(t) = 0.5 + \text{sign}\left(u_i^j(t) - u_i^k(t)\right) \cdot \max\left(u_i^A(t), u_i^B(t)\right) \cdot \frac{\alpha^{EX}}{\beta^{EX}} \quad (3.24)$$

in which the parameter $0 < \alpha^{EX} < 0.5$ now signifies the amount of probability that is added for each good experience with that action.

Both ways of evaluating the payoff record of the strategies is consistent with the notion of monotonicity as defined by Sarin (2000). Sarin shows that the application of such processes to stationary probabilistic environments (that is, bandit problems) also eventually leads to the exclusive play of the maxmin strategy. For common interest games Aumann and Sorin (1989) have shown that the efficient cell is reached. They also show that efficiency cannot be ensured, if memory is allowed to be infinite.[10]

Sarin and Vahid (SV)

A completely different approach is that of using past payoffs to generate approximates for the expected payoffs of the respective alternatives. Not the first, but probably the simplest, approach in this line is the one by Sarin and Vahid (1999). They assume that the expected payoffs (and not the choice probabilities) follow a reinforcement process with the difference equation being linear in the difference between previous expectation and current payoff. The decision is then a stochastic process depending on these payoff expectations.

Formally stated, the payoff expectation for action j evolves according to

$$u_i^j(t+1) = u_i^j(t) + \alpha^{sv}\left(\pi_i(t) - u_i^j(t)\right) \cdot 1[a_i(t) = j]$$ (3.25)

Before players choose their action these assessments are perturbed by a random variable Z that may depend on time, that is,

$$\tilde{u}_i^j(t) = u_i^j(t) + Z(t)$$ (3.26)

Players then choose the one alternative that promises the maximum payoff according to the perturbed assessments, that is,

$$a_i(t) = \arg\max_{j \in \{A,B\}} \tilde{u}_i^j(t)$$ (3.27)

As Sarin and Vahid (2001) argue, this scheme is much more in the tradition of economists' models of behaviour. It contains two elements that psychologists did not deem relevant. First, players are assumed to form beliefs or expectations about future payoffs and, second, subjects are assumed to make use of maximisation. Sarin and Vahid (2001) even use the deterministic process, that is, $Z(t)$ assigns probability 1 to the value zero, which means that players always choose the action with the highest expected payoff. However, we will stick to the original model (Sarin and Vahid 1999) with the time-independent random variable Z and specify it to have normal distribution with zero mean and standard deviation σ^{sv}. The standard deviation of the perturbation constitutes our second parameter of the model, that is, $\beta^{sv} = \sqrt{\sigma^{sv}}$.

Matsushima (1998a; 1998b) simultaneously analysed such processes in a much broader context. However, the basic result is the same as derived in Sarin and Vahid (1999): behaviour according to the Sarin–Vahid rule will lead to the maxmin strategy. Within stationary environments (that is, bandit problems) and under fairly general conditions this leads to the maximisation of expected payoffs. However, as Matsushima (1998b) shows, in simple symmetric 2×2 games this process will most often lead to inefficiencies.

3.4   BENCHMARK MODELS

Because of their adaptive nature and their sometimes crude-looking assessments of choice probabilities, the above learning rules have often been viewed as involving very little sophistication. Compared to approaches known from macroeconomic modelling, such as Bayesian updating or least squares learning, this is certainly true. However, there are even less sophisticated models of adaptive behaviour. In Chapter 6, we will compare the above rules with these benchmarks on qualitative grounds. In Chapter 8, such a comparison will tell us how much improvement parameterised learning rules yield over the rudimentary rules that involve no sophistication whatsoever.

Win–Stay Lose–Change (WSLC)

Consider, first, the rule win–stay lose–change. This rule has been shown to be very successful in settings involving dilemma situations, sometimes even outperforming tit-for-tat (see Nowak and Sigmund 1993). This simple learning rule is related to the learning direction scheme developed for larger strategy spaces by Selten and Stoecker (1986) while analysing Prisoner's Dilemma supergames, and has further been investigated by Selten and Buchta (1994) on auction data. The idea is simply that whenever the individual fails to reach the optimal goal he or she will compute the direction of ascent and adjust his or her decision accordingly. Our data sets all come from games involving only two strategies and two levels of payoffs. For such games this scheme translates into staying with one's strategy if it yielded a payoff of 1 and changing if it resulted in a payoff of zero. Formally, the rule simply postulates

$$p_i^j(t+1) = 1[a_i(t) = j] \cdot 1[\pi_i(t) = 1] + 1[a_i(t) \neq j] \cdot 1[\pi_i(t) = 0] \quad (3.28)$$

Win–Stay Lose–Randomise (WSLR)

As we see in Chapter 6, for the games under consideration, a randomisation after receiving zero payoff is much more effective in pursuing the efficient cell than is the strict change of action. Therefore, we also investigate the rule win–stay lose–randomise, whereby the randomisation is assumed to occur with equal probability over both actions.

$$p_i^j(t+1) = 1[a_i(t) = j] \cdot 1[\pi_i(t) = 1] + 0.5 \cdot 1[\pi_i(t) = 0] \quad (3.29)$$

As can easily be verified, this rule is nested within the Karandikar et al. scheme.

Randomisation (RAND)

Learning rules have often been compared with the theoretical equilibrium strategy of a one-shot game. In our set of games, equilibria will involve either games with pure-strategy equilibria and/or the mixed-strategy equilibrium in which both actions are chosen with equal probabilities (0.5, 0.5), or games with a continuum of equilibria. For this reason, the only strictly mixed-strategy of interest will be the strategy that assigns equal probability to each of the two actions. That is,

$$p_i^j(t) = 0.5 \tag{3.30}$$

3.5   OMITTED MODELS

There are some models of adaptive learning that are applicable to the environment of little information, but which we are not dealing with in the following.

Gilboa and Schmeidler

Gilboa and Schmeidler (1995; 1996) also formulated an adaptation rule that assesses approximates to expected payoffs of choice alternatives. However, they do not let approximates evolve according to a reinforcement process. Rather they let subjects compare their actual aspiration level with the past payoffs of the alternatives. The cognitive requirements for this rule are substantial. Players are assumed not only to keep all past payoffs readily available for the recalculation of the expected value of each strategy, but also to actually use all past historical data in each period. Furthermore, the player is assumed to perform dual maximisation: the aspiration level follows a linear adjustment using the maximum of past average payoffs, while the actual choice is the action that has the highest value, this value being calculated as the sum of differences between actually received payoffs in the past and the current aspiration level.

In order to formalise this in a mathematical way we, first, denote the set of time periods until time t in which action j was played by player i:

$$T_i^j(t) = \left\{ \tau \in \{1,...,t\} \middle| a_i(t) = j \right\} \tag{3.31}$$

The average past payoffs are given by

$$u_i^j(t) = \frac{1}{\#T_i^j(t)} \sum_{\tau \in T_i^j(t)} \pi_i(\tau) \tag{3.32}$$

and aspirations evolve according to

$$b(t+1) = (1 - \lambda^{GS})b(t) + \lambda^{GS} \max_{j \in \{A,B\}} u_i^j(t) \qquad (3.33)$$

while expectations for payoff margins are determined by

$$\widetilde{u}_i^j(t+1) = \sum_{\tau \in T_i^j(t)} \left(\pi_i(\tau) - b_i(t+1) \right)$$
$$= \#T_i^j(t) \cdot \left(u_i^j(t) - b_i(t+1) \right) \qquad (3.34)$$

Choice is finally determined according to

$$a_i(t) = \arg\max_{j \in \{A,B\}} \widetilde{u}_i^j(t) \qquad (3.35)$$

Gilboa and Schmeidler (1996) show that a sufficiently high aspiration level or an aspiration level that is regularly adjusted upwards over time, leads to the maximisation of expected payoff in a stationary environment with probabilistic rewards. Because this result runs counter to that by Börgers and Sarin (2000), who show that the addition of the consideration of an aspiration level to the Cross-dynamic leads to suboptimal decisions in the same environment, the latter authors devote considerable space to explaining the similarities and differences of the two rules. It seems as though the basic difference lies in the role of the aspiration level. In Gilboa and Schmeidler's framework a higher aspiration level leads to increased experimentation among the alternatives, while in Börgers and Sarin's scheme high initial aspiration levels preclude sufficient experimentation at the beginning.

Gilboa and Schmeidler (1997) further consider a possible similarity of actions, which translates into the expected payoff margins. But, since we are confined to only two actions, we might have simply assumed a similarity of zero between action A and action B. The scheme as presented here is deterministic in nature and therefore would have been difficult to compare with all the other probabilistic learning rules. Furthermore, a maximum likelihood estimation of parameters would not have been possible, since the likelihood function becomes degenerate whenever choice probabilities of 0 are predicted. But we easily could have rendered choice probabilistically by introducing an error term, such as the one for the Sarin–Vahid scheme. The main reason not to include this process in those being investigated in our study is its complexity. We would need at least three parameters (initial aspiration level, adjustment speed of the aspiration level and the variance of choice) in order to fit all crucial aspects of the decision rule. And, more importantly, the process is computationally too demanding to have a chance of attaining a reasonable model of actual cognitive processes.

Variant to Experienced Weighted Attraction Learning

Until recently, reinforcement-like models and belief-based models of learning were dealt with separately. Camerer and Ho (1999) were the first to present a more general model that incorporated the most prominent learning rules from both classes as special cases.[11] Just like the Roth–Erev model, Camerer and Ho regarded propensities assigned to each available action as the basis for the subsequent choice. The main innovation was to allow the updating of propensities not only for the previously chosen strategy (or those 'near' the previously chosen strategy, see Roth and Erev 1995) but also to update propensities of unchosen strategies according to the payoff they would have obtained had they been chosen. This processing of fictitious payoffs could be parameterised in such a way so as to model fictitious play.

In order to be able to update propensities in this way, players need to know their own payoff matrix in advance and observe opponents' choices. Both kinds of information, however, are not provided to subjects within an environment characterised by little information. Chen and Khoroshilov (2001) presented a modification of Camerer and Ho's (1999) model that fits into our restricted informational settings. Since Chen and Khoroshilov use a larger space of available actions, we simplify their model to accord to the two-action case.

The evaluation of an action j follows the same weighted sum of past payoffs obtained from playing that strategy as has been used for the Sarin–Vahid scheme, that is,

$$u_i^j(t+1) = u_i^j(t) + \alpha^{CK}\left(\pi_i(t) - u_i^j(t)\right) \cdot 1\left[a_i(t) = j\right] \qquad (3.36)$$

Different to the Sarin–Vahid scheme, there is a variable that keeps track of the amount of experience gained up to period t,

$$N(t) = \rho^{CK} \cdot N(t-1) + 1 \qquad (3.37)$$

with ρ^{CK} being the depreciation rate of previous experience.

For convenience, we further define the fictitious payoff of an action j as

$$\tilde{\pi}_i^j(t) = \begin{cases} \pi_i(t) & \text{if } a_i(t) = j \\ \delta^{CK} u_i^j(t) & \text{otherwise} \end{cases} \qquad (3.38)$$

that is, the attraction of the chosen strategy is assumed to be updated using the payoff actually received from that period, while the attraction of the strategy that has not been chosen is updated using a discounted value of the payoff expectation. The level of attraction of a strategy j to player i is then given by

$$\widetilde{u}_i^j(t) = \frac{N(t-1)\widetilde{u}_i^j(t-1) + \widetilde{\pi}_i^j(t)}{N(t)} \tag{3.39}$$

and the choice probabilities are determined by the exponential transformation

$$p_i^j(t) = \frac{e^{\lambda^{ck}\widetilde{u}_i^j(t)}}{e^{\lambda^{ck}\widetilde{u}_i^A(t)} + e^{\lambda^{ck}\widetilde{u}_i^B(t)}} \tag{3.40}$$

As with Gilboa and Schmeidler's rule, we dismiss this rule mainly for reasons of complexity. We deem it unrealistic that subjects in the laboratory keep track of two, or even three, intermediate variables that only indirectly influence actual choices. And even if one allows for this to be the case, the stochastic nature of choice would render the updating behaviour so complex that experiments with a moderate number of rounds are hardly able to provide sufficient data for the statistical analysis of each of the features. We postpone further discussions of this topic to Chapter 6.

NOTES

1. See Skinner (1938) for classical operant conditioning.
2. See Bush and Mosteller (1955, pp. 188f).
3. See Bush and Mosteller (1955, pp. 37ff).
4. See Cross (1973, p. 246).
5. The properties of the replicator dynamics are discussed for example in a recent survey by Mailath (1998).
6. Early studies discussing the impact of aspiration levels on behaviour comprise Lewin et al. (1944) and Merton (1957).
7. This process has first been presented by Harley (1981) as a solution to the problem of finding an evolutionary stable learning rule. Arthur (1991; 1993) also considers a model very similar to the basic one-parameter Roth–Erev scheme.
8. See Roth and Erev (1995) for a discussion of this parameter. Recall from Section 3.2 that this parameter models the degree to which the rule conforms to the power law of practice.
9. Erev et al. (1999) call it the *reference point*.
10. Lehrer (1988) also studies such processes but focuses on the asymptotic properties as memory grows.
11. Camerer and Ho (1999) named their model 'experience weighted attraction learning', which is now widely addressed by its abbreviation EWA.

4. Related Experimental Literature

Early Work

The early experiments on dynamic decision-making were centred on individual choice tasks. They were usually limited to the repeated choice between two alternative actions. Because, early on, psychologists were first interested in the unconscious processes of the mind, they often resorted to experimental subjects whose cognitive capacity was rather limited and, thus, promised to exhibit simple patterns and regularities that could be extended to fit the more complex processes of humans. Apart from human subjects, psychologists showed particular interest in rats and pigeons. An extensive survey on experiments with rats can be found in Dember and Fowler (1958). This article focuses on the win–stay lose–change dynamics. For rats, a few robust regularities could be found. T-maze experiments showed that rats are able to learn which way to choose in order to reach the place with high reward probability. However, it also became evident that rats never choose one alternative with certainty, even when this alternative is always reinforced and the others are never reinforced. Very similar patterns of behaviour are reported for pigeons (see, for example, the overview by Shimp 1966). Biologists attribute this kind of behaviour to the need to experiment among alternatives in order to keep a positive chance of finding a better choice alternative than the currently reinforced alternative. This kind of experimentation has proved successful for the global optimisation of non-algebraic functions (see, for example, Hinton and Sejnowski 1986 for the method of simulated annealing).

Interestingly, early qualitative tests on learning theories rarely made use of fixed environments against which the subject had to play repeatedly. Rather, subjects had to adapt to an environment that responded according to a fixed rule that was based on the subjects' responses. Estes (1954) gives a brief overview of such experiments involving human subjects. The basic result is the amazing accordance with probability matching. Estes points out the fact that the use of probability matching is irrational. It does not serve the purpose of maximising one's payoff. It was further shown that this result is in line with predictions derived from the early mathematical learning model by Bush and Mosteller (1951; 1953). As already indicated in Chapter 3, later experimental work, of which Cross (1973) gives a brief account, this pattern of behaviour could be attributed to several elements of the experimental design. Longer runs of repetitions and true monetary payoffs, in particular, seem to eliminate subjects' disposition to match the probabilities of occurrences.[1]

The early analysis of learning in games was conducted in a very similar fashion. Probably because, at that time, the mathematical and computational techniques were not very much advanced, learning in repeated games was analysed mathematically and experimentally using simple artificial agents. Due to the association with rats used in laboratory experiments, that exhibited a similarly limited amount of cognitive capacity as was typical of the early theories of learning, such artificial agents were called *stat-rats*. Predictions of learning in games were derived from asymptotic properties of the Markov chains defined by the dynamic rules (Flood 1954). Accordingly, subjects in the laboratory were not playing repeated games against each other, but interacted against a stat-rat, usually under little information (though being told that they played against a stat-rat).

Suppes and Atkinson

Suppes and Atkinson's (1960, ch. 3) experiment may be regarded as the first experiment whose design comes close to our notion of little information. They studied controlled two-player repeated games under little information. Still, there was a marked difference compared with today's experimental methodology in economics. They used probabilistic payoff incentives, that is, a pair of decisions did not result in deterministic payoffs for both players but in probabilities of reward and non-reward. Suppes and Atkinson used the expected values of payoffs to derive asymptotic predictions for subjects' play, without knowing that such a transformation may result in different dynamics than the true stochastic process (see Börgers and Sarin 1997 for a discussion of this on the Cross-dynamic).

Apart from using a probabilistic payoff matrix, their design also differs from ours in that they did not tell subjects that they were actually involved in a two-person game. Instead, subjects were made to believe that the payoff scheme was determined by a stationary probability distribution. The presence of a second subject in the laboratory was said to be purely a matter of convenience for the experimenter.[2] Subjects played 2 × 2 repeated games without knowledge about one's own payoff matrix, nor the payoff matrix of the other player. The game was zero-sum in that each pair of actions determined a certain probability of win to player 1 and a loss to player 2, that is, in each round one player gained one point and one player suffered a loss of one point. Monetary rewards to players were independent of their pointscore. Each pair played the task for 200 repetitions.

Under these circumstances Suppes and Atkinson assigned pairs to one of three payoff matrices. The first payoff matrix was designed such that, according to the Nash-equilibrium of the stage game, each player should play a strictly mixed strategy, that is, player 1's equilibrium profile is (1/3, 2/3), and player 2's profile is (5/6, 1/6). The second payoff matrix can be solved via iterated elimination of weakly dominated strategies (in expected payoffs) and, therefore, assigns pure equilibrium strategies to each player (player 1: (1,0), player 2: (1,0)). The third payoff matrix even allows for elimination of strictly dominated strategies (in expected payoffs) and leads to the same predictions as the second payoff matrix.

Based on block-averaged data, Suppes and Atkinson show that relative frequencies of play at the end of the 200-period encounter are, on average, very close to predictions derived from asymptotic play by agents that accord with Estes's (1950) linear association scheme and far from the standard game-theoretic equilibria. Even though they admit that graphs of relative frequencies of play reveal considerable variation, they are able to show that during the last 60 periods relative frequencies of occurrences of outcomes had not changed significantly. They, thus, state their confidence in their conclusion that subjects had settled to a stationary probabilistic distribution over their respective sets of actions.[3]

At the end of the 1950s and at the beginning of the 1960s the psychological literature on simple interactive experiments was growing quite rapidly. Apart from studies of games with unique mixed-strategy equilibrium, interest focused on coordination games. Since these experiments are closely related to the experiment we report on in Chapter 5, we postpone a detailed account of this literature.

Mookherjee and Sopher

Since experiments in economics mainly served to test game theory's predictions and, for a long time, game theory used to operate on the common knowledge assumption, experiments on repeated games under limited information had not been performed until recently. The first such experiment we know of that was run by economists is Mookherjee and Sopher's (1994) matching pennies game. Their study was inspired by the wish to confirm game theory's Nash-equilibrium prediction in the realm of little information, at least for an extremely simple two-player zero-sum game. They compared subjects' play between two informational treatments: (i) full information, that is, conditions as usual, with the payoff matrix being common knowledge and feedback about not only one's own payoff but also on the payoff received and the action taken by the opponent, and (ii) little information, that is, players not knowing which game they were playing, and not being informed about other players' actions and payoffs at any point in time.

Their results clearly show that, for both treatments, average relative frequencies conform to the Nash-equilibrium prediction, that is, they are close to the equal distribution among the two alternative actions. However, while subjects in the full-information treatment show negative serial correlation (an observation often observed in single-person decision problems and usually attributed to subjects' inability to produce true random sequences),[4] subjects in the little-information treatment showed a considerable amount of inertia. Mookherjee and Sopher conclude that subjects are employing equilibrium-like strategies when sufficient information is provided, but processes similar to routine learning govern behaviour under little information.

Nagel and Vriend

Unlike Mookherjee and Sopher's aim at specifying the nature of adaptive play in an extremely simple environment under little information, Nagel and Vriend (1999) try to discern the adaptive nature of behaviour in extremely complex situations. Their working hypothesis is that, as soon as optimal behaviour can only be reached using complex mathematical devices, subjects will automatically resort to simple dynamics to solve the task. Subjects in the experiment were organised in groups of six players who competed in an oligopolistic market. Choices in one period not only had effects on the other player's payoffs, but also on future demand of the market. This demand was simulated via a fixed algorithm and did not involve additional players. Subjects, hence, were interacting in a dynamic environment, whereby interaction between players involved simultaneous choices of output *and* signals. In addition, subjects were told neither the number of competing firms, nor the payoff function, so that the calculation of the equilibrium strategy was effectively impossible.

Nagel and Vriend confine themselves to the comparison between two area theories, that is, learning direction theory (Selten and Stoecker 1986; Selten and Buchta 1999) and a variant of gradient learning (also called method of steepest ascent, or hill climbing). The results clearly favour learning direction theory over gradient learning. The authors are thus led to conclude that, in complex and highly uncertain environments, subjects prefer to stick to simple adaptive dynamics, rather than try to calculate locally optimal adjustment behaviour. This observation is shown to be true even for experienced players. Their results seem to support Mookherjee and Sopher's implicitly stated hypothesis that uncertainty about the environment promotes the use of simple adaptive rules.

Huck, Normann and Oechssler

A somewhat similar experiment that preceded that by Nagel and Vriend is that by Huck et al. (1999). They studied four-player Cournot-oligopoly markets under various informational conditions and specified the degree of competition in each of the treatments. Information was varied along two dimensions: first, information about the structure of the market and, second, information about opponents' play and payoffs. The authors report two neat results: first, more information about the market yields less competition (as measured by average output levels) and, second, more information about behaviour and profits of the other players leads to more competition. Under little information (their 'NOIN'-treatment) subjects already perform fairly competitively, which is even amplified when subjects are given feedback on actions and profits of the other players.

Similar to Nagel and Vriend, analysis of individual behaviour was performed on a qualitative level. Under little information subjects accord fairly well to trial-and-error behaviour, that is, subjects continue with expanding or reducing output, if that had led to higher profits in the past, and subjects change direction, if reduction or expansion of output resulted in a reduction of own profits.[5] As one might expect, increasing the information about the market causes an increase in the use of best-response dynamics, and increasing the information on other players' actions and profits increases imitative behaviour.

Even though it is an area theory, Huck et al.'s trial-and-error learning is quite similar to some probabilistic point predicting learning rules that we consider. In fact, in cases where no information on the payoff function is given, their trial-and-error learning process corresponds to the learning direction theory (Selten and Stoecker 1986). And where each player has only two alternative actions available, both theories coincide with the win–stay lose–change dynamics.

Van Huyck, Battalio and Rankin

A study that, at first sight, seems to contradict the analyses above is Van Huyck et al. (2001). They conducted two median coordination games with five players per group. Each game contains only one equilibrium that is stable under the myopic best response dynamic. They also show that the Cross dynamic does not converge to any state within a reasonable number of repetitions and a reasonable set of parameters. Subjects played the same game in fixed groups for 75 periods. After each period, subjects got to know the median choice and their own payoff. So, there was slightly more information provided than what we call 'little information'.

In their experiments, behaviour of the subjects always showed quick convergence to the stable equilibrium. Convergence is not only faster than in the Cross dynamic but sometimes even faster than predicted by the myopic best-response dynamic. Van Huyck et al. are led to conclude that subjects in their experiments formed effective anticipatory beliefs that helped to coordinate more quickly than simple adaptive behaviour. However, we believe that the information about last round's median choice provided subjects with enough information to get an approximate idea of the best-response structure of the game. This was facilitated by the payoff function, which is a smooth quadratic function of the median choice. Moreover, the information about the median choice may have served as a subjective focal point which in this game is always close to the best response.

The failure of the reinforcement models to predict the speed of convergence can easily be attributed to the size of the strategy space. While most learning models had been developed for few alternative actions, the strategy space of Van Huyck et al.'s experiment consisted of 101 alternative actions. Assuming that subjects are able to simplify the strategy space using cognitive maps such as metrics or topologies around prominent numbers, adaptive behaviour is likely to reach stable equilibria more quickly than is shown by the simulations.

Still, Van Huyck et al. report that subjects in their experiment exhibit much noisier behaviour than in a similar experiment with full information about payoff incentives. Unfortunately, the authors do not investigate this aspect further. The studies below show that higher variance of subjects' behaviour under little information is not merely unstructured noise. It shows certain regularities that can be traced further.

Chen and Khoroshilov

Chen and Khoroshilov (2001) use the data from the experiment by Van Huyck et al. and the data from Chen (2000) on average cost-pricing and serial mechanisms for the provision of a public good under limited information. All experimental games involve large strategy spaces. For this reason Chen and Khoroshilov extend known learning models to perform adaptations on whole intervals of the strategy space, instead of applying adaptations only to the action that has been chosen in the last round.[6] The learning models they use are Roth–Erev, Sarin–Vahid, and the modification of Camerer and Ho's (1999) experienced weighted attraction learning (EWA) we presented at the end of Chapter 3.

After estimating the learning models (RE and SV use two parameters, EWA uses three parameters) their predictive success is analysed on a separate data set via a comparison between observed individual actions and one-period ahead predictions. Predictions are implemented through simulations of the probabilistic predictions. The metric that was used was the mean squared deviation (MSD).[7] Their results indicate that the type of game that people are repeatedly playing influences behaviour in a substantial way. While for the data on the serial mechanism and the coordination game one is able to put the learning rules in a unique order of predictive success, neither learning rule is able to predict behaviour significantly better than random choice in the average cost-pricing mechanism. The conclusion one is bound to draw from these observations is that, even when the environment looks equivalent (that is, in all cases the feedback on the own payoff is the most informative piece of information), subjects react differently to the dynamics that were imposed via the structure of the underlying game.

Friedman, Shor, Shenker and Sopher

Based on Chen's (2000) design, Friedman et al. (2000) conducted an elaborate experiment on little information. They initially provided subjects with even less information than we did. In addition to foreclosing the nature of the underlying game, Friedman et al. did not even provide subjects with information about the number of the players involved (including the possibility that they may actually play a single-person decision task), and they allowed for changes in parameters or even in the whole structure of the game without further notice to the subjects. The reason for this design was to investigate the ability of the subjects to adapt to a 'silently' changing environment. In fact, subjects had to, first, play a monopoly situation with parameters changing once after a certain period of time (seven minutes) and, after a further period of time had elapsed, either a Cournot-oligopoly or a serial cost-sharing game had to be played. The parameters of these latter games again changed once during the course of play. In contrast to that, our design abstracts from any problems of structural changes during play, and our subjects are informed of this prior to playing.

Some other features also depart from our setting. Most of these are motivated by the authors' desire to implement a situation that approximates as closely as possible the situation an individual faces when using the Internet. Players were playing in (approximately) continuous time, with varying updating intervals. That is, in the 'asynchronous' treatments, some players were allowed to change strategies more often than other players. Moreover, the strategy space consisted of 101 alternative actions, that is, an almost continuous strategy space that gave rise to considerable search activities on the part of the subjects. Otherwise, feedback after each update interval was limited to the same piece of information as we provide in our experiments, namely one's own payoff from the last round.

Due to the abundance of alternative strategy profiles, the computer programme (that assisted subjects in their decisions) provided a lot of visually processed summary statistics. The most prominent summary statistic was the average past performance of each strategy. In our experiments, since we restricted subjects' strategy space to only two alternative actions, we do not have the need for such potentially biasing tools. As an example of why such helping tools may bias results, consider the finding that in a Cournot-duopoly those subjects who may change their action rather slowly tend to act as Stackelberg-leaders over time. From the point of view of the subjects with larger response frequency, the environment stays fixed for a number of periods, so the provision with aggregate information over alternative strategies steers their focus onto the short-run best response structure.

Likewise, the slower subjects only get information about performance over longer intervals, and so they will make use of the aggregate information, which is readily available on the screen. So, they are led to figure out the long-run best-response. Considering both biases together, behaviour is naturally driven into Stackelberg-leadership.

Friedman et al. also report that, in the monopoly environment, subjects quickly learn to choose the payoff-maximising strategy. Furthermore, sufficient experimentation among strategies ensures that almost all subjects fairly quickly detect the structural change that occurs after seven minutes has elapsed, even though for those who would continue playing the previously payoff-maximising strategy, payoffs would remain constant. In the serial cost-sharing game subjects quickly coordinate on the equilibrium outcome and also quickly detect a structural change that occurs during play. The authors attribute this stability in the cost-sharing game to the fact that the game is solvable not only by iterated deletion of dominated strategies, but also by iterated deletion of overwhelmed strategies.

More interesting for us is Friedman et al.'s (2000) finding on experimentation behaviour. The authors report that 'subjects experiment frequently and in a methodical, autocorrelated fashion' (ibid., p. 16). They even specify typical experimentation patterns, which they call 'arrhythmic heartbeat patterns'. Many subjects tend to deviate substantially from the equilibrium action in small and, over time, evenly scattered intervals of several periods in a row. In order for such exploratory patterns to be detected, one needs a large strategy space in which strategies can be cognitively ordered. In our study, we provide subjects with only two available strategies. We are, hence, unable to record similar heartbeat patters. Yet, we are able to show that in our experiments experimentation behaviour also plays an important role.

Slembeck

A different study on little information is that by Slembeck (1999). He studied the sequential two-player ultimatum game under little information. In a random matching design, subjects had to propose divisions of a pie or to respond to such offers (in fixed roles) over 20 periods. In one treatment the responders were left uninformed about the nature of the game and were foreclosed information about the payoff to the proposer. They were even left uninformed about being involved in a game; so, the environment rather resembled a two-armed bandit, the two arms representing the alternatives to reject or accept the (unknown) offer. Proposers, on the other hand, knew all details of the game.

Slembeck reports two important results. First, the less information the responders are provided with, the lower are the offers by the proposers. Proposers, hence, try to exploit their informational advantage (see also Kagel et al. 1996 and Yang et al. 2001 for similar results). Second, even uninformed responders exhibit positive rejection rates until the end of the 20-round sequel, even though they must have found out that one response most often yields a positive payoff, while the other always yields zero payoff. Just as in Friedman et al. (2000), Slembeck considers experimentation behaviour, which aims at detection of possible structural changes, as one possible explanation for the phenomenon.

NOTES

1. See also Winter (1982) and Vulkan (2000).
2. A more elaborate discussion of the experiment designs in early studies follows in Chapter 5.
3. O'Neill (1987) criticised all psychologists' experiments that preceded his study, on the grounds that foreclosure of information, the lack of monetary incentives and the anonymity among players all promoted behaviour that led to the non-optimising result of probability matching. Using an ingenious design with full information, face-to-face encounter, and a repetition of an asymmetric zero-sum game in which cash was shifted among players after each round, O'Neill showed that subjects accorded to the unique mixed-strategy Nash-equilibrium rather well. Alas, even his analysis was criticised (see Brown and Rosenthal 1990; and O'Neill's 1991 reply).
4. See for example Camerer (1995, pp. 602–4).
5. Huck et al. (1999) refrain from presenting a probabilistic or point-predicting version of their theory. Similar to Selten and Buchta (1999), they state it as an area theory.
6. A more elaborate discussion of this aspect follows in Chapter 9.
7. For a definition and discussion of this measure see Chapter 8.

5.   A Preliminary Experiment[1]

This chapter reports on an experiment that is devoted to elicit general features of learning behaviour of subjects under little information. It is a preliminary study in that it tries to replicate past results from psychology within a setting that conforms to the more rigorous standards of the methodology that is currently applied among experimental economists. Using this new set of data, the purpose will be to investigate primarily the qualitative virtues of the previously very successful RE reinforcement learning scheme. The guiding question will be whether the RE model is able to make good predictions of individual behaviour in a rather favourable setting. As a by-product, we directly compare our results with the results from earlier psychological experiments.

We take one of the simplest possible social games and impose our little-information setting. This setting provides just enough information in order to allow subjects to act according to this learning scheme. For the moment, we do not apply the global-game approach we outlined in Chapter 2. The reason for this is that we first want to replicate past results in a manner that is consistent with today's experimental practice. However, the analysis of this preliminary experiment will make clear that the shape of the whole game environment helps in explaining some of the behavioural phenomena. We thereby introduce the consideration of a global game which will be dealt with extensively in the next chapter.

This chapter starts with the presentation of the game that was implemented in the experiment. We then discuss previous results from psychological experiments. After that, we turn our attention to learning rules and present results from simulations that indicate that reinforcement learning seems to predict different behaviour than had been observed in the earlier studies. Therefore, we also present simulations on an alternative learning scheme (EX) that seems to perform better in accounting for the results.

After explaining the exact experiment design, we present and discuss the data. We see that behaviour in our experiment differs from what has been observed in psychological studies. Furthermore, none of the two proposed learning schemes successfully describes all broad qualitative features of actual behaviour. The general result is that subjects' play is much more complex than can reasonably be traced by simple adaptive learning schemes. For this reason the game of mutual fate control provides an environment in which simple dynamics would lead to efficiency, but subjects are handicapped by the complexity of their own thoughts.

5.1   GAME AND PREDICTIONS

The game that is being used in the following experimental analysis has the property of being one of the simplest conceivable games that allows for a distinction between different learning rules. It is a 2 × 2 game that allows for only two possible values of payoff, 0 or 1. The characteristic of this game is that each subject controls the payoff of the other player. For this reason it is also known as *mutual fate control*. Psychologists are more familiar with this game than are economists, since it served as the basic game representing a *minimal social situation* (see, for example, Thibaut and Kelley 1959), that is, one of the simplest situations in which at least two persons are involved and in which at least one strategy of one player affects the payoff of at least one other player. The players might be unaware of being involved in an interactive situation. However, psychological experiments date back as far as 1981, with the peak of interest having been during the early 1960s. This is why we decided, first, to replicate the experiment in a modern style, using current economic experimental methodology and, second, to describe the game in more detail in the next subsection. We also give a brief survey of the psychological results.

The Game

The game under consideration is an extremely simple 2 × 2 game with payoffs being either 0 or 1. The essence of the game is that each player's payoff is solely determined by the action taken by the opponent. In our simple two-value 2 × 2 version this means that each player decides upon whether to give 0 or 1 to the other player. The according payoff bimatrix is shown in Figure 5.1.

An extension to continuous strategy spaces is straightforward. For three reasons we deliberately chose the simplest version of this game. First, we wanted to avoid possible sampling processes arising from a complex strategy space. Second, the more simple the game is the more likely it is that the underlying structure of the game is quickly revealed by repeated play. Third, using this design we can rule out that subjects sample actions with the aim of identifying the set of possible payoffs. As can easily be seen, under complete information any mixed-strategy profile is a weak Nash-equilibrium, that is, whatever my own (pure or impure) mixed-strategy is, my payoff is solely determined by the action chosen by the other player. Players are, hence, faced with an extreme multitude of equilibria. However, since there is only one efficient cell (which also gives the same payoff to both players) any motivational theory will suggest that individuals will prefer this cell (B,B).[2]

Player 2

		A	B
		0	1
Player 1	A	0	0
		0	1
	B	1	1

Figure 5.1: Mutual fate control

In case players are left uncertain about the payoffs, however, they first have to investigate the underlying payoff structure before being able to coordinate on cell (B,B). Since no information of either actions or payoffs of the opponent is given to the players, coordination has to emerge *silently*, that is, individual calculus does not suffice for coordination, while joint action can lead to efficiency. In the next two subsections we show that both divergence and silent coordination are possible under different individualistic learning rules. But before turning to this analysis, we briefly review earlier psychological literature on this game.

Earlier Results

Psychologists have found strong evidence in favour of successful cooperation (Sidowski et al. 1956; Sidowski 1957; Kelley et al. 1962; Rabinowitz et al. 1966; Arickx and Van Avermaet 1981). The authors report that usually, coordination after 100 rounds of repeated play was reached by approximately 75 per cent. However, they usually did not tell the subjects that they were actually playing a two-person game[3] and, second, incentives were generally non-monetary; instead, electric shocks provided negative payoffs while points (not converted into money) provided positive incentives.

In more detail, Sidowski et al. (1956) first conducted mutual fate control under a free-timing scheme, that is, subjects could choose among strategies at any time they wanted. The result of each choice was immediately forwarded to the opponent. The common observation was that cooperative play rose gradually over time, despite players not being aware of participating in a social environment. Sidowski (1957) replicated this finding.

Experiments by Kelley et al. (1962) showed that the timing scheme seems to be crucial. They found that mutual fate control leads to successful cooperation, if responses are made simultaneously. However, cooperation does not evolve, if responses have to be made in alternating order, that is, the outcome of one player's response is showed to the other player before he/she is allowed to make his/her own choice. Kelley et al. argue that cooperation is the result of a win–stay lose–change learning scheme, which is successful in a simultaneous-move environment (or an environment in which simultaneous moves are frequent), but yields misleading incentives in an alternating-move environment. Furthermore, after analysing individual behaviour Kelley et al. conclude that the win–stay part of the learning scheme is strong while the lose–change part cannot be confirmed. Rabinowitz et al. (1966) report confirming results from similar experiments on mutual fate control and a variant, termed *fate control–behaviour control*, by using a framing in which subjects' choices were presented as predictions of a bivariate random variable and the other players' responses were presented as successes or failures.

From the point of view of today's accepted methodology all experiments suffer from severe shortcomings. First, the early ones gave incentives to opponents to maximise one's own positive payoffs (points), while negative payoffs (electric shocks) were seen as negative stimuli per se. Given the fixed time limit (usually five minutes) and no restrictions on the speed of responses, subjects tended to hit the buttons as often as possible, yielding response frequencies of several hundred times within the time interval of up to five minutes. Second, response frequencies were recorded 'on the fly', that is, every 30 seconds the experimenter had to take down four numbers simultaneously, each number representing the number of hits on one key. At the given response speed this task was certainly lacking accuracy. Third, because of the free-timing scheme it is not credible that subjects were not aware of interacting in a social environment. Subjects must have quickly found out that no random variable was determining their responses but a human person, even more so because, at that time, electronic techniques were not very advanced.

The problem of making subjects believe that they do not interact with other subjects was not solved by introducing simultaneous or alternating moves, because there is no reason to control for the timing of responses other than coordinating responses with responses of other subjects. However, the controlled schemes allowed for more detailed individual analyses and are much closer to today's experimental practice in economics. We basically build on the simultaneous-move experiment by Rabinowitz et al. (1966) with some modifications that make our experiment adhere to current experimental designs in economics. In particular, we do not try to conceal the social interaction. Instead, we tell subjects in advance that they are going to play a two-person game. Furthermore, we give true monetary incentives by paying subjects according to their payoffs gathered during play. Finally, we took great care to make interaction anonymous, so subjects, first, cannot make use of known personal characteristics of their opponent, second, communication during play is not possible and, third, personal attitudes towards their opponent do not play a role.

Predictions of the Roth–Erev (RE) Model

The results from former experiments on the simultaneous-move mutual fate control game are quite favourable for the prediction that eventual cooperation is quite probable. We now check whether the RE scheme yields the same predictions. The RE scheme is probably the most prominent learning scheme that is applicable to the given little-information environment. We also check on the performance of the more general scheme ADR as described in Chapter 3.

We investigate the characteristics of the RE model by using simulations of repeated play when both players keep to this rule. Since the implemented experiment uses 100 repetitions of the game, we accordingly stop simulations after 100 rounds.

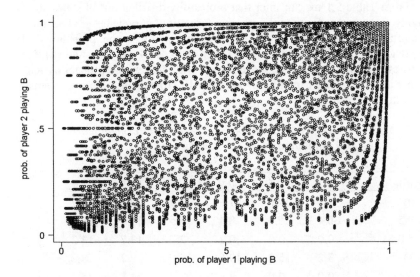

Figure 5.2: Profiles (σ_1^B, σ_2^B) after 100 rounds with RE reinforcement learners

One of the most prominent features of reinforcement learning is the adherence to the *power-law of practice*. Recall from Chapter 1 that this effect states that learning is fast at the beginning of play and gradually diminishes as time proceeds. For our 2×2 game this means that after an initial phase of rapid adjustment, subjects will slowly settle to some mixed-strategy profile. As we see from simulations, this process results in extremely diverse strategy profiles covering almost all of the set of mixed strategies. Figure 5.2 depicts 10 000 profiles resulting from 100 periods of repeated play by reinforcement learners. We set initial propensities equal to 1 for each strategy and each player and the forgetting (or depreciation) parameter[4] $\varphi = 1$. Each dot in the figure represents the probability of either player to play strategy B in the 101st period, (σ_1^B, σ_2^B).

We see that our virtual subjects have a slight tendency either to move to the efficient state $(1,1)$ or to remain near the Pareto-worst state $(0,0)$. However, after 100 rounds behaviour is extremely diverse.[5]

Things change when considering forgetting, that is, when $\varphi < 1$. We summarise our findings from simulations in Table 5.1. For convenience we classify choice probabilities in those with $\sigma^B \approx 0$, $\sigma^B \approx 0.5$, and $\sigma^B \approx 1$, where σ^B denotes the probability to play action B. What cannot be seen from Table 5.1 is that for any value $\varphi < 1$ the classifications are very precise, that is, the virtual subjects eventually converge to either of the classes. For $\varphi = 1$, however, we get the diverse picture as illustrated in Figure 5.2.[6]

From Table 5.1 we can infer that probability distributions of states show highly non-linear dependence on the forgetting parameter φ. The most important characteristics to be observed are (i) that the probability of approaching the efficient state $(1,1)$ never exceeds 33 per cent, and (ii) that profiles in which at least one player mixes with 50 per cent probability look rather unstable. They can only survive after 100 rounds, if forgetting is small enough.

Table 5.1:   Profile classification (per cent) for reinforcement learning: 1000 simulations with 100 rounds each

	φ					
Profile	0.1	0.5	0.9	0.95	0.99	1
(0,0)	3.8	19.0	31.6	27.7	20.9	18.2
(0,0.5)	60.4	35.0	8.4	7.5	15.8	19.0
(0.5,0.5)	0.0	0.0	0.2	2.7	13.7	14.2
(0,1)	3.2	15.9	19.5	15.9	9.7	8.2
(0.5,1)	0.0	0.0	9.6	22.3	24.1	25.3
(1,1)	32.6	30.1	30.7	23.9	15.8	15.1

Simulations on the ADR variant of the reinforcement scheme (see Table 5.2, values for φ, w, and α are taken from Erev and Roth 1996) show that more elaborate reinforcement models are indeed able to predict convergence to the efficient cell. The crucial point, however, is not the size of the weighing parameters but the consideration of an aspiration level[7] and the allowance for the reference point to eventually become large. With forgetting being small (that is, φ near 1) the aspiration level cannot sufficiently quickly adjust upwards from its initial pessimistic value of 0. So, the variable experience of the first rounds determines the final strategy profile of the pair to a large extent. Only when the aspiration level is allowed to rise significantly above 0.5 and propensities are allowed to adjust sufficiently quickly, can payoffs of zero cause the individual to react with increased experimentation behaviour.[8] In this case, the process resembles more the EX process we analyse in the next section and convergence to the efficient cell is predicted to a fairly high degree.

Table 5.2: *Profile classification (per cent) for the ADR model with w = 0.98 and α = 0.5: 1000 simulations with 100 rounds each*

	φ					
profile	*0.1*	*0.5*	*0.9*	*0.95*	*0.99*	*1*
(0,0)	0.0	0.2	0.6	10.7	21.9	20.9
(0,0.5)	5.2	15.2	47.8	28.1	15.3	16.2
(0.5,0.5)	2.5	2.3	0.2	3.5	14.1	13.1
(0,1)	0.0	0.1	3.5	11.8	8.7	7.5
(0.5,1)	0.0	0.6	5.1	18.8	23.8	24.2
(1,1)	92.3	81.6	42.8	27.1	16.2	18.1

Predictions of the Experimentation (EX) Model

We next present results from simulations on the EX model that captures the crucial characteristics of the ADR model in a more compact way. Here, we will deal only with the variant that allows for three levels of probabilistic response. We will see that the EX scheme succeeds in predicting convergence to the efficient cell. Depending on the parameters, convergence may occur to a higher or lower degree.

A very interesting extreme case occurs when the probability of choosing an action after experiencing a full record of positive feedback is $\alpha^{EX} = 1$, that is, experimentation occurs with equal probability until one strategy gets a full record. The crucial property of this learning process is that play among two players eventually converges to the efficient state. The reason for this is simply that random play by both players will never cause both players simultaneously to commit to some pure strategy, unless both players have a record with complete successes. Under the 2×2 mutual fate control game this is only possible if both players have reached the state at which they are playing strategy B with certainty. Furthermore, since probability distributions under non-commitment are assumed to stay fixed over time and to have full support, the outcome (B,B) will eventually occur with probability 1.[9]

By way of illustration we ran simulations with $\alpha^{EX} = 1$ in order to assess the distribution of the probability of convergence over time. Probabilities of convergence strongly depend on the size β^{EX} of memory. Figure 5.3 shows the cumulated distributions of date of convergence. They are composed of 10 000 simulations for each $\beta^{EX} \in \{1,2,3,4\}$.

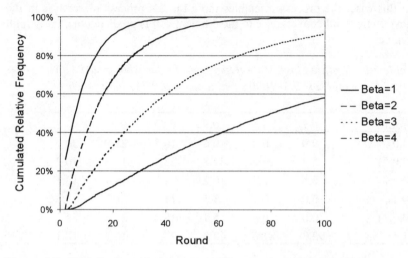

Figure 5.3: Distribution of convergence for experimentation learning

Not surprisingly, the probability of convergence quickly shifts to the later rounds as β^{EX} increases. We will have to bear this in mind when interpreting our data. However, for $\beta^{EX} \leq 3$ convergence until period 100 is quite likely.

After relaxing the parameter of choice probability of successful strategies to values lower than 1, the process no longer exhibits an absorbing state, since there is always a positive probability of a player choosing the unsuccessful strategy over the successful one. However, as long as players have high values for α^{EX} the process will eventually stay in the efficient cell (B,B) most of the time.

5.2   EXPERIMENTAL PROCEDURE

The experiment was conducted in four sessions at the MaxLab.[10] In each session eight to ten subjects, most of them business and economics students at various levels, were randomly allocated to computer terminals, which were separated by mobile cardboard devices. By internal computer assignment, subjects were then randomly matched to pairs. A custom-made computer program, written in Java, helped to make decisions conveniently and to view all information gathered during play. There were 17 pairs (34 subjects) participating in the experiments. Below we describe the information given.

Each pair played 100 repetitions of the stage game shown in Figure 5.1. Players did not receive any fixed amount of money for participation. Instead, their entire payoff was determined during the game. A payoff of 0 lab dollars was converted into 0 Deutschmark and a payoff of 1 lab dollar was converted into 0.30 Deutschmark. Participants were paid at the end of the experimental session, whereby fractions of Deutschmarks were rounded to the next higher integer. So minimum and maximum payoffs that could be earned were 0 Deutschmark and 30 Deutschmarks, respectively. On average subjects earned 18.25 Deutschmarks, whilst a session lasted for 45 to 60 minutes. However, large differences between individual total payoffs indicate that considerable payoff incentives were given. The maximum total payoff was 30 Deutschmarks, while the minimum total payoff was only 2 Deutschmarks.

In contrast to many psychological experiments, we followed the economic convention to inform subjects, before starting to play, about them being involved in a two-person game. We did this mainly in order to avoid uncontrolled beliefs on the part of the subjects about the interaction they were going to participate in. Furthermore, this procedure is consistent with almost all economic experiments. After that, subjects were also told that each participant received the same instructions. In addition, subjects knew about playing a game in a pair with an opponent staying fixed for the entire duration of the experiment. They knew that they would never get any information about their opponent, his or her payoffs, his or her choices, or his or her identity.

The information about the payoff structure of the game was minimal. Subjects were left ignorant about the entries of the payoff matrix. However, the instructions clearly indicated that payoffs were calculated with reference to a payoff table that remained fixed over time. Furthermore, it was common knowledge that payoffs for any strategy combination of a pair could take on either of the two values, 0 or 1.[11]

Without prior announcement, a questionnaire was handed out at the end of each session (but before subjects were paid out) that asked for verbal descriptions of, first, the process (German: 'Verfahren') according to which the participant had chosen his or her actions at the first and the last few rounds, second, the reason for a change in process, if this had occurred and, third, what the subjects believed was the underlying payoff scheme. Subjects were explicitly told that their comments had no effect on their earnings and that the questionnaire was purely meant to serve as additional information for the experimenter on a voluntary basis.

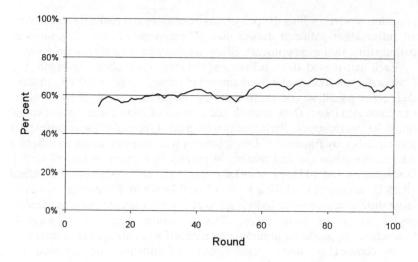

Figure 5.4: Ten-period moving average of rate of B-moves (all players)

5.3   DATA ANALYSIS

Summary Statistics

Average choice frequencies, at first sight, seem to be in line with the former findings of the psychological literature. As Figure 5.4 shows, the ten-period moving average of the rate of *B*-moves shows a slight upward trend over time, while choices obviously contain a large amount of variance. This is confirmed by a simple linear regression of mean choices on time, where the coefficient for the time variable is positive and significant to the 1 per cent level. The rate starts at around 54 per cent and approximates roughly 66 per cent towards the end. Final coordination is not as high as in Kelley et al. (1962), but it is considerably more than the benchmark case of complete randomisation, that is, 50 per cent. So far, it looks like a slow adjustment process and a gradual awareness of the coordination scheme are confirmed by the data. Below, we will see that both conjectures are falsified by the structure of individual play.[12]

We start our more detailed analysis by having a look at the number of pairs that show successful coordination: seven pairs (pairs 2, 3, 9, 10, 13, 16 and 17) eventually coordinate to the efficient cell while ten pairs fail to do so. This is a clear rejection of the hypothesis that people use experimentation learning with high α^{EX} and low memory (that is, $\beta^{EX} \leq 3$).[13] The rate of successful coordination is simply too low. Furthermore, a similar rate of convergence is what has been expected by the basic RE learning model with slight forgetting (that is, $\varphi = 0.9$).

A closer look at those pairs, which eventually coordinate on playing the efficient cell, again draws a different picture. Five of the seven pairs agree on playing the efficient profile (B,B) no later than the ninth round (pairs 2, 9, 10, 13 and 17). One pair starts playing (B,B) as late as round 65 (pair 3), while only one pair shows a gradual adjustment towards the efficient cell. From this, we may infer that a slow adjustment process, as is predicted by reinforcement learning, is not typical of actual play. Having another look at the one pair that converges rather late in the game we find that a subtle harmony of choices, assumedly born out of pure chance, preceded coordination. The sequence of actions from round 58 to 65 was (B,A), (A,A), (A,A), (B,B), (A,A), (B,B), (A,A), (B,B), on which (B,B) followed thereafter. And even in pair 16 which does not show any explicit point of coordination, B-play seems to have come up rather suddenly. This can be seen from Figure 5.5 which shows the empirical frequencies of choices as a moving average of ten rounds for each player. Hence, in case pairs do coordinate, we find hardly any evidence for slow adjustment behaviour as is predicted by reinforcement learning.

In fact, slow adjustment cannot be found in those pairs that did not converge. As can be seen from Figure 5.5, behaviour is rather volatile over time, within subjects and across subjects. Furthermore, for eight out of the ten pairs that do not coordinate to the efficient outcome, empirical frequencies over all periods show a tendency towards equal frequency for either strategy. This is contrary to what we observed in our simulations on reinforcement learning in the section above.

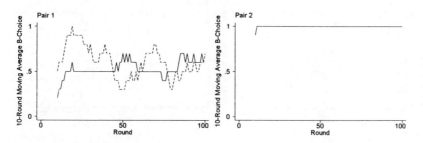

Figure 5.5a: Individual ten-round moving averages of B-frequencies (pairs 1 to 2)

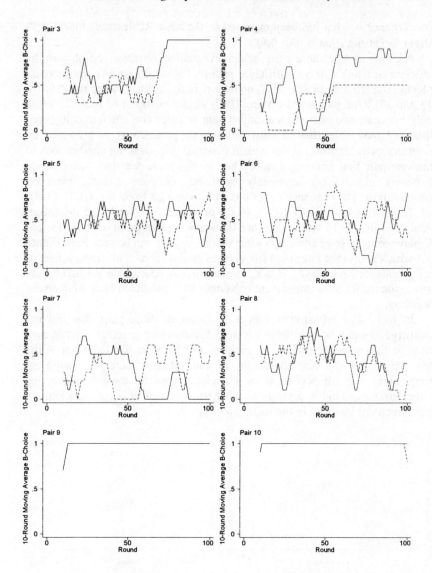

*Figure 5.5b: Individual ten-round moving averages of B-frequencies
(pairs 3 to 10)*

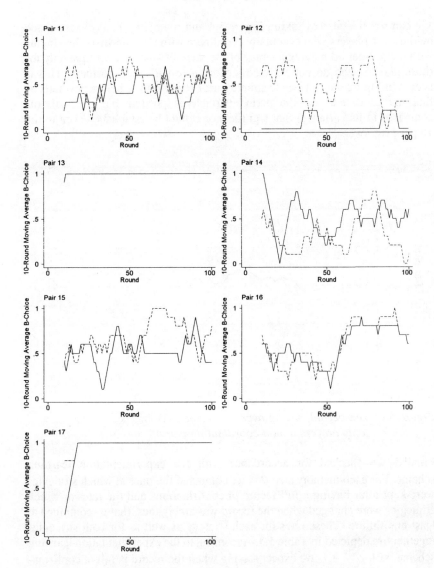

Figure 5.5c: Individual ten-round moving averages of B-*frequencies
              (pairs 11 to 17)*

We can see this also by taking Figure 5.4 and removing the decisions made by those 14 players who eventually coordinate with their partners, leaving us with the ten-period moving average of the rate of *B*-moves over time only for those players who do not eventually coordinate with their partners. This is shown in Figure 5.6. The same simple linear regression as before now tells us that the coefficient for the period variable is positive but so small (as compared to its variance) that significance cannot be established even to the 10 per cent level.

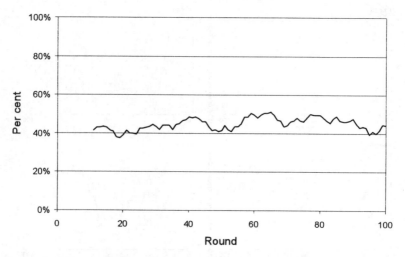

Figure 5.6: Ten-period moving average of rate of B-moves
(only players in non-coordinating pairs)

Finally, we checked for accordance with the experimentation learning scheme. For each memory size β^{EX} we computed the rates at which strategies were kept after having a full record of confirmations and the rates at which strategies were changed when the record was ambiguous, that is, contained at least one failure. These rates for each strategy as well as for both strategies together are depicted in Table 5.3. According to the experimentation learning scheme with $\alpha^{EX} = 1$, we expect staying when the record is full of confirmations to occur with probability 1 and changing when the record is ambiguous to occur with probability 0.5. Note that for $\beta^{EX} = 1$ we can directly compare behaviour with the win–stay lose–change strategy (WSLC) which has, as yet, been proposed to account best for behaviour in the mutual fate control game (see Kelley et al. 1962; Rabinowitz et al. 1966). As in the experimental learning scheme, the WSLC scheme would predict a win–stay rate of 1. However, the lose–change rate would also be predicted to be 1.

Table 5.3: Accordance with response dynamics of experimentation learning (averages over all subjects in non-coordinating pairs)

Dynamic	Response	$\beta^{EX}=1$	$\beta^{EX}=2$	$\beta^{EX}=3$	$\beta^{EX}=4$
Full record-stay rate	Both	0.63	0.63	0.57	0.54
Ambiguous record-change rate	Both	0.42	0.40	0.40	0.40
Full record-stay rate	A	0.65	0.65	0.60	0.62
Full record-stay rate	B	0.47	0.52	0.44	0.29
Ambiguous record-change rate	A	0.42	0.41	0.40	0.40
Ambiguous record-change rate	B	0.45	0.44	0.44	0.44

From the figures for both responses taken together we clearly see that players are far from being in according with experimentation learning. Best approximation is reached for $\beta^{EX} = 1$ and $\beta^{EX} = 2$, while higher values of β^{EX} seem to predict even worse. In line with earlier observations, we find that staying with a strategy after it has been confirmed is much more likely than changing one's strategy after failure. However, contrary to former studies, changing after failure occurs with considerably lower frequency than 0.5, which is a complete rejection of the lose–change prediction and is even significantly lower than predicted by random play.[14] Furthermore, for $\beta^{EX} = 1$ and $\beta^{EX} = 2$, the sum of the first two rows only marginally exceeds 1 which indicates that staying and changing behaviour is almost independent of whether the strategy's record is confirmatory or not. We conclude that our subjects show a significant amount of inertia, but the amount of inertia is almost independent of whether strategies have a confirmatory record or not.

Looking at the data for each action separately, we see that, ironically, a confirmatory record for action A causes subjects to stay with larger probability than a confirmatory record does for action B. We have no account for this observation. The sudden drop of the rate of staying when the record is full at strategy B is due to few observations.[15]

The discouraging results from Table 5.3 stand in sharp contrast to results from earlier studies in which the WSLC strategy was put forward to account for observed behaviour. Rabinowitz et al. (1966) showed that in their experiment, as time proceeds, subjects increasingly accord to win–stay and to lose–change. We recalculated their table 2 with our own data and found no such adjustment behaviour (Table 5.4).

In fact, rather the opposite can be found. All categories show a downward trend from the first half to the second half of the experiment, though some trends are only small in size. We may, hence, conclude that gradual adjustment to the WSLC rule can neither be observed. However, we have no account for the general trend to move away from both the win–stay part and the lose–change part of the strategy.

Table 5.4:   Rates of accordance to win–stay lose–change strategy (averages over all subjects in non-coordinating pairs)

		Rounds	
Tendency	Response	2–50	51–100
Win–stay	Both	0.62	0.57
Lose–change	Both	0.42	0.38
Win–stay	A	0.68	0.63
Win–stay	B	0.55	0.52
Lose–change	A	0.39	0.38
Lose–change	B	0.47	0.38

Using maximum-likelihood estimation we calculated the best-fitting parameters for both learning schemes, the RE scheme and the EX scheme (Tables 5.5 and 5.6). We did separate analyses for the full set of pairs and only for those pairs that do not converge. We estimated the learning schemes over all 100 rounds.

Table 5.5:   Maximum-likelihood estimation for RE

	All pairs		
Restrictions	$u^A(1) = u^B(1) = 1$	$u^A(1) = u^B(1)$	None
$u^A(1)$			1.53
$u^B(1)$		1.97	2.43
φ	0.984	0.976	0.977
−2 LL	3361.9	3345.8	3328.4
	Non-converging pairs		
Restrictions	$u^A(1) = u^B(1) = 1$	$u^A(1) = u^B(1)$	None
$u^A(1)$			8.32
$u^B(1)$		6.92	7.50
φ	1.003	0.984	0.983
−2 LL	2688.5	2626.2	2625.0

The analysis shows for the reinforcement learning scheme that – taking all pairs into account – we get results very close to our initial assumptions, that is, $u^A(1)$ and $u^B(1)$ at approximately 1 and φ very near 1, allowing for only 2 to 2.5 per cent forgetting. Exclusion of the converging pairs yields similar values for φ but much higher values for the initialisation parameters. This is plausible since higher initial propensities mean more variation of play. Consequently, fixing the initial parameter at 1 yields an implausible value for φ. Not surprisingly, if considering all pairs and initial propensities are kept equal, then we suffer a significant loss of explanatory power. The propensity of B naturally is much larger than the one of A. Interestingly, when excluding the converging pairs this restriction does not have a significant impact. This is one more piece of evidence in favour of the hypothesis that those subjects who do not coordinate with their partners have no systematic tendency towards either of the actions.

For the experimentation learning we first find that when excluding the converging pairs $\beta^{EX} = 1$ again fits the data best. The small values for β^{EX} indicate that the win–stay part of the strategy is not very pronounced. Considering all pairs, values for β^{EX} are naturally much higher, since at the point of convergence the win–stay part is fully met. As for the performance, it might seem surprising that $\beta^{EX} = 4$ is best and most probably higher values for β^{EX} would yield even better results. The reason is simply that, because of the value for β^{EX} being predicted much higher, those strategies perform better which allow for more random play in pairs that do not converge.

Table 5.6: Maximum likelihood estimation for EX

	All pairs		
β^{EX}	1	2	3	4
α^{EX}	0.83	0.84	0.90	0.92
-2LL	3732.3	3798.9	3697.7	3657.8
	Non-converging pairs		
β^{EX}	1	2	3	4
α^{EX}	0.64	0.60	0.60	0.57
-2LL	2707.3	2746.5	2759.6	2768.7

A comparison between the two learning schemes shows that we can add this study to the list of those that favour the RE model. In order to put the comparison on equal footing we compare the best likelihood value from the experimentation learning scheme with the likelihood value for the one-parameter reinforcement model. This shows that for both categories the reinforcement model performs much better than the experimentation learning scheme. This is so even though the experimentation learning scheme has the advantage of one more discrete variable (namely β^{EX}). However, we have to point at two drawbacks of such a comparison. First, a straightforward comparison of likelihoods is only one of several possible ways to assess the relative goodness-of-fit (see Chapter 8 for a detailed discussion). Second, qualitative features force us to say that none of the algorithms does a particularly good job.[16]

Game Space

One may argue that, since people do not know which game they are actually going to play, they will simply imagine one and start playing according to that game. However, this does not cause trouble to our interpretations of subjects' play, because, given subjects' prior information, there are only four games that can possibly occur. In particular, if one writes down all 256 possible 2 × 2 games resulting from payoffs that can take either value 0 or 1 and subsequently eliminates all games that involve a weakly dominated strategy for at least one player, then one is left with the following four games: (i) the matching pennies game, (ii) the symmetric coordination game, (iii) our mutual fate control game, and (iv) fate control–behaviour control,[17] in which, for one player, giving is identified with one action and the other player's giving action depends on the action chosen by the first player. For all cases experimentation learning (EX) eventually leads either to behaviour almost indistinguishable from the unique mixed-strategy Nash-equilibrium or to an outcome that maximizes both individual as well as joint payoffs.

Furthermore, the only game not containing the prospect of eventual coordination is the game of matching pennies.[18] In Chapter 4, we reported on the experimental analysis by Mookherjee and Sopher (1994), who conducted this game under little information. They found little evidence for deliberate mixing behaviour. We investigated whether subjects in our experiment exhibited similar patterns of behaviour.

We first checked for the consistency of mixing between the two strategies. Assuming that, in the first periods, subjects learn about their environment and, after a sufficient amount of time, they converge to a more or less stable mixed strategy, we expect to observe a mix of strategies that conforms to an independent and identically distributed (i.i.d.) play. Taking the observed rate of occurrence of strategy B to be the approximation to the probability of playing B, one can conduct a Wald–Wolfowitz One-Sample Runs test to check whether the number of runs (that is, the number of sequences in which the same action has been played) is similar to the expected number of runs under the i.i.d. hypothesis. We perform this test for the last 40 rounds of each subject and exclude subjects of pairs that do coordinate. The results are shown in Table 5.7.

As can be seen, for eight out of 20 subjects the i.i.d. hypothesis can be rejected to the 10 per cent level. For the 5 per cent level the number of rejections is still six out of 20. This is in line with what Mookherjee and Sopher (1994) have found for their low-information treatment. In our study five out of eight rejections are based on too few runs, which is not an immediate indicator for some sort of inertia in subject's play. But, two of the rejections that are caused by too many runs (players 8 and 27) are due to the players obviously alternating between the two strategies. For further analysis of inertia in subject's play we have to look at the individual dynamics.

Table 5.7: Wald–Wolfowitz One-Sample Runs test for last 40 periods

Player	Freq. B	No. of runs	Exp. no. of runs	p-value
1	22	27	20.80	0.05 *
2	23	19	20.55	0.63
7	33	15	12.55	0.30
8	20	40	21.00	0.00 **
9	21	19	20.95	0.63
10	21	20	20.95	0.88
11	18	11	20.80	0.00 **
12	19	19	20.95	0.63
13	3	3	6.55	0.00 **
14	19	7	20.95	0.00 **
15	13	19	18.55	1.00
16	11	14	16.95	0.30
21	18	17	20.80	0.26
22	21	26	20.95	0.11
23	2	3	4.80	0.05 *
24	17	11	20.55	0.00 **
27	21	27	20.95	0.04 **
28	16	8	20.20	1.00
29	22	13	20.80	1.00
30	32	9	13.80	0.99

Notes: * 10 per cent significance; ** 5 per cent significance.

For this purpose we follow Mookherjee and Sopher (1994) and adopt the concept of vindication of strategies, which is close to the MS scheme described in Chapter 3. According to them, a strategy is vindicated whenever either, it has been chosen and yielded a success, or, the alternative strategy has been chosen and yielded a failure. For the following, we denote the strategy chosen by player i at time t again by $a_i(t)$ and the resulting payoff by $\pi_i(t)$. The vindication of player i's strategy 1 will be denoted by $v_i(t)$, thus,

$$v_i(t) = \begin{cases} 1 & if \ [(a_i(t)=1) \wedge (\pi_i(t)=1)] \vee [(a_i(t)=0) \wedge (\pi_i(t)=0)] \\ 0 & otherwise \end{cases} \quad (5.1)$$

Mookherjee and Sopher now use a logistic regression to analyse the impact of own lagged actions and lagged vindication of action B (up to four periods before the current period) on the probability to choose action B, the rewarding strategy. Table 5.8 shows the coefficients of the respective regressands and the corresponding p-values. For obvious reasons we excluded pairs that eventually coordinate on the efficient outcome.

Table 5.8: Logistic regression on probability of choosing strategy B for last 40 rounds

	Coefficient	p-value
Constant	−1.26	0.00
$a(t-1)$	0.80	0.00
$a(t-2)$	0.52	0.00
$a(t-3)$	−0.27	0.01
$a(t-4)$	0.69	0.00
$v(t-1)$	0.04	0.73
$v(t-2)$	0.31	0.00
$v(t-3)$	−0.37	0.00
$v(t-4)$	0.57	0.00

Notes: $n = 1920$; $\chi^2(8) = 198.74$; $p = 0.00$.

Large positive coefficients and strong significance for the one- and two-period lagged own choices signify a strong tendency towards inertia. However, three-lagged own choices are significantly negative. Furthermore, vindication is not immediately responded to as can be seen from the insignificant coefficient for the one-period lagged vindication. Former vindication, however, does have a significant impact, though with alternating sign. We conclude that subjects exhibit a significant amount of inertia and respond variably to the vindication of the rewarding strategy. We also find positive auto-correlation of subject's choices. In this respect behaviour differs from mainly negatively autocorrelated choices in the matching-pennies game. However, the volatile response to vindication is a similarity found in both games within the setting of little information. Neither the RE scheme nor the EX scheme can account for this latter observation.

Individual Patterns

Under little information it is likely that subjects exhibit varying strategies in order to explore their environment. Furthermore, the task looks similar to playing a two-armed bandit, so it is likely that subjects use individual exploration strategies before playing a certain action. As noted earlier, some of the subjects deliberately chose to play certain patterns. In Table 5.9 we give an overview of broad characteristics of the subjects.

Table 5.9: Characteristics of subjects' play

No.	Characteristic
1	Alternating play in rounds 11 to 48 and 50 to 73
2	Some long sequences of the same action until round 45, no pattern thereafter
3	Coordination starting in round 2
4	Coordination starting in round 2
5	Alternating play in rounds 32 to 45, coordination starting in round 65
6	Coordination starting in round 65
7	Many long sequences of the same action, in later rounds more sequences of Bs
8	Sequence of As in rounds 6 to 30, alternating play from round 46 onwards
9	No specific pattern
10	A few short sequences of small patterns like ($AABBAA$) or (ABA)
11	Some long sequences of the same action at the beginning and towards the end, alternating play in rounds 46 to 60
12	No specific pattern
13	Very long sequences of the same strategy at the beginning and during the whole second half, alternating play in rounds 18 to 40
14	Many long sequences of the same action throughout
15	Less changes than predicted by independent draws, though no specific pattern
16	One larger sequence of As towards the end, otherwise no specific pattern
17	Coordination starting at round 4
18	Coordination starting at round 4
19	Coordination starting at round 2
20	Coordination starting at round 2, deviation in the last 2 rounds
21	Less changes than predicted by independent draws, though no specific pattern, more changes towards the end
22	No specific pattern
23	Almost always As
24	Many long sequences of the same action
25	Coordination starting in round 2
26	Coordination starting in round 2
27	Less changes than predicted by independent draws, though no specific pattern, more changes towards the end

No.	Characteristic
28	Many long sequences of the same action
29	No specific pattern
30	Some alternation patterns in the intermediate term, rather long sequences towards the end
31	No pattern at the beginning, almost always *B*s starting in round 53
32	No pattern at the beginning, almost always *B*s starting in round 53
33	Coordination starting in round 9
34	Coordination starting in round 9

As can be seen from Table 5.9, only four out of the 20 subjects that do not succeed in coordinating with their partner do not show any sign of inertia or a deliberate application of a dynamic pattern. In the post-experimental questionnaire many of them explicitly mentioned the purpose to be an exploration of their environment. The most popular patterns are long sequences of the same strategy (ten subjects) and the alternation between the two strategies (six subjects). There is very little evidence in favour of gradual adjustment towards action B. Only one subject (player 7) can be categorised in this class. Players 31 and 32 (constituting the coordinating pair 16) rather suddenly switch to almost always play B.

Most striking is the persistent play of action A by player 23. This subject obviously was not willing to deviate from his favourite action even after long sequences of non-rewarding feedback. Only twice did the subject feel driven to play action B for two times before falling back to play A. In the questionnaire this subject wrote: 'Although I always tried to choose the same strategy I did not succeed in always getting a payoff of 1; possibly because the other [player] misinterpreted the situation and chose this and that' (translated from German; insertion by the author). The remark clearly indicates that this person had a pure coordination game in mind and did not think of any other possible payoff scheme. In fact, five out of the 20 subjects who did not coordinate with their partner stated that they had the impression they were playing a coordination game. Most of the remaining 15 players stated that they did not have a clue as to what the payoff matrix must have looked like or indicated a repeating multi-period scheme that should have given them the desired payoff of 1, despite our care to indicate in the instruction sheet that payoffs only depended on the decisions of the stage game.

It seems that within an environment with little information, subjects are tempted to believe they are involved in a single-person experiment or to focus on a coordination task. However, none of these beliefs justifies the renunciation of the EX scheme.

5.4   SUMMARY

We summarise our findings as follows. In our 40-round experiment on mutual fate control under little information we could observe little coordination, and convergence appeared to be triggered by extreme chance events. Moreover, compliance with simple dynamics, such as the win–stay lose–change scheme, cannot be found. Our impression is that even the simultaneous-move environment that Kelley et al. (1962) consider as particularly favourable for coordination is still not sufficient to enforce this learning dynamic. There are two events that have to coincide in order to trigger coordination. First, both players have to choose *B* simultaneously and, second, none of the players deviates in the next interaction. If one player deviates, an immediate vindication of *A* follows. Without a device that coordinates timing this task seems to be difficult to accomplish. Furthermore, the more flexible EX scheme leads to the desired result, only if we may expect the partner to accord to this dynamic, too. As we have seen from the data, there is good reason for subjects to doubt this.

Generally, the results are unfavourable for all learning schemes presented so far. Convergence to the efficient outcome is much slower than can reasonably be traced by the experimentation learning scheme. The basic win–stay lose–change scheme is not accorded to, either. Furthermore, subjects do not show any sign of slow adjustment behaviour. Rather, subjects seem to follow an exploratory scheme, much in the way Kalai and Lehrer (1995) describe it by using the concept of the environment response function. Subjects use different multi-period patterns in order to explore the response of their individual environment. However, Table 5.9 clearly shows that they obviously do not conform to any simple dynamics and stick to complex exploration schemes, even if these do not lead to a significant improvement in payoff. Hence, mutual fate control provides an environment in which subjects' behaviour is more complex than it should be. Such behaviour results in avoidable inefficiencies.

We have seen that to withhold any information on the payoff scheme generally deprives subjects of the ability systematically to coordinate on the efficient cell, even though, theoretically, there exists a simple learning scheme that does the job. Had subjects known the payoff matrix, without doubt they would have coordinated instantly. Hence, there must be a certain amount of information in between that just suffices for people to coordinate, which is the subject of Chapter 7. But before turning to this topic Chapter 6 will be concerned with two further questions. First, does the way the environment is presented to the players influence behaviour and the ability to coordinate? This question is investigated by transforming the foreclosure of the game into a probability distribution over a set of games, that is, into a global game. Second, does experience enhance the ability to coordinate? We check this by letting subjects repeat the whole repeated game. As a by-product we further investigate the ability of all learning rules that were introduced in Chapter 3 to account for observed behaviour.

NOTES

1.   This chapter is based on Mitropoulos (2001a). Permission by Elsevier to reprint the contents is gratefully acknowledged.
2.   However, different motivational theories might tell a different story. Theories based on intentions (see Rabin 1993; Dufwenberg and Kirchsteiger 1998; Falk and Fischbacher 2000) say that, to assume the goodwill of the other player and, at the same time, to give a point to the other player is an equilibrium in positively reciprocal intentions. Theories of inequality aversion (see Fehr and Schmidt 1999; Bolton and Ockenfels 2000) predict that players' utility is always maximised when one's own payoff is maximal and the allocation assigns equal payoff to all players (fairness). The only theory allowing for alternative actions when there is a single mutually payoff-maximising, efficient and fair outcome is the theory of spite (Levine 1998). However, we consider it as highly improbable that people exhibit so much spite as to deliberately harm the opponent without any positive return from such an action. Note also that in mutual fate control coordination coincides with cooperation.
3.   So subjects had the idea of playing against a two-armed bandit.
4.   Note that, in this chapter, in order to incorporate the ADR process we will use the conventional names of parameters (that is, φ, w, α, and so on).
5.   Due to the power-law of practice simulations with a longer time horizon reveal the same diverse picture. See Mitropoulos (2000) for more details.
6.   For the case $\varphi = 1$ it is important to know that the boundaries of the classes were defined at 0, 0.33, 0.67, and 1.
7.   Indeed, the results are fairly stable against variations of w and α.
8.   Starting with an optimistic aspiration level, that is, $\rho(1) = 1$, causes experimentation after zero-payoffs to start immediately and the process converges even for rather high values of φ.
9.   From the point of view of Markov chains the argument is that the state, at which both players have a full success record for strategy B, is the only absorbing state of the game.
10.   The Magdeburg Experimental Laboratory, Germany.
11.   Instructions are given in Appendix A.
12.   For the raw data, see Appendix B.
13.   In their corresponding treatment Rabinowitz et al. (1966) find less complete coordination. The number of coordinating pairs was 3 out of 19. However, in a slightly different experiment Kelley et al. (1962) had coordination rates similar to ours, namely 11 out of 30 pairs in a first experiment and 12 out of 22 pairs in a second experiment.
14.   The detailed analysis runs as follows: for each player participating in a non-converging pair we use the binomial test to determine whether the lose–change decision is (to the 5 per cent level) significantly lower or higher than 0.5. For those players showing significance we find that seven players change less often

than 0.5 and two players change more often than 0.5. According to the binomial test this distribution is (to the 5 per cent level) significantly biased towards lower frequencies than 0.5.

15. A detailed table on an individual level is given in Appendix C.
16. We also did simulations and maximum likelihood estimations for the REL scheme and the SV scheme. The results are not much better. The REL scheme shares the problem of slow adjustment towards the efficient cell, which is regularly counterbalanced by reinforcement of the wrong action, and the scheme by Sarin and Vahid simply predicts small adjustment of the reference point with small variation in subjects' play for coordinating pairs and large adjustment of the reference point with large variation in subjects' play for the non-coordinating pairs. While the two-parameter REL model performs approximately as well as the original one-parameter reinforcement learning our two-parameter variant of SV does even worse.
17. For a more detailed description of fate control–behaviour control, see for example Arickx and van Avermaet (1981) or Chapter 6 in this volume.
18. Note that the crucial difference in dynamics between mutual fate control and matching pennies lies in the impact of opponent's play. In matching pennies the opponent's action determines which of my own actions is vindicated and which is refuted, while in mutual fate control the opponent's action determines whether my currently active action is vindicated or refuted.

6.   The Global-Game Experiment[1]

In the previous chapter we argued that the inability of subjects to figure out the whole set of possible games may considerably complicate coordination tasks for a purely technical reason. Subjects may not be able to work out the whole set of potential games and might focus on one or a few types of games. And the game which they are actually playing may not enter their minds. Thus, when subjects fail to coordinate in the repeated mutual fate control game, we are unable to attribute this to misled beliefs or to inefficient choice among adaptive rules.

Since the topic of this book is learning behaviour and not the construction of beliefs, we would like to fix beliefs about the set of possible games and to allow the unrestricted choice among decision rules. We achieve this by thoroughly introducing the set of possible games and thus depart from previous studies in that we do not simply foreclose information on the underlying payoff scheme.[2]

We extend the previous design along one more dimension. We allow subjects to gather experience with the learning task. That is, pairs of subjects will play a certain randomly assigned game for a fixed number of periods and will repeat this task with a different randomly assigned game and a different randomly assigned opponent. Such a within-subject replication of the learning task (also called *supergame*) has, as yet, rarely been investigated in experimental economics.[3]

Otherwise, the experimental setting remains in the general line of research. In particular, just as in most previous studies on little information, a simple learning rule – if applied by all players simultaneously – would lead players to an optimal solution. Moreover, groups will again consist of only two players. So, from the point of view of the number of interacting players, the learning task is kept rather simple.

This chapter, however, also differs from most previous studies in its methodological approach to the study of behaviour. We focus on the identification of structural characteristics within subjects' play and refrain from ranking theories on purely quantitative grounds, such as the mean squared deviation or the log-likelihood of predictions.[4] We will use estimation results only for the purpose of tracking behavioural changes as experience with the task rises.

Our main focus will rest on the coordination task which subjects have to solve within three of the four possible games. In Section 6.1 we discuss the set of possible games and show that a simple learning rule (that is, win–stay lose–randomise) is able to achieve almost complete efficiency. We take this result as our benchmark. Section 6.2 is devoted to presenting the experimental design while Section 6.3 contains the general data analysis. As it turns out, compared with the benchmark, subjects in our experiments suffer a considerable amount of loss of efficiency. They earn up to 30 per cent less than the benchmark payoff. We find the main determinant to be whether subjects succeed in coordinating or not. Since we allowed subjects to repeat the 40-round repeated game with randomly assigned opponents and games, we further investigate for an experience effect and, indeed, we find such an effect: as subjects repeat the learning task they obviously succeed in coordinating more quickly, even though the number of successfully coordinating pairs does not increase.

In search of the reason for the improved speed of coordination, we analyse the nine parameterised learning rules which we introduced in Chapter 3. The characteristics of all rules are shown by way of expected motion as well as simulations. We then compare the dynamics with the actual data. We further fit the learning models to individual as well as aggregated data. The discouraging result from our efforts is that none of the rules is able to capture any effect that might be due to experience. Finally, we show one reason for the failure of all rules to uncover important determinants of behaviour: while adaptive rules always focus on round-by-round adaptation, we show that subjects make frequent use of multi-round patterns.

6.1 THE GAMES

Let us, first, reconsider how little information is perceived from the point of view of the subjects that play an unknown repeated game. Imagine subjects not being told which repeated game they are actually going to play. A Bayesian approach would be, first, to collect the given constraints and, subsequently, to derive the complete set of possible games. Having determined this set, one is able to construct one's own optimal strategy in much the same way as should be done under complete knowledge of the game, the only difference being in the consideration of a distribution of games instead of only one game.

A typical situation of Knightian uncertainty,[5] however, is that of a subject not having a clue as to what the underlying game is. The game is only revealed gradually by actually playing the game repeatedly. The usual way of implementing such a situation is the one we used in the experiment we reported in the preceding chapter, that is, we simply withhold the actual payoff matrix. We argue that the drawback of this approach is that beliefs of subjects about the set of possible games may vary and may substantially influence behaviour.

Experimental research on decision-making under risk and uncertainty has tackled this problem long ago. As mentioned in Chapter 2, risk has usually been modelled by way of providing subjects with a probability distribution over the set of possible states of nature, while uncertainty has typically been modelled by providing subjects with a probability distribution over probability distributions over the set of possible states. Camerer and Weber (1992) call this the *second order probability distribution.*[6]

We, therefore, choose to give subjects a complete characterisation of the distribution of possible games while keeping the situation as close as possible to that of Knightian uncertainty about the underlying payoff matrix. Our instructions are almost equivalent to saying that the payoff matrix may be any, the only restriction being that payoffs take values of either 0 or 1. As has been argued in the previous chapter we may select all those two-player, two-action normal-form games that contain only the values 0 or 1 and do not involve a weakly dominated strategy for either player. What we are left with is a set of 12 different payoff matrices, which, due to some matrices being structurally the same as others (the sole difference lying in the permutation of labels), leaves us with four structurally different payoff matrices, which we subsequently call stage games and which we now describe in more detail.

For convenience we redraw mutual fate control (henceforth MFC) in Figuer 6.1. The game represents the situation in which each player's action determines the payoff of the opponent.

Figure 6.1:   Mutual fate control

Recall that this game contains a continuum of Nash-equilibria. In particular, every mixed-strategy profile of the players constitutes a Nash-equilibrium. However, cell (*B,B*) is the only cell that allows for mutual payoff maximisation. The experiment reported in the previous chapter showed that, under little information, pairs of players may have considerable difficulties in coordinating on this cell.

The next game, fate–control behaviour–control (FCBC), is in a way very similar to MFC. Again the actions of both players determine the payoff of the opponent. In FCBC, however, the action with which one player (in Figure 6.2 it is player 2) gives the payoff to the opponent is determined by the action of the opponent. So, one player has some influence on his or her own payoff while the other one has not.

		Player 2	
		A	B
Player 1	A	1 0	0 0
	B	0 1	1 1

Figure 6.2: Fate–control behaviour–control

As similar as MFC and FCBC look from the point of view of the stage games, they are different from the dynamical point of view. The simple rule of win–stay lose–change illustrates this point. Given that both players fully accord to the win–stay lose–change rule, in MFC the pair will converge to the efficient cell within two rounds and stay there for ever, no matter where the starting point lies. This is different in FCBC. After starting in the efficient cell, players will stay with their actions forever. If starting in any other of the three remaining cells, players will be involved in an endless cycle. In order to avoid the inefficient cycling a substitution of the lose–change part, for example into a lose–randomise behaviour would be advisable. We will return to this point later in the text when studying efficiency and the adaptation behaviour of the subjects.

		Player 2	
		A	B
Player 1	A	1 1	0 0
	B	0 0	1 1

Figure 6.3: Coordination game

In the coordination game (CO) players have mutual interest to coordinate on one or the other combination of actions in order to yield the efficient outcome. In case they do not succeed to coordinate they both get a payoff of zero. Schelling (1960, pp. 53–8) and Mehta et al. (1994) have played this game before. However, their setting, and thus their primary interest in this game, was different from ours. They used the frame of a coin to implement this game as a one-shot interaction. Subjects had to write down either 'head' or 'tail' on a sheet of paper and were rewarded only if both players stated the same word. These experiments differed from our implementation of the pure coordination game in two respects. First, they did not play this game repeatedly, either in groups with random matching or as a two-player repeated game. Second, the two alternative actions were deliberately labelled with names having common connotation. The point of study was whether one or other of the two labels shared particular salience[7] within the group of people among which the subjects were chosen. On the contrary, in our study we allow for the case that labels had different meanings, so that it is not clear from the beginning whether subjects are rewarded for choosing the same labels or for choosing opposite labels.

Still, this game looks more or less trivial. We choose to include it in our set of games, because, in the debriefing of our preliminary experiment (see the previous chapter) some of the participants clearly indicated that they assumed this game to have been the underlying game. Later we will see that a non-trivial number of pairs did not reach coordination until the end, which suggests that, given little information, CO is not as trivial a game as it seems.

Figure 6.4: Matching pennies

The matching-pennies game (MP) has earlier been studied by Mookherjee and Sopher (1994) and Ochs (1995). It is the constant-sum game in which each action allows for both winning and losing. Game theory implies that subjects will end up playing each strategy with equal probability. However, players have no positive incentive to do so. Instead, giving equal probability to both strategies is the sole mixed strategy that impedes exploitation.[8] Because of this, it is far from obvious that subjects will accord with the Nash-equilibrium. Recall that the analysis by Mookherjee and Sopher (1994) showed that subjects approximate the Nash-equilibrium fairly closely when being informed about the game, but do not conform to stochastic play when left ignorant about the payoff matrix. Ochs (1995) further investigated play under complete information and found that, even when knowing the payoff matrix and when being allowed to issue mixed strategies, the accordance with the Nash-equilibrium in the MP game is mainly due to the extreme symmetry of the game.

The distribution over the four games placed equal probability on each of them. Given the game, the distribution placed equal probability on each of the payoff matrices belonging to each game. Subjects were not informed of which player position (player 1 or player 2) they were assigned. This was again determined via a random draw giving equal probability to each position.

In the previous chapter we indicated briefly that, despite the simplicity of the games the environment is comprised of and despite subjects repeatedly playing in fixed pairs, the task is not at all easy. Coordination in the first three games is beneficial but, in order to coordinate, there is a need to extract valuable information from the feedback provided. Payoffs, however, can take on values of only 0 or 1, and, since in each game for each player and each strategy both values are possible, feedback does not immediately help in reducing the set of possible games. Valuable information can only be gathered by interpreting the dynamics of the payoffs received. Subjects' strategies, thus, have to take into account the informational problems of their opponents. As a consequence, successful coordination in the first three games can only be achieved by a harmonisation of dynamic choice.

6.2   EXPERIMENTAL PROCEDURE

We again conducted the experiment at the MaxLab. In each session ten subjects – most of them first-year business and economics students – were randomly allocated to computer terminals, which were separated by mobile cardboard devices. A custom-made computer program, written in Java, helped to make decisions conveniently and to view all information gathered during play. In total, there were 120 subjects participating in the experiments.

At the beginning of each session, subjects were handed the instructions on paper.[9] The experimenter (always the same person) read aloud the instructions. Subjects were then given the opportunity privately to ask questions to the experimenter. Most questions could be answered by simply repeating the corresponding sentences from the instructions. After that, trial rounds were played. Subjects played against a computer opponent for four rounds of each of the four games. Prior to playing the trial rounds, subjects were informed of exactly what the computer was going to play. They were also told that these decisions were not going to be paid and that these trial rounds were intended to make subjects familiar with the computer program, the decision task and the set of possible games. After finishing the trial rounds subjects again were given the opportunity to ask questions. This part of the experiment took 30 to 45 minutes.

By internal computer assignment, subjects were then randomly matched to pairs and payoff matrices. Subjects played 40 repetitions of the stage game. They were not told which of the possible payoff matrices or which of the possible games they actually played. They were also left ignorant of their player position. In order to leave the focus on payoff maximisation and to avoid subjects playing for the revelation of the underlying game, we decided not to tell subjects which game they had been playing, even after the games were ended. For the same reason we refrained from debriefing the subjects during or after the experiment. The only feedback they got was their own payoff of the last round stated in lab dollars. On the screen, a separate window stored all information they got until that round (round number, action, payoff), so subjects did not need to take down any notes. The same procedure was repeated four times. We term these repetitions of the 40-round repeated game as *runs*. Hence, games and opponents were assigned randomly to the subjects in each run. Pairs were matched so that no subject played with the same opponent more than once. Subjects were informed of all this in the instructions.

At the end of the experiment the experimenter separately and privately paid off subjects. Each lab dollar was converted into 0.30 Deutschmarks. A show-up fee of 5 Deutschmarks was added. Money earnings varied between 25 Deutschmarks and 50 Deutschmarks with the average lying at 38 Deutschmarks, while sessions lasted for 90 to 120 minutes. At the time the experiments were run students' wages were approximately 14 Deutschmarks per hour.

In the instructions, subjects were presented with all relevant payoff matrices, that is, all four payoff matrices as described above as well as all payoff matrices with all possible permutations of actions. They were explicitly told that each of the games could occur with equal probability and each of the permutations of a game again could occur with equal probability. We restricted the random assignment only in the way that in each run each game was played by exactly 15 pairs. In order to make the games more comprehensible we provided a brief verbal description of the games. We took great care to design the description as neutrally as possible.

We deliberately chose a smaller number of repetitions of the stage game as compared to the preliminary experiment we reported in the preceding chapter, for two reasons. First, the 40-round limit allowed us to perform four runs and, thus, to have a reasonable database for the investigation into the experience effect. Second, the preliminary study has shown that under the given learning task pairs of subjects most often either coordinated early on, or failed to do so until the end. We, hence, deem 40 rounds as sufficient to elicit the coordination abilities of the pairs.

6.3   DATA ANALYSIS

The analysis of this extended experiment is considerably more voluminous than that of the previous chapter. We, therefore, decided to organise the results in explicitly stated *observations*. This section is devoted to the analysis of aggregated data. The first subsection deals with the ability of the subjects to coordinate, while the second lays its focus on the achieved payoffs. Individual data are analysed in the next section.

Coordination

We start the analysis with the coordination rate within games and runs. The large data set does not allow for a single simple definition that captures all the details of the individual coordination dynamics. There were some pairs that succeeded in coordinating very late in the run, while others coordinated rather soon and exhibited some deviations from the efficient cell towards the end. In order to capture the former as well as the latter, we decided to use a stepwise criterion (requiring an appearance rate of roughly 80 per cent) to discriminate between coordinating and non-coordinating pairs:

> *Definition 1:*
> A pair coordinated on the efficient cell, if
> 1. within the last seven rounds at least six rounds, or
> 2. within the last ten rounds at least eight rounds, or
> 3. within the last 20 rounds at least 16 rounds
> resulted in the efficient cell.

Implicitly, we exclude the consideration of the MP game in which the term 'coordination' may be interpreted as joint play of the Nash-equilibrium which consists of both players using mixed strategies that give equal probability to both actions. For the moment, we also do not take into account those pairs that fulfilled the above definition for other than the efficient cell. We only mention that there were two such pairs. Both pairs were playing FCBC games wherein player 1 for a very long sequence continuously played action *A* while player 2 showed some variable behaviour.

We now turn to the analysis of the coordination success of the pairs between games and runs. Table 6.1 provides an overview of coordination frequencies, whereby each inner cell contains a set of 15 observations.

Table 6.5: Frequencies of coordinating pairs

	Run				
	1	2	3	4	Sum
MFC	6	9	9	6	30
FCBC	4	7	12	8	31
CO	12	15	14	12	53
Sum	22	31	35	26	114

We notice that, not surprisingly, the coordination rate for CO is very high. However, there is a non-trivial amount of non-coordinating pairs (seven out of 60). For MFC as well as FCBC we find that the overall coordination rate is almost exactly 50 per cent. A reasonable comparison with the results of the preceding chapter, however, requires that we consider only the first run, since subjects' degree of experience is different in the later runs. The coordination rates for MFC and FCBC are a bit lower for run 1 and, so, they are rather similar to what has been observed in previous experiments with complete uncertainty about the set of possible games. We summarise this as

Observation 1:
As compared to complete uncertainty about the underlying game, the coordination rate of pairs playing MFC or FCBC is roughly the same as prior to playing the game when the probability distribution over games is given.

For both MFC and FCBC we further find a single peaked curve of coordination rates over runs; however, neither a chi-square test nor a Kolmogorov–Smirnov test can find a significant (to the 10 per cent level) difference to a flat distribution (that is, 7.5 coordinations for each game in each run) for either of the games or even for the sum of both. Somewhat astonishing is that even for CO we observe the single-peaked coordination rate; this, however, is a very weak observation and may very well be due to chance events.

We further checked for the correlation of successes among subjects and did not find any sign of concentration of successes. In more detail, we ran Monte Carlo simulations for the success of subjects. We checked for two different distributional assumptions: we took the true rate of coordination for each game and each run and we took coordination to be a 50/50 chance event. Via a chi-squared test, we then compared the resulting simulated distributions of the number of subjects over the number of successes with the relevant actual distribution. The results are displayed in Table 6.2.

Table 6.2: Actual numbers of subjects with the relevant number of successful coordinations and average numbers from simulations

	Number of coordinations					
	0	1	2	3 or 4	Chi-square	p-value
Actual observation	33	60	19	8		
Expectation 1	35.41	54.03	24.28	6.28	3.4517	0.4853
Expectation 2	37.55	51.65	24.44	6.37	4.7247	0.3167

The comparison of actual observations with the expected numbers calculated from 10 000 simulations of populations using the empirical frequencies (row titled 'Expectation 1') is not significant. Likewise, the observed distribution is not significantly different to a distribution calculated from 10 000 simulations of populations using the uniform distribution of success (row titled 'Expectation 2'). We, hence, cannot reject the hypothesis that subjects' successes to coordinate were determined with equal probability over all subjects. Note that the above tests are rather strict, since we did not take into account that subjects' successes were determined within pairs.

For the understanding of how people got to coordinate to the efficient cell it is equally important to have a look at the *starting round* of coordination. Since for some pairs play turned out to be quite variable, we had to fix some rule according to which the first encounter of a large number of coordination outcomes can be uniquely identified. Notice that we separate the general definition of coordination from the time at which coordination starts. The reason is that a joint definition appeared to result in a very complicated rule that would have impeded interpretation. For the definition of the starting round of coordination we took the following rule.[10]

Definition 2:
The starting round of successful coordination of a coordinating pair is determined by the first round of the first sequence of successful coordinations whose length is neither eventually exceeded by a sequence of non-coordination nor is exceeded by three times the length of the directly following sequence of non-coordinations.

We are aware of the fact that this definition does not include sequences in which a large number of coordination outcomes have been interrupted regularly by single non-coordinating outcomes. However, it does include sequences in which pairs had a sequence of five or six coordination outcomes early on, then had a long sequence of variable outcomes and, finally, returned to regularly coordinate. Both types of pairs, however, have been observed only rarely.[11] Given our above definition Table 6.3 summarises the data.

Table 6.3: Average starting round of coordination

| | Run | | | | |
	1	2	3	4	All
MFC	11.83	10.44	9.78	2.83	9.00
FCBC	18.75	13.14	10.00	4.25	10.35
CO	9.00	5.07	4.86	7.92	6.55
All	11.55	8.45	7.89	5.60	8.20

Recall that Table 6.1 did not show evidence in favour of an experience effect. The hypothesis stating that as experience grows subjects learn to coordinate more *often* could not be confirmed. As we see from Table 6.3, however, the starting round of coordination is persistently declining over runs; the only exception being run 4 in CO. A Jonkheere test for samples ordered by runs gives us asymptotic two-tailed p-values below the 5 per cent level for each game separately as well as for all games combined. We may, hence, conclude

Observation 2:
As experience grows, subjects tend to coordinate more quickly.

Coordination was clearly easiest in CO. The figures in Table 6.3 also suggest that there is a distinction to be made between FCBC and MFC. It looks as though the average starting round of coordination is lower for MFC. However, a custom-made randomisation test fails to show significance ($p = 0.27$).

Efficiency and Payoffs

We now turn our attention to the efficiency issue. We first have to determine what efficiency actually is. Since, at the beginning of a game, subjects were not aware of how to gain their payoffs and naturally needed time to learn about the incentives of the game, we deem it unjustified to compare actual payoffs with the maximum payoff available. We prefer the benchmark to be defined by the average payoff that could have been gained had both players applied the most efficient simple adaptive rule. For our games it turns out that, among all simple adaptive rules we could think of, the win–stay lose–randomise (WSLR) dynamics[12] yields the maximal payoff. We take WSLR as the ideal model and calculate the according benchmark payoffs for the games MFC, FCBC and CO to be 69.8, 68.3 and 78, respectively. This benchmark also functions as a moderator between the games. That is efficiency requires a higher payoff in those games in which coordination is easier. The actual average payoffs for experimental pairs over runs are shown in Figure 6.5.

We, first, notice that there are considerable inefficiencies in all three games. As expected, efficiency is generally highest in CO, lying between 83 per cent (run 4) and 96 per cent (run 2). However, owing to the higher benchmark, the difference to the other games is not very pronounced. We further notice that

Observation 3:
The expected increase in efficiency over runs can only be observed for FCBC (Jonkheere-test, $p < 0.01$).

This test includes the data from run 4, meaning that the rise from run 1 to run 3 (62 to 93 per cent) overcompensates the drop to 83 per cent in run 4. For MFC and CO we cannot find a significant over all runs. However, for CO we find a significant rise in efficiency over runs 1 to 3 (Jonkheere-test, two-tailed, $p < 0.01$). For MFC even this cannot be found.

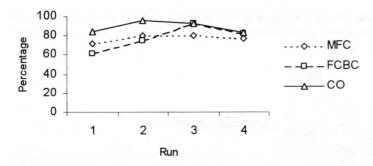

Figure 6.5: Efficiency rate over runs based on benchmark payoffs

When comparing efficiency rates between games we only find significant differences between CO and the other two games, while a difference between MFC and FCBC cannot be confirmed. Separate Mann-Whitney-U tests for runs show that differences between MFC and CO cannot be attributed to single runs, as for none of the runs the p-value lies below 0.1. However, the overall significance is p = 0.04. Tests on the difference between FCBC and CO show that efficiency is significantly higher in CO only for runs 1 and 2 (p = 0.000 and p = 0.023, respectively).

In addition to the payoff for a whole pair, we are also interested in the development of aggregate payoffs over individuals. Figure 6.6 provides information on this issue. Each diagram shows the development of average payoffs for one game over eight blocks of five-round averages. Each line stands for one run.

In addition to Observation 3 we can state that, not surprisingly, payoffs always slightly increase over time, while the marginal rate of payoff gain roughly declines.

As for the development of average payoffs over runs, we checked whether there are differences within the first ten rounds, rounds 16 to 25 and the last ten rounds of each run. For MFC we do not find any significant differences at any of the investigated time intervals. Hence, experience does not lead to higher payoffs in this game. In contrast, for FCBC we find that, within the first ten rounds, average payoffs rise with experience (Jonkheere test, p < 0.01, two-tailed), though differences between successive runs cannot be detected (corresponding Mann-Whitney-U tests always yield p > 0.1).

Towards the end, however, average payoffs appear to converge. In particular, no significant differences between any two runs can be detected and the corresponding Jonkheere test for a trend with experience yields insignificance (p = 0.67, two-tailed). In CO differences in average payoffs between runs can only be found for the first ten rounds, where Mann–Whitney-U tests show differences between runs 1 and 4 on the one hand and runs 2 and 3 on the other hand (significances always with p < 0.01). A

Jonkheere test for a trend over runs is not significant when considering all runs, but yields significance for runs 1 to 3 (p = 0.452 and p < 0.01, respectively).

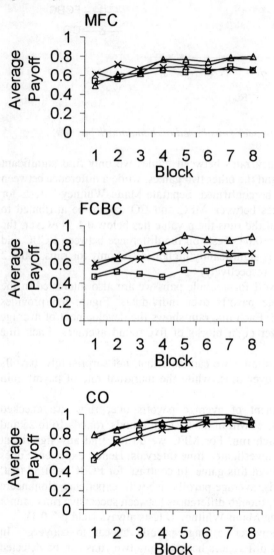

Notes: □ Run1   △ Run 2   – Run 3   × Run 4

Figure 6.6:   Individual average payoffs over eight blocks of five-round averages

Summing up we may state

Observation 4:
Significant experience effects on average payoffs are rarely noticeable. The only ones we could detect were limited to either the first rounds (CO) or the intermediate part of play (FCBC). These can be explained by the number of successfully coordinating pairs and the corresponding starting round of coordination.

For the game FCBC, we also examined whether there are specific differences between the player roles, that is, those players having a unique strategy with which they give a point to the opponent and those whose given strategy depends on the action played by the opponent. We did not find any such difference.

6.4 ANALYSIS OF LEARNING

We now turn to the analysis of individual play. We divide the analysis into three subsections. In order to get a rough idea of how and to what extent subjects changed actions over runs and within runs, the first subsection provides analysis of the accordance with the basic win–stay lose–change (WSLC) adjustment scheme. The second subsection then discusses the properties of the learning rules we introduced in Chapter 3 for the four games. The comparison between theoretical predictions of learning rules with the actual data is worked out in the third subsection.

Basic One-Period Adaptation Behaviour

In terms of learning, we first investigate compliance to the win–stay lose–change scheme. The numbers on rates of staying and changing help to get a first impression of the individual dynamics of play. Figure 6.7 shows aggregate data on the win–stay part of the learning scheme. We separated aggregation between those pairs that did converge and those that did not converge. Win–stay rates for coordinating pairs are calculated only for the rounds until the coordination phase sets in.

We first note that all win–stay rates (that is, the rates of staying after succeeding in getting a point) always lie within the range of 0.5 and 0.8, which is rather low compared with the theoretical prediction of 1. One may argue that, since subjects did not know which game they were actually about to play, they may have assumed that the underlying game was MP in which a win–stay rate of 0.5 is just a Nash-equilibrium. However, considering that MP had a 0.25 chance to occur, the win–stay rates are too close to 0.5 to be justified by this argument. We further do not find any correlation between experience (as expressed in the run) and win–stay rates.

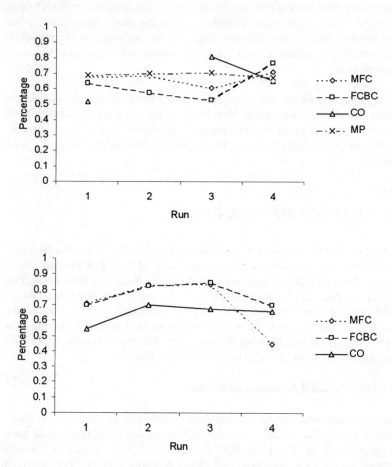

Figure 6.7:   Average win–stay rate over runs (top: non-coordinating pairs; bottom: coordinating pairs)

We, hence, state

Observation 5:

Subjects' decision to stay after winning a point does not depend on the experience gained.

What we do find, however, is that subjects in pairs that eventually coordinate do have a slightly stronger tendency to accord with the win–stay rule. In particular, Mann–Whitney-U tests show that win–stay rates are higher for subjects in coordinating pairs in MFC ($p < 0.01$) and in FCBC ($p < 0.1$). However, a closer look reveals that for both games this significant difference is solely caused by the observations within run 3. We therefore do not dare to state this finding as an assumedly stable observation and, hence, cannot confirm that accordance with the win–stay rule is a major vehicle for coordination. We further note that in MP the rate to stay after winning a point persistently lies at about 0.7. This is much higher than the theoretically predicted 0.5. At this stage we may suspect that this effect is caused by a significant amount of inertia. However, we also have to look at dynamics within each run in order to finally assess this. This is done below.

Before turning to the dynamics within a run, we have a brief look at the aggregate data on the compliance to the lose–change part, which is summarised in Figure 6.8.

Again we find that compliance is rather low, lying at about 0.5 on average. Note that, contrary to the win–stay part of the strategy, randomisation after losing may well be more advisable in all games except MFC. So, we are not surprised to find lose–change behaviour to roughly accord with randomisation. We also do not find any tendency that is dependent on experience. The same is true for subjects in coordinating pairs. However, we are surprised to find the lose–change rate to lie highest for MP (pairwise Mann–Whitney-U tests, $p < 0.01$, two-tailed), since the game dynamics of MP should favour randomisation more than in other games. We suspect that this phenomenon is a consequence of over-randomisation on part of the subjects, which has been found to be frequent in games with unique mixed-strategy equilibria (see, for example, Brown and Rosenthal 1990).

We summarise our findings in

Observation 6:
Compliance with changing action after losing is rather low, lying at about 0.5. No dependency on the amount of experience can be found. The lose–change rate is highest for MP.

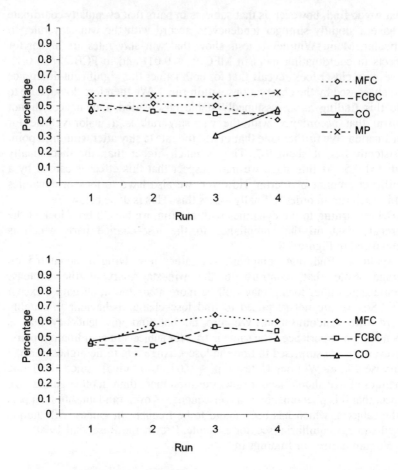

*Figure 6.8: Average lose–change rate over runs (top: non-coordinating
           pairs; bottom: coordinating pairs)*

We next examine the win–stay lose–change dynamics within runs. For this
purpose we subdivide the 40 rounds of play into two blocks of 20 rounds
each. We then analyse differences between the first and the second half of a
run. We again start with the win–stay analysis (Table 6.4).

The first thing to notice is that none of the games shows a tendency
towards more compliance with the win–stay process from one half of the run
to the second. This is contrary to what Rabinowitz et al. (1966) have found
but in line with the findings of the previous chapter. The decline is strongest
for MP and may partially be due to the incentive to play stochastically.
Nevertheless, the findings suggest a disprove of the win–stay assumption.
Table 6.5 shows the aggregate data for the lose–change part of the theory.

*Table 6.4:   Average win–stay rates over 20-round blocks (only non-
coordinating pairs)*

	Rounds 2–20	Rounds 21–40	Observations
MFC	0.67	0.67	60
FCBC	0.67	0.63	58
CO	0.60	0.60	14
MP	0.72	0.67	120

*Table 6.5:   Average lose-change rates over 20-round blocks (only non-
coordinating pairs)*

	Rounds 2–20	Rounds 21–40	Observations
MFC	0.50	0.49	60
FCBC	0.52	0.47	58
CO	0.47	0.46	14
MP	0.59	0.59	120

Even for the lose–change part of the theory we cannot find any shift towards more compliance with the simple dynamics. The rates are rather stable. In Table 6.5 the most dramatic decline can be observed for FCBC. This time, for MP we find neither more nor less accordance with the lose–change process. We summarise the findings in

Observation 7:
None of the games shows an increase in either the win-stay rate or the lose-change rate from one half of a run to the second.

We checked the robustness of this observation in two ways. We, first, replicated Table 6.4 and Table 6.5 using the first and the last ten-round blocks instead of the first and last 20-round blocks. We came to the same conclusion, the only difference lying in the lose–change rate within MP that slightly increases over the two blocks. Second, we also looked at the same rates for each run separately and found only few instances where there were increases in either the average win–stay rate or the average lose–change rate over the two 20-round blocks. Overall, we were confirmed in the finding that a decline in both win–stay and lose–change rates is the rule.

Predictions from Learning Rules

Observation 2 indicates that, as subjects repeat the 40-round task, they obviously improve skills in coordination. The question now is how subjects manage to do this. A natural hypothesis is that subjects in the first run of the experiment start with the application of a certain adaptive rule and adapt to their experiences in the past by changing the shape of adaptation in later runs of the experiment. This calls for an analysis of meta-adaptive behaviour, which, as yet, has rarely been studied in experimental games.[13] Our approach is to take a large set of adaptive rules, all of which are applicable to our low-information environment, and to compare characteristics of the rules with actual play.

The predictions of the learning models are based on simulations that assume that both players always use the same rule. We additionally provide diagrams showing the expected motion of pairs within the set of mixed strategies. For those learning rules that contain parameters both types of diagrams are drawn for specific sets of parameters. Even though, in principle, the choice of parameters is arbitrary, we tried to fix parameters in a way that is both close to the estimated values and reasonable for illustrative purposes, showing the basic dynamics of the processes. In case there are distinct differences in the predictions of a single learning rule depending on the exact values of the parameters, we provide several diagrams for different values. We start off, however, with the more intense discussion of the parameter-free rule, win–stay lose–randomise.

Win–stay lose–randomise (WSLR)

Consider first the rule win–stay lose–*change*. This rule has been shown to be very successful in settings involving dilemma situations, sometimes even outperforming tit-for-tat (see Nowak and Sigmund 1993). This simple learning rule is related to the learning direction scheme developed for larger strategy spaces by Selten and Stoecker (1986) while analysing Prisoner's Dilemma supergames and further investigated by Selten and Buchta (1999) on auction data. The idea is simply that whenever the individual fails to reach the optimal goal he or she will compute the direction of ascent and adjust his or her decision accordingly. In our two-strategy two-outcome space this scheme translates into staying with one's strategy if it yielded a payoff of 1 and changing if it resulted in a payoff of zero.

One can easily see that in our game space this adaptation rule is not very efficient. Even when assuming that both players are strictly following the win–stay lose–change rule we get into inefficient cycles of adjustment. Applying this rule to both players of a pair, the MFC game is solved rather quickly (certainly within three rounds of play). However, in CO starting in one of the two inefficient cells would lead this process into an infinite cycle between these two cells and, similarly, in FCBC they are quite likely to get stuck in the inefficient cycle (A,A), (A,B), (B,A).

Such cycles can be avoided by introducing randomisation. Since the win–stay part is necessary for lasting coordination in MFC, FCBC and CO, randomisation is better introduced by replacing the lose–change part with lose–randomise. As a consequence the time needed to coordinate in MFC and

CO increases slightly, but in turn FCBC is solved almost as quickly as MFC. In order to accept win–stay lose–randomise as a good benchmark in our setting we still have to clarify the dynamics within MP.

From the outset, it is clear that in MP the sole Nash-equilibrium is for both players in each round to choose each strategy with equal probability. It remains the sole equilibrium within a finitely repeated task. Since in all other games this is not a good rule we have to dismiss this trivial adaptation rule as an optimal strategy for our game-space. Playing best-response strategies to both win–stay lose–change as well as win–stay lose–randomise, however, result in best-response cycles. Using the obvious abbreviations we get (i) WSLC → WCLC → WCLS → WSLS → WSLC, and (ii) WSLR → WRLC → WCLR → WRLS → WSLR. Still, there is good reason to become involved in cycle (ii) rather than in cycle (i). While payoffs from strategies in cycle (i) are completely eradicated by the best-response strategies, payoffs are diminished only partially in strategies involving the lose–randomise part. Hence, win–stay lose–randomise has the virtue of being an almost optimal strategy in MFC, FCBC and CO whilst also being part of a small best-response cycle within MP.

Bush and Mosteller (BM)
The dynamics resulting from the BM scheme are shown in Figure 6.9. The first row shows the transition dynamics for each of the four stage games, whereby the x-axis denotes the probability of player 1 playing action B and the y-axis denotes the probability of player 2 playing action B. The arrows indicate the direction and the relative strength of the expected adjustment of the mixed-strategy profile. Note that the sizes of the arrows are normalised, so that no comparison on the strength of adjustment can be made between diagrams. In order to show the predicted speed of adjustments and to capture the impact of time-varying influences we added one more row showing simulations of representative pairs of players. In more detail, we first divided the unit space of mixed-strategy profiles into four quadrants and then printed the average path resulting from all pairs starting in the respective quadrant. We used average profiles of 1000 simulated pairs at each round to approximate the path.[14]

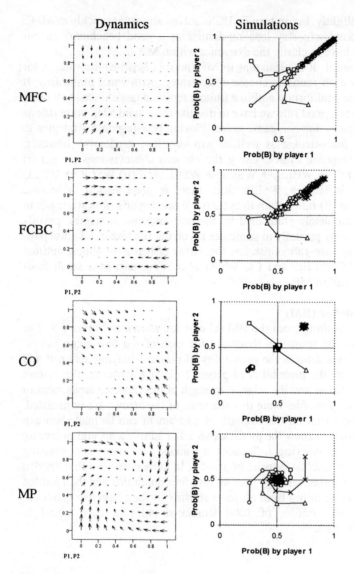

Note:

Key for right-hand side figures:

Average path for pairs starting in respective quadrant:

O Quadrant 1; △ Quadrant 2; □ Quadrant 3; × Quadrant 4

Figure 6.9: Dynamics of the Bush–Mosteller (BM) learning scheme ($\alpha^{BM} = \beta^{BM} = 0.5$)

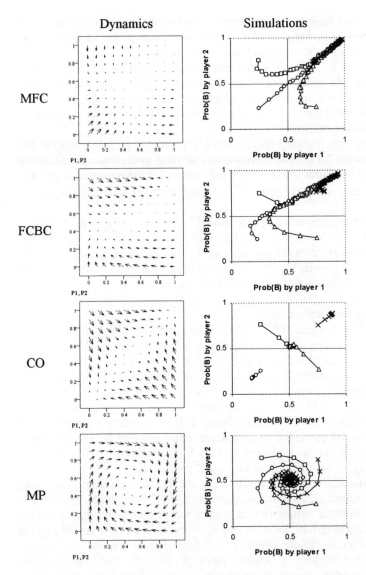

Figure 6.10: Dynamics of the Bush–Mosteller (BM) learning scheme (α^{BM} = 0.8, β^{BM} = 0.2)

Because of the BM-scheme describing a Markov chain, it is no surprise that the dynamics look very similar to the simulated pairs. In MFC quick adjustment towards the efficient pair of strategies $(p_1^B, p_2^B) = (1,1)$ can be observed. In FCBC there is a tendency to adjust much more slowly towards $(1,1)$. In the CO game there is quick guidance towards the diagonal from where there is no incentive to adjust further, and, in MP, pairs cycle clockwise towards the only Nash-equilibrium $(0.5;0.5)$ whereby convergence is reached rather quickly.

Since the next learning rule by Mookherjee and Sopher MS and the BM scheme coincide for the above parameters we need to illustrate the difference between the two rules using asymmetric values for the parameters. For this purpose we take $\alpha^{BM} = 0.8$ and $\beta^{BM} = 0.2$ and show the corresponding Figure 6.10.

The main difference compared with Figure 6.9 is that convergence of profiles is reached more slowly. Additionally, in FCBC there is a slight drift towards the upper left quadrant, reflecting the influence by player 1's action on his/her own payoff. Finally, in CO we observe a slight tendency to drift towards the efficient states $(0,0)$ and $(1,1)$.

Mookherjee and Sopher (MS)

We take $\alpha^{BM} = 0.8$ and $\beta^{BM} = 0.2$ as before and draw the dynamics of this process for two players always using the same rule (Figure 6.11).

Compared with the figures within the Bush–Mosteller scheme, we see that in MFC incentives to adjust towards the efficient $(1,1)$ are identical in shape but stronger, as the simulations show. A similar, but slightly deranged picture is drawn for FCBC. In the CO game, despite its symmetry concerning the two actions, the Mookherjee–Sopher scheme suggests a drive towards $(1,1)$. For the MP game we again observe a clockwise cycle, but one that is shifted towards player 1 playing B with high probability, while player 2 keeps up playing both strategies with equal probability.

The dynamics obviously result from the parameters simply implying stronger adjustment for vindictive experience with B than with A, which is a rather unreasonable assumption in a situation in which the names for the actions are nothing but labels. In our environment players start off playing the repeated game without knowing the labels of one's actions. Unless there is evidence that subjects try to match labels (for example, due to focal points) which they quickly identify while playing, there is little sense in assuming anything other than $\alpha^{MS} = \beta^{MS}$. From this point of view, the Bush–Mosteller scheme looks richer in structure, since it allows for different reinforcements depending solely on the feedback rather than on combinations of feedback and label. We may thus be interested in the comparison between the two rules on grounds of their ability to predict behaviour. This is what we turn to in Chapter 8.

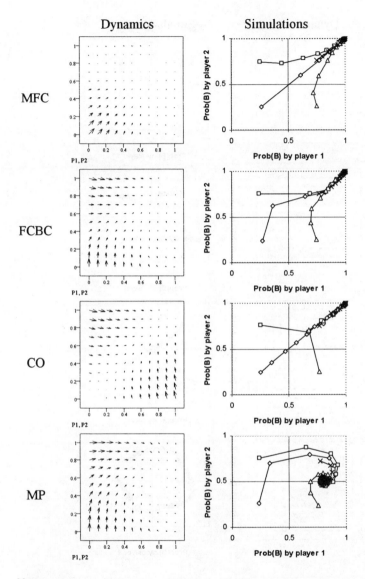

Figure 6.11: Dynamics of the Mookherjee–Sopher (MS) learning scheme
$(\alpha^{MS} = 0.8, \beta^{MS} = 0.2)$

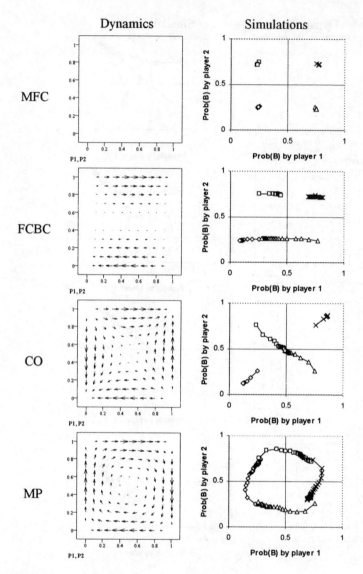

Note:
Key for right-hand side figures:
Average path for pairs starting in respective quadrant:
O Quadrant 1; △ Quadrant 2; □ Quadrant 3; × Quadrant 4

Figure 6.12: Dynamics of the Cross (CR) learning scheme ($\alpha^{CR} = 0.9$, $\beta^{CR} = 0$)

Cross (CR)

Recall that the scheme proposed by Cross (1973) was derived from the idea by Bush and Mosteller to model adaptation as reinforced by payoffs. It is intriguing that the slight modification of their model leads to distinctly different dynamics, as is illustrated in Figure 6.12, where we use $\alpha^{CR} = 0.9$ indicating a rather strong tendency to adjust, and $\beta^{CR} = 0$.

While in MFC there is no drive towards any direction, that is, pairs will wander around according to chance events, in FCBC there will be a simple adjustment by player 1 only, the one player who has some influence on his/her own payoff. In CO there are symmetric drifts towards the efficient pairs (0,0) and (1,1), while the strength of the drifts diminishes the closer the pair gets to the diagonal or the anti-diagonal. Finally, in MP one again observes a clockwise cycling around the unique Nash-equilibrium. However, differently to Bush–Mosteller and Mookherjee–Sopher the cycling does hardly show any attraction towards the centre.

Börgers and Sarin (BS)

Recall that β^{BS} determines the speed of adjustment of the aspiration level. The second parameter denotes the initial aspiration level, that is, $\alpha^{BS} = b_i(1)$. The evolving aspiration level b causes the stationary look at the dynamics to neglect certain time-dependent aspects. For illustration we, hence, provide dynamics and simulations for two distinct cases, namely $\alpha^{BS} = 0.9$ (that is, initially optimistic agents) in Figure 6.13 and $\alpha^{BS} = 0.1$ (that is, initially pessimistic agents) in Figure 6.14.

The main difference between optimistic and pessimistic players is that pessimists adjust more smoothly to vindictive experiences. For pessimists, vindictive experience causes the chosen strategy to be reinforced strongly, while refuting experience causes small adjustments of choice probabilities. For optimists the opposite is true; vindication has small effects and refutation has large effects on choice probabilities. As a consequence, the volatile behaviour of optimists in the game FCBC causes them to get stuck in intermediate choice probabilities until the aspiration level has decreased to values in the order of expected payoffs. However, pessimists show steady adaptation in the direction of efficient play. The rising aspiration level causes the reinforcing effect of vindication to decrease at much higher choice probabilities for action B than is observed for optimists.

Similarly for the game MP we find that the Börgers-Sarin scheme with optimistic aspiration levels resembles that of the cycling Cross dynamic, while the Börgers-Sarin scheme for pessimists looks more similar to the converging symmetric Bush-Mosteller scheme. The differences vanish as the aspiration levels approach levels near 0.5.

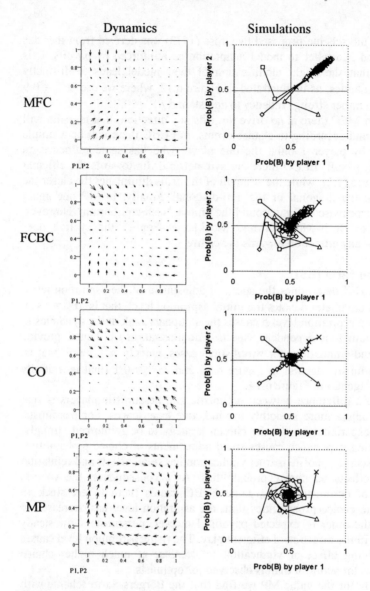

Note:

Key for right-hand side figures:

Average path for pairs starting in respective quadrant:

O Quadrant 1; △ Quadrant 2; □ Quadrant 3; × Quadrant 4

Figure 6.13: Dynamics of the Börgers–Sarin (BS) learning scheme ($\alpha^{BS} = 0.9$, $\beta^{BS} = 0.9$)

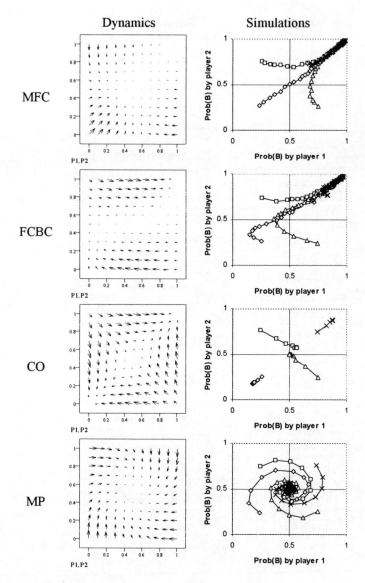

Note:
Key for right-hand side figures:
Average path for pairs starting in respective quadrant:
O Quadrant 1; △ Quadrant 2; □ Quadrant 3; × Quadrant 4

Figure 6.14: Dynamics of the Börgers–Sarin (BS) learning scheme ($\alpha^{BS} =$ 0.1, $\beta^{BS} = 0.9$)

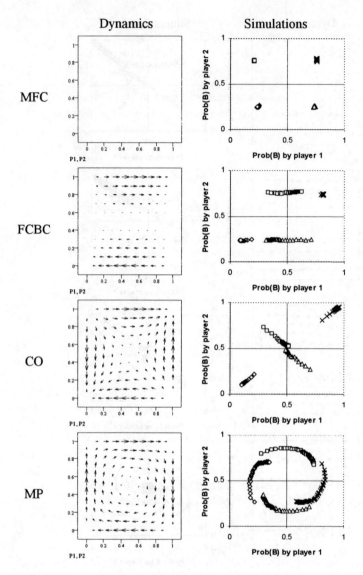

Note:
Key for right-hand side figures:
Average path for pairs starting in respective quadrant:
O Quadrant 1; △ Quadrant 2; □ Quadrant 3; × Quadrant 4

Figure 6.15: Dynamics of the Roth–Erev (RE) learning scheme ($\alpha^{RE} = 1$,
* $\beta^{RE} = 0.95$)*

In sum, the adjustment of the aspiration level allows for a subtle synthesis of the Bush–Mosteller idea on the one hand, and the Cross idea on the other. We are curious whether this structure is able to tell us more than each of these two rules separately.

Roth and Erev's reinforcement learning (RE)

The basic dynamics are depicted in Figure 6.15. In fact, the diagrams show little difference to the ones for the Cross scheme, the reason being that the only difference lies in the introduction of diminishing effects of feedback via increasing values for the propensities. Hence, the basic difference lies in the process tending to slow down after a while, that is, structurally it adds the consideration of the power-law of practice.

Apart from the apparent slowing down of the process as play advances, the process shares all characteristics of the Cross scheme. The more forgetting is assumed, that is, the lower β^{RE} is chosen, the quicker the process converges to the Nash-equilibrium in the MP game.

Karandikar et al. (KA)

The dynamics for this scheme are depicted in Figures 6.16 and 6.17. Recall that, for the purpose of exposition, we fixed $\gamma^{KA} = 0.2$ and $\delta^{KA} = 0.1$, so that $h(.)$ shows reasonable sensitivity as its argument varies between 0 and 1. The basic characteristics of the process do not depend on slight variations of these parameters. As with the Börgers–Sarin scheme, we show the dynamics for players with initially optimistic aspiration levels and the dynamics for players with initially pessimistic aspiration levels.

From the figures we see that for the Karandikar process the initial aspiration level has a markedly different impact than on the Börgers–Sarin scheme. Here, starting with a low initial aspiration level easily causes players to get stuck in actions that regularly yield zero payoff, because the difference between the low aspiration level and the payoff of zero is not large enough to induce a change in choice. This observation uncovers one of the weaknesses of this scheme: even if we introduce small shocks in aspiration levels the process would need a large amount of time to leave a strategy that returns low payoff, if such a payoff is being expected. Experimentation with the parameter α^{KA} showed that, for our game environment, values of about 0.3 suffice to make lock-ins sufficiently improbable so that the dynamics follow the trajectory.

Somewhat surprising is the fact that the Karandikar scheme, when initialised with optimistic players, roughly yields the same dynamics as the Bush–Mosteller scheme, even though it does not make use of last round's choice probabilities.

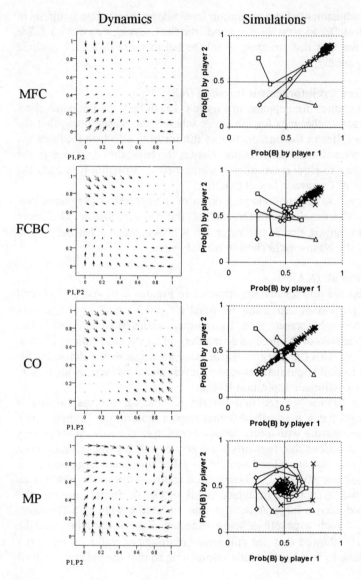

Note:
Key for right-hand side figures:
Average path for pairs starting in respective quadrant:
O Quadrant 1; △ Quadrant 2; □ Quadrant 3; × Quadrant 4

Figure 6.16: Dynamics of the Karandikar et al. (KA) learning scheme (γ^{KA}
= 0.2, δ^{KA} = 0.1, η^{KA} = 0, α^{KA} = 0.9, β^{KA} = 0.9)

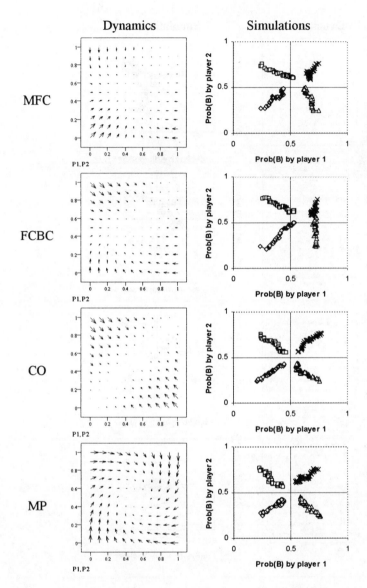

Note:
Key for right-hand side figures:
Average path for pairs starting in respective quadrant:
O Quadrant 1; △ Quadrant 2; □ Quadrant 3; × Quadrant 4

Figure 6.17: Dynamics of the Karandikar et al. (KA) learning scheme (γ^{KA} = 0.2, δ^{KA} = 0.1, η^{KA} = 0, α^{KA} = 0.1, β^{KA} = 0.9)

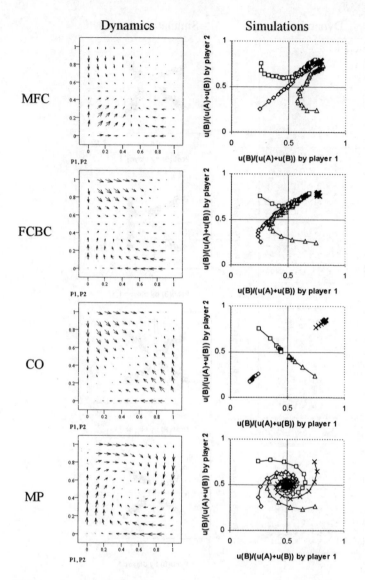

Note:
Key for right-hand side figures:
Average path for pairs starting in respective quadrant:
O Quadrant 1; △ Quadrant 2; □ Quadrant 3; × Quadrant 4

Figure 6.18: Dynamics of the Sarin–Vahid (SV) learning scheme ($\alpha^{SV} = 0.5$, $\beta^{SV} = 0.2$)

Sarin and Vahid

Recall that this process was different from the others in that it assumes that players adaptively construct beliefs about expected payoffs from actions. The first parameter α^{SV} denoted the adjustment speed of the beliefs, while the second parameter β^{SV} specifies the standard deviation of the error that slips into the maximisation process. For the dynamics diagrams we had to restrict expected payoffs so that $u_i^A + u_i^B = 1$ for all i. Since the u_i^j's evolve over time, the dynamics diagrams again do not tell us the whole story of the process. In fact, the simulation results in Figure 6.18 turn out to be strikingly similar to the ones of the Bush–Mosteller scheme with asymmetric parameters. We do not have a proper account for this phenomenon.

Summing up, we may state that the simulations revealed certain similarities and some differences between rules which we might not have detected from simple inspection of the difference equations. In particular, we may expect the aspiration level of the Börgers–Sarin scheme to reflect either the similarity to the Bush–Mosteller process or rather the similarity to the Cross model. We expect the Cross scheme to produce roughly the same results as the Roth–Erev scheme. The Karandikar et al. scheme also may give valuable insights via its aspiration level. Optimists show similarities to the Bush–Mosteller scheme, while pessimists get stuck in inefficient play. Finally, we are curious whether the Sarin–Vahid scheme correctly predicts players to slow down in their motion towards the efficient cell.

Aggregate Paths and Results from Player-Based Estimations

Our approach is different from many other studies on adaptation behaviour in that it does not focus on quantitative comparisons between learning rules, such as the goodness of fit or the predictive success. We prefer to use methods that reveal structural characteristics of learning rules and compare them to the characteristics of the data. The first such analysis concerns the path of play. For this purpose we redraw the figures that show the average paths of pairs for actual data. We proceed in the following way: first, we classify each pair of players according to the choice frequencies within the first ten rounds. Pairs for which both players played action B four times or less were classified into quadrant 0; pairs for which player 1 played B four times or less and player 2 played action B five times or more often were classified into quadrant 1. Likewise, the classifications for quadrants 2 and 3 were determined. By this procedure we classified each pair into one starting quadrant. Figure 6.19 shows, separately for each game, the average paths of all pairs that fall into the respective starting quadrant. Since variance of play was quite large, the pictures show only four data points per path, each one relating to the average choice within a ten-round block.

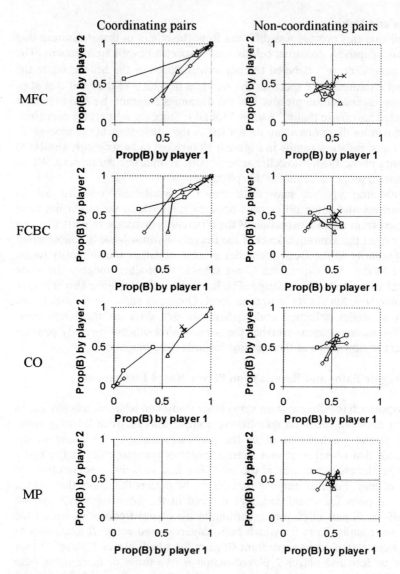

Note:

Average path for pairs starting in respective quadrant:

O Quadrant 1; △ Quadrant 2; □ Quadrant 3; × Quadrant 4

Figure 6.19: Forty-round path of average choice proportions by game and coordination

The figures clearly show that subject behaviour of coordinating pairs was quite different from behaviour of non-coordinating pairs. For the game MFC it is no surprise to see all paths of coordinating pairs leading to the efficient outcome (1,1), that is (*B,B*), since we selected the pairs to contain only those that did approach this outcome. The same is true for the graphs of coordinating pairs for the game FCBC. The figure for MP by definition does not contain any data. However, the figure for the CO game is worth looking at in more detail. Those pairs that start in quadrant 0 quickly make their way through to the NE at (*A,A*). By way of contrast, pairs that start in quadrant 3 do not always reach the coordination at (*B,B*). Three pairs out of 15 starting in quadrant 3 coordinate on (*A,A*). Finally, there is only one coordinating pair that starts in quadrant 1 and only two coordinating pairs that start in quadrant 2. Thus, it is no surprise, either, that paths for both classes of pairs follow a straight line towards one of the pure strategy Nash-equilibria.

Overall, the essence of Figure 6.19 is that for the non-coordinating pairs there is no trend towards efficient play to be observed. On average, play always amounts to allocate roughly equal frequency to each strategy. This is independent of the game and the number of rounds already played. Variance looks smaller for the MP game, but this is mainly due to the significantly larger number of pairs over which aggregation has been performed. Our conclusion is

Observation 8:
Subjects within pairs that do not succeed in coordination show no sign of a trend towards efficient play.[15]

One way to find out whether subjects show a difference in adaptation behaviour between having experienced the learning task and behaviour in run 1 when they are not familiar with the learning environment, is to estimate separately the parameters of learning rules for the four different runs. Since different games give rise to different dynamic processes we also perform estimations for each game separately. Figure 6.20 shows the path of estimated parameters over runs for each learning rule and each game. Each point in each diagram represents one estimation performed on all data from coordinating pairs until coordination sets in. The underlying idea is that the learning rules may be able to capture qualitative characteristics of play until coordination sets in by way of a corresponding sensitivity of the parameters. The game MP is not included since coordination is not an issue there.

The results are rather discouraging. None of the learning rules is able to elicit any steady trend of parameters. No conclusions from estimations can be drawn on the cognitive processes of subjects over parts. We also did the same analysis with all non-coordinating pairs as well as with estimations for all pairs combined. The same conclusion was reached.

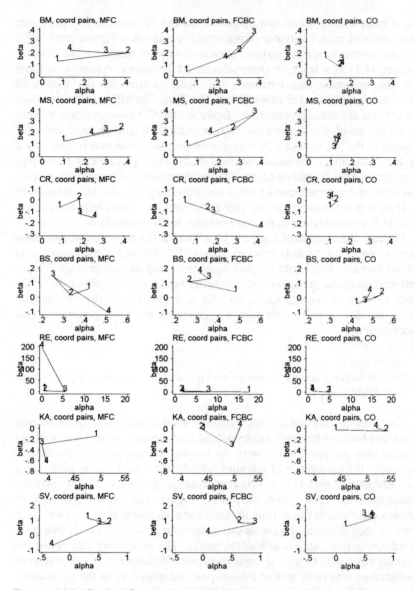

Figure 6.20: Paths of estimation parameters over runs by learning rule and game using data from coordinating pairs until coordination sets in

One criticism related to the method of analysis concerns the representative agent approach. There may very well be a trend over parts, which, however, is obscured by the heterogeneity of subjects' behaviour. From a static point of view the maximum likelihood procedure weighs those predictions more for which prediction is difficult to achieve (that is, to get a high likelihood). Likewise those subjects are given more weight whose path is difficult to fit by the respective learning rule. A more rigorous analysis would thus involve estimation of parameters for individual players, and this is what we present next.

We, therefore, leave the standard approach of the analysis of subject play which is usually based on the representative agent assumption. We rather estimate separately parameters of learning rules for each agent. This is one of few studies to perform this task.[16]

Our hope to get more insight as to which changes in adaptive behaviour cause the improved ability to coordinate on the efficient cell was disappointed. Figure 6.21 gives an account of individual estimations for coordinating pairs. Each graph shows confidence ellipses around the mean for individual parameter estimations of one learning rule. Ellipses are drawn for estimations of a single run over all games.[17] Each ellipse depicts the 90 per cent confidence ellipse[18] around the mean of all estimated parameter points excluding outliers according to Hadi's (1992; 1994) algorithm and excluding players for which the estimation algorithm did not converge.[19] Estimations were done via a maximum-likelihood estimation for one-period ahead predictions.[20]

Similar to Figure 6.20, Figure 6.21 shows that none of the learning rules is able to capture any behavioural trend over runs. The estimations fail to answer the question as to why or how subjects were able to coordinate more quickly as they gained experience with the task. This overall picture does not change when depicting the same graphs for non-coordinating pairs. The ellipses for non-coordinating pairs typically show slightly smaller variance, which is probably due to the larger number of observations. They are very similar otherwise. We summarise these results in

Observation 9:
None of the learning rules is able to capture a change of adjustment behaviour as is suggested by observation 2. This is independent of whether estimations of parameters are done using the representative agent approach or for each individual separately.

It is informative to look at the number of observations that comprise a confidence ellipse. Since estimations for different learning rules were performed for the same data, the numbers reflect the ability of the respective learning rule to produce reasonable estimation results. After eliminating all those subjects that coordinated with their partner before period 10, those for

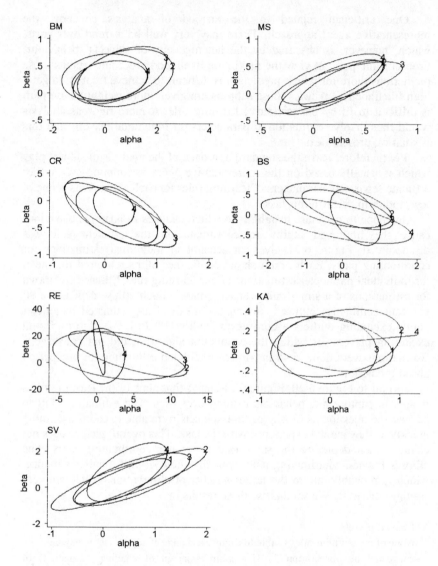

*Figure 6.21: Confidence ellipses for estimation parameters by runs and
             rules*

which the estimation procedure did not converge, and those who were classified as outliers according to Hadi's criterion, we obtained the numbers of successful estimation of individual learning parameters depicted in Table 6.6.

The results clearly depend on the way parameters were specified for the learning rules. They also depend on the particular estimation procedure.[21] Nevertheless, the numbers give a rough impression of how stable estimations were. From Table 6.6, and much more so when including the numbers on non-coordinating pairs, we get the impression that the RE and the KA schemes were much worse in producing useful results than were the other learning rules.

Table 6.6: Number of successful estimations for players in coordinating pairs by runs and rules

	Run			
Rule	1	2	3	4
BM	19	17	22	7
MS	19	14	19	8
CR	13	9	14	6
BS	15	12	21	6
RE	6	7	6	5
KA	9	10	15	2
SV	13	17	17	9

6.5   PATTERNS

All adaptation rules considered so far only capture round-by-round adjustments. However, they fail to account for another aspect that has been put forward to be crucial in any learning process, namely the investigation and understanding of the game environment. As has already been observed in the previous chapter, subjects appear frequently to be involved in stationary patterns that supposedly serve to find an understanding of the feedback that subjects get from the environment. We now have sufficient data to systematically investigate subjects' use of patterns. We will make use of the following

Definition 3:
A pattern played by a subject is identified by one of the following sequences of actions that occurs before and until coordination of the corresponding pair sets in:
1. A sequence of at least six consecutive rounds with the same action, that is, ...AAAAAA... or ...BBBBBB...

2. A sequence of at least five consecutive alternations of actions, that is, ...ABABABA... or ...BABABAB...
3. A sequence of at least seven consecutive alternations between staying and changing, that is, ...ABBAABBA... or ...BAABBAAB...

In order to assess whether subjects used these patterns more often than randomly playing agents we run the following procedure. We, first, add up all rounds that lie within a sequence identified as a pattern. We then use artificial agents to simulate play. Each agent corresponds to a subject playing a 40-round repetition. The agent chooses the actions with fixed probabilities that were determined by the relative frequency of play by the actual subject. Of course, we limit the simulation to the number of rounds until coordination sets in in the actual play. Finally, we calculate the number of rounds captured by one of the above patterns just in the same way as we did for the actual subjects. In order to approximate the distribution of the simulated results we repeat simulations for the whole of the 12 sessions 1000 times. The results are given in Table 6.7. They show that each pattern is played significantly more often than is suggested by random play.

Table 6.7:   Observed and simulated mean number of rounds captured by patterns (p-values are determined using t-tests)

Pattern	Observations	Simulated mean	p-value
1	1941	1824	0.000
2	633	529	0.000
3	683	406	0.000
Sum	3257	2759	0.000

Figure 6.22 shows that the occurrence of patterns is a rather stable phenomenon. Playing patterns is common in all games and over all runs.

Patterns always account for more than 20 per cent of the total number of rounds before coordination sets in (except for run 2 in CO where there are only few observations) and reach up to 41.8 per cent in run 3 with FCBC as the underlying game. There is neither a clear difference between the games nor a trend over runs to be observed.

We further investigated whether playing patterns is typical for a rather small subpopulation of the subjects, and found that 113 out of the 120 subjects who participated in our experiments showed an identified pattern within the 160 rounds of play.

Summarising we state

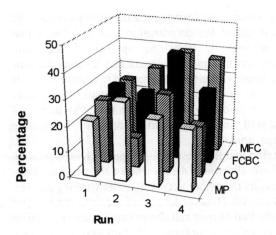

Figure 6.22: Frequency of rounds falling into patterns in per cent of all rounds before coordination

Observation 10:
The use of patterns is a stable phenomenon throughout all games and independent of the previous experience with the forty-round task. Ninety-four per cent of all subjects eventually play an identified pattern.

6.6 SUMMARY

The experiment we described in this chapter was designed to shed light on the acquisition of information in environments in which players are provided little information about the underlying game. We confronted subjects with a set of simple 2 × 2 games and let them play anonymously with the same opponent for 40 rounds. By this means subjects had the opportunity to work out the incentives of the underlying game without knowing the exact shape. Three of the four games had one or two efficient outcomes that were also individually payoff maximising. Despite the large number of repetitions, subjects had considerable difficulty in coordinating. In the simple coordination game (CO) there was a non-trivial number of pairs that did not reach coordination after 40 rounds. In the more subtle games of mutual fate control (MFC) and fate–control behaviour–control (FCBC) only half of the pairs finally reached coordination. Foreclosure of structural information obviously has a considerable effect on the success of efficient coordination.

Experience is the second variable we investigated in our experiment. We let subjects play four repetitions of the coordination task and found that experience does not significantly increase the number of successful coordinations. However, there was a significant experience effect on the time of coordination. Experience helps reduce the time needed to coordinate. This observation is a clear sign in favour of the hypothesis that with experience subjects gain sophistication. It conforms to Levenson's (1998) notion of learning as improvement of skill, and goes beyond the definition of learning as some form of adaptive algorithm.

In terms of learning, we find that the most popular approach to explaining learning, behaviour in such two-alternative decision tasks, the win–stay lose–change strategy, does not predict behaviour very well. After winning a point, subjects repeat the same action only 50 to 80 per cent of the time. An analysis of the first half and the second half of each run shows that, even in the course of learning subjects do not increasingly conform to the win–stay lose–change rule. In some cases, rather the opposite can be observed. Changing the action after experiencing a payoff of 0 is even less likely. In this case, subjects appear to accord with randomisation, which in three out of the four games is indeed superior to the strict change of action.

A more elaborate consideration of adaptation rules that have been put forward for accounting for behaviour in more recent studies shows that these learning rules are not able to reveal structural differences of adaptation behaviour. Thus, no learning rule was able to give us theoretical insights into what drives subjects to coordinate more quickly as experience increases. This finding complements Salmon's (1999a) result that standard experiments on learning are generally incapable of discriminating among the most prominent learning rules. He found that even if the true processes follow simple adaptive rules, experiments of moderate length (for example 100 rounds) and a moderate number of players (for example 60) will hardly suffice to support statistically significant differences between the standard learning rules. Our study extends this finding on the quantitative deficiencies of the experimental design to qualitative aspects of data fitting.

The preceding section gives a hint as to why adaptation rules may not be able to tell the most important part of actual behaviour under little information. Subjects appear to use patterns of play that last for considerably more than one period. These patterns seem to fulfil an exploratory purpose with which subjects approach tasks of decision-making involving an uncertain environment. Subjects seem to study the reaction of the environment to their specific patterns and draw some conclusions after terminating their exploration time. For our environment, in which subjects often had to coordinate on an efficient cell, this complicated cognitive approach leads to a disabling of the timing of exploratory phases. The result is a massive loss of efficiency as compared to a simple adaptive rule such as win–stay lose–randomise.

Salmon's (1999b) answer to the problem of statistical data fitting and the possible change of learning rules during the course of play is to modify the experiment design. He puts forward the use of frequent questionnaires. In his experiment, questionnaires are used to ask players to describe their updating process at different points in time. (Salmon asks subjects every ten rounds.) By this means he seeks verbally to reveal the underlying adaptive rule and possibly the change in rule over time. Our opinion of this design is that such questionnaires may give valuable hints as to which adaptive processes are typically considered by experimental subjects. This is why we, too, used such a questionnaire, but only in our preliminary study. However, we believe that the frequent questioning of subjects during play causes a severe bias. By anticipating the question about their underlying decision rule, subjects may only implement rules they can easily verbalise. Many subjects may be led to implement simple dynamics, otherwise, they would have used more complex rules. For this reason we chose a more cautious experimental design for our study. It may be that exactly for this reason we found that simple adaptive dynamics did not explain our data.

NOTES

1. This chapter is based on Mitropoulos (2001b). Permission to reprint parts of the material by Anthony Courakis is gratefully acknowledged.
2. Independently, Shachat and Walker (2000) conducted an experiment in which they, too, provide subjects with the whole set of possible games. Unlike us, they show subjects their own payoff matrix and provide a distribution over all possible payoff matrices for their opponents only. Feltovich (2000) is similar, but still different in so far as initial information about the distribution is relevant for both stages of a two-stage game.
3. Replications of learning tasks are more common in single-person decision problems (see, for example, Slonim 1999). An early example of an experimental supergame is Selten and Stoecker (1986).
4. The discussion of the quantitative comparison between learning rules is delayed until Chapter 8.
5. Our notions of risk and uncertainty follow Knight (1921), that is, risk captures all situations in which states of nature are known to occur with certain probabilities, while uncertainty is the situation in which no probabilities over states can be assessed. Note that Ellsberg's (1961) terminology is different. Our notion of uncertainty is equivalent to his ambiguity, while he used uncertainty as a more general term.
6. For a more intense discussion of the methodological concerns on the experimental investigation of individual decision-making under risk and uncertainty, see Hey (1997).
7. The authors also distinguish between primary, secondary and Schelling salience. For more details on these notions, see Mehta et al. (1994).
8. This point has extensively been discussed by Fudenberg and Kreps (1993).

9. The instructions for this experiment are given in Appendix D.
10. A formal definition requires some notation, and therefore is given in Appendix E.
11. We checked for the robustness of the following results by varying definition 2 in several ways. In all cases we came to the same conclusions.
12. A more elaborate justification of the choice of win–stay lose–randomise is given in the next section.
13. An exception is Stahl (1999), who includes a parameter in his maximum likelihood estimation that measures the extend to which adaptation rules from one part of a repeated game with full information are transferred to another repeated game.
14. Similar figures for the average path of play of simulated players can be found in Feltovich (2000).
15. We found this statement also to be true independent of the experience gained over runs.
16. Shachat and Walker (2000) and Stahl (2000) also do individual estimations of updating behaviour.
17. There are not enough data points to perform separately the same analysis for each game.
18. As approximated by the ellipse with two times the standard deviations of the parameters as respective radii and the correlation coefficient indicating the angle.
19. The exclusion of those players for which the estimation procedure did not lead to sensible results leads to a slight bias in data selection. Typically, those players were excluded for which few changes in behaviour were recorded.
20. Apart from the renunciation of the representative agent assumption this procedure is fairly standard in the literature; see for example Camerer and Ho (1999) and references therein.
21. Estimations were performed using Stata 6.0. According to its manual the procedure uses the BFGS method with some modifications as to the rescaling and the initialisation of the search algorithm. Control estimations using the implementation of the BHHH and BFGS methods within TSP 4.5 produced similar results.

7.   The Value of Information[1]

7.1   MOTIVATION

Until recently, the value of information has most often been dealt with in management studies. Typically, additional information that is available to investors or optimisers of production processes improves their performance.[2] In the past, the point of greatest concern has been the question of how the performance of an individual is affected by additional information. Less often, economic analyses were devoted to elicit the effects on allocation.

Our previous analysis showed that the exclusion of information about the underlying payoff matrix severely affects the joint payoff of a pair. Had the subjects known that they were playing one of the coordination games, they quickly would have been able to reach an efficient state. A natural question arising from this observation is: how much information do subjects need in order to be able to coordinate quickly? Is there an intermediate level of information that constitutes a threshold after which coordination is easily established by repeatedly playing partners?

As we noticed in Chapter 5, subjects make use of complex patterns of behaviour even though a simple updating rule would have quickly guided them to the desired result. The behaviour we detected in the experimental data in Chapter 6 supported the view that subjects lack the ability to coordinate when structural information is diffuse or lacking. However, Chapter 6 also taught us that subjects are able somewhat to improve their performance as experience with the task rises. The experience gained from repeating the multi-round learning task might be considered as an improvement in their perception of the structure of their environment. The experiment we present in this chapter provides subjects with slightly more information about the structure of their interaction. We were curious to see whether subjects are now able to use more efficient learning schemes that guide them into successful coordination.

7.2   EXPERIMENTAL PROCEDURE

Since we are now interested in the impact of initial information on behaviour, we relate our design to the design used in Chapter 5. That is, we match pairs only once at the beginning of the experiment and let them play 100 repetitions of the mutual fate control game. The difference comüared to the design in Chapter 5 is that, this time, subjects are informed about playing the mutual fate control game. Subjects are only left ignorant about which action causes the other player to receive the positive payoff and which action causes the other player to receive zero payoff. In the instructions, this crucial difference between the designs reads as follows:

> In each round two persons are playing with each other. Each player may choose among two alternative actions, A or B. The actions of the two players determine the payoffs to both players. The following payoff scheme applies: Each person has one action available which assigns one point to the other player, and one action which assigns zero points to the other player. (The author's translation from German)

By reading aloud the instruction sheet, this information was (almost) common knowledge to the subjects. Note that this information is equivalent to saying that the underlying payoff matrix may be any of the four payoff matrices that result from interchanging the labels of the actions. Compared to the design in Chapter 6, we, thus, reduce the set of possible payoff matrices to the four (out of the 11) that correspond to the mutual fate control game. We did not provide subjects with probabilities on the occurrence of the matrices. However, the design makes fairly clear that, in order to avoid possible biases owing to one label being perceived as more salient than another,[3] we are forced to implement each payoff matrix with roughly the same frequency.

Otherwise, the design of the experiment remained the same as in Chapter 5. We conducted three sessions with a total of 28 participants. We thus have 14 independent observations from pairs. In the following, we compare these observations with the observations on the 17 pairs from Chapter 5. By referring to the *little-information treatment* we address the data from the experiment in Chapter 5, and we name our new data as the *experiment with prior structural information*.

7.3   DATA ANALYSIS

We make use of Definitions 1 and 2 in Chapter 6 in order to, first, classify pairs of subjects into those that coordinate and those that do not coordinate, and second, in order to specify the starting round of coordination. Recall that we may also use Definition 2 as determinant of whether a pair succeeds in coordinating or fails to do so. For example, if the starting round of coordination is found not to occur before period 100, then this pair may have been classified as non-coordinating. Even though some numbers may change depending on which definition we use, all the results remain the same. We indicate changes due to the definition throughout this chapter.

Table 7.1:   Frequencies of successful and unsuccessful coordinations over treatments

Treatment	Successes	Failures	Total
Little information	7	10	17
Structural information	13	1	14

The number of pairs that successfully coordinate on the efficient cell draws a fairly clear picture. Table 7.1 depicts the corresponding numbers from the little-information treatment of Chapter 5 and the treatment with prior information on the structure of the environment. A Fisher-exact test rejects the hypothesis of equal distributions between treatments (to the 1 per cent level, two-tailed).[4]

Table 7.2:   Starting round of convergence for the coordinating pairs over treatments

	Little info.	Structural info.
Starting	2	1
round of	2	3
coordination	2	7
	4	9
	9	12
	65	13
		13
		14
		31
		44
		50
		52
		93
Mean	14.0	26.3

Restricting our attention to the pairs that coordinate, we find that the starting round of coordination seems to differ between the experiments. Table 7.2 depicts all numbers on the starting round of coordination.[5] We find the means differ considerably between the experiment with little information and the experiment with structural information, the mean for the pairs of the former treatment (14.0) lying lower than the mean for the pairs of the latter (26.3). However, Monte Carlo permutation tests on the equality of medians and means fail to be significant ($p = 0.28$, $p = 0.38$, respectively, two-tailed).

Table 7.3: Individual win–stay and lose–change rates until coordination

	Win–stay		Lose–change	
	Little info.	Structural info.	Little info.	Structural info.
	0.00	0.00	0.25	0.25
	0.00	0.00	0.33	0.25
	0.00	0.00	0.33	0.33
	0.00	0.00	0.50	0.33
	0.00	0.14	0.56	0.38
	0.00	0.25	0.69	0.39
	0.00	0.29	1.00	0.40
	0.00	0.33	1.00	0.43
	0.00	0.38	1.00	0.44
	0.24	0.42	1.00	0.50
	0.61	0.50	1.00	0.50
	0.86	0.50	1.00	0.50
		0.60		0.52
		0.67		0.54
		0.67		0.55
		0.71		0.56
		0.75		0.57
		0.75		0.57
		0.78		0.60
		0.80		0.66
		0.80		0.71
		0.82		0.83
		0.83		
		0.88		
Mean	0.14	0.49	0.72	0.49
Std dev.	(0.29)	(0.31)	(0.31)	(0.14)

We then try to find differences in behaviour between those subjects that coordinate in the two information treatments. We calculate the win–stay and the lose–change rates for each individual and compare the rates between the two treatments. We suspect that subjects that are given more information behave more in accordance with the win–stay lose–change dynamics, since this scheme would guide players quickly to the efficient cell. Table 7.3 reports the individual mean win–stay and lose–change rates of subjects until coordination sets in.[6]

Each column shows rates for all subjects that coordinated in the corresponding treatment. Numbers have been ordered from low to high. By inspection, one already notices that the variance is quite high, and is higher for the little information treatment than for the treatment with structural information. The reason for this is simply that, in the little information treatment, pairs coordinated rather soon (see Table 7.2) and, thus, individual averages were computed from few within-subject observations. Monte Carlo permutation tests on the equality of medians and means across treatments reject the null hypothesis for the win–stay rates ($p = 0.02$, $p < 0.01$, resp., two-tailed) as well as for the lose–change rates ($p < 0.01$ for both, two-tailed).

We also tried to estimate learning theories for the data on coordinating pairs. By this means, we hoped to find indicators for structural differences between the two differently informed subject groups. However, probably due to the small data sample, the estimation results were similarly uninformative as the ones we conducted in Chapter 6.

7.4   QUESTIONNAIRES

The questionnaires handed out after the experiments ended were much more informative. As indicated in Chapter 5, these questionnaires asked for information on strategies and possible motives for the way the subjects made their decisions. Three questions were asked. First, subjects should briefly describe verbally which process they had used to make their decisions in the first rounds. The second question asked the same for the last rounds. And the third question asked whether subjects had changed their strategy in between and, if they had, why they had changed their strategy. The experimenter made explicit that the subjects were free to answer the questions or to leave the whole sheet blank, and that, in any case, their payoff would not be affected. Nevertheless, most subjects gave enough information to allow us a rough classification of their strategies. In order to avoid artificial play by players who, in anticipation of the questionnaire, restrict behaviour to only those strategies which they can verbalise, subjects were left uninformed about the questionnaire until the end of the experiment.

We classified responses to the questionnaires according to the seven most prominent patterns of play. Table 7.4 shows the aggregate numbers of players who, at some point in time, appealed to the corresponding pattern. Since some subjects changed strategies several times, the numbers within one column may sum to more than the total number of players who responded to the questionnaire in the respective treatment.

Table 7.4 shows that the subjects' intended play differs greatly between treatments. Even though in some cases our interpretation of the vague descriptions are oversimplifying, we may state that a general trend can be observed. Without information on the payoff scheme, subjects make extensive use of simple exploratory multi-round patterns (randomisation, alternation between actions and staying with one action for multiple rounds). Prior structural information drives subjects to accord much more to the win–stay lose–change dynamics. In the treatment with structural information, two subjects even had the idea of using punishment strategies, that is, after losing a point these subjects intended to signal discontent by changing their strategy only once and returning back to their original strategy immediately afterwards. These subjects ignored that they might start off with the action that gives zero points to the opponent, thus, initiating a cycle in punishment signals. Yet, these strategies indicate that subjects were much more determined in their search for the goal than are the rather 'confused' subjects of the experiment on little information.

Table 7.4: Classification of responses in the questionnaires

	Little information	Structural information
Win–stay	7	16
Lose–change	3	9
Lose–change–return	0	2
Randomise	16	7
Alternate	9	2
Stay with one action	8	4
Total number of responses	32	25

While, in the little-information treatment, none of the subjects dared to state a definitive solution concept, several did so in the little-information treatment. One subject who clearly stated to have used the win–stay lose–change dynamics, also wrote: 'Whoever, after 20 rounds, still does not know which action to press, in order to be "rewarded" by the other player, cannot think logically' (translation from German by the author). Obviously, with the inclusion of prior structural information, some subjects perceived the task as trivial. Yet, considering that a substantial number of subjects still made use of randomisation and multi-round patterns, it seems astonishing that almost all pairs eventually managed to coordinate.

7.5   SUMMARY

This small experiment on the impact of structural information prior to repeatedly playing a game in which otherwise little information is provided to the players, led to one clear statement: those subjects who are not informed of the structure of the environment encounter difficulties in coordinating on the single efficient and individually payoff-maximising cell. Few pairs attain coordination, and those who do most often reach coordination very early in the sequence. To the contrary, subjects who are informed about the structure of the interaction most often succeed in reaching coordination, even though pairs sometimes need a considerable amount of repetitions.

We failed to attribute the increased success of the informed subjects to characteristics of individual play. In both treatments, play looks extremely variable. Also, in both treatments subjects repeatedly use multi-round patterns, which may be conceived of as investigation of the environment. This use of complicated structures of behaviour, together with the fact that data on behaviour of successful uninformed subjects is scarce, impeded a firm distinction of adaptive behaviour. Our speculation that we might find a difference between differently informed groups when looking at the data on a round-by-round basis, was partly confirmed. Informed subjects, after encountering a win, seem to stay with their action more often than the uninformed counterparts. The opposite is true for the lose–change dynamics. Informed subjects seem to accord closer with the lose–randomise scheme than the uninformed players who change after losing rather often. While the scarcity of data on decisions impeded firm statistically safe statements, we found further support for our hypothesis in the questionnaires that were handed out after the repeated game was ended.

Following Smith's (1990) tentative early statement that the most important piece of information is one's own payoff from past play, most researchers – theorists as well as experimentalists – have focused on the use of feedback. Our results indicate that there is a need to complement earlier studies with a closer look at the impact of prior information on adaptive play.

NOTES

1. This chapter is based on Mitropoulos (forthcoming). Permission for reprint of the material by Elsevier is gratefully acknowledged.
2. If it does not come at a cost. Indeed, some studies show that even in individual optimisation tasks that do not impose informational cost, additional information may be disadvantageous to the decision-maker (see, for example, Sulganik and Zilcha 1996). A simple game-theoretic model in which information is socially undesirable can be found in Green and Stokey (1980). However, in our game environment, additional information can always be expected to be beneficial.
3. Schelling (1960, pp. 53ff) already reports on the natural salience of certain labels in certain choice tasks.
4. If we use the alternative definition, based on the starting round of coordination, only six pairs in treatment 1 would be classified as coordinating. Rejection of the null hypothesis of equal frequencies of coordination across treatments would then become even stronger.

5. Note that, according to Definition 2 in Chapter 6, the one pair of the experiment with little information, which we classified as slowly coordinating, cannot be assigned a definitive starting round of coordination.
6. Note that two subjects never lost before their coordination phase started.

8.   Measurement of Predictive Success[1]

8.1   INTRODUCTION

Our previous analyses of experimental data deliberately avoided the question of whether any of the adaptive learning rules of Chapter 3 is able to predict actual behaviour better than any other of these rules. One reason for our caution is the fact that we found all rules to suffer from qualitative deficiencies. Obviously, in our game environment subjects followed a more complicated behaviour than any of these rules is able to model. Thus, we would perform a ranking among rules even though we already know that the estimated rules are severely misspecifying the true generating process. Such a ranking would leave us with little insight into learning behaviour, since we would not have confidence in the robustness of the results towards slight variations of the experimental environment. Special environments may be more appropriate for the application of such simple adaptive rules.[2]

The second reason is that a comparison among learning rules can be performed in many different ways, and the way with which learning rules are compared with each other may also influence the resulting ranking. In the past experimental literature on learning, many different researchers have applied many different measures but rarely stated concern about the impact of their choice of measure on the result. At the same time, authors most often selected one or two measures without checking their results on further robustness against variation of the measure that was applied. As far as we are aware, Feltovich (2000) and Erev and Haruvy (2000) are the only works that use more than two different measures. This practice neglects the abundance of conceivable methods of evaluation. This chapter is devoted to showing that the choice of method of evaluation does have an impact on the result of the comparison.

Evaluations consist of different components. We specify three components:

1. the *measure* that implements the comparison between observations and predictions,[3]
2. the *method* of comparing observations with predictions, and
3. the way observations are defined.

Each of these components can be filled in various ways. The combinations of the elements of these components result in a large number of alternative methods of evaluation of the predictive power of learning rules. We apply all these methods of evaluation to all our 12 learning rules that we presented in Chapter 3 and analyse the impact of each component on the ranking of learning rules. The ranking will be based on the ability of the rules to predict behaviour within the four games of our global-game experiment from Chapter 6.

The Mean Squared Deviation

In the past, the measure that has most often been used to compare the success of learning rules in predicting experimental data is the *mean squared deviation* (*MSD*). This measure sums the squared deviations of prediction probabilities from occurred events and normalizes this value by finally taking the square root. Selten (1998) has argued in favour of this measure, since it is the only one that can be generated via a scoring rule that simultaneously fulfils symmetry, elongation invariance, incentive compatibility and neutrality. As noted earlier by Friedman (1983) the *MSD* also has the virtue of being 'effective' with respect to the Euclidean metric, that is, the measure produces larger (that is, less favourable) values as the Euclidean distance between prediction and observation increases. The *MSD* has often been applied to experimental data by way of computing the sum of squared deviations between probability vectors and the relevant unit vectors describing the observations that were made, thereby ignoring the fact that the favourable properties apply only to comparisons between probability distributions and probability distributions. We will argue in this chapter that the applicability of the *MSD* to dependent realisations of random variables causes several problems, the most important of which is that, among two learning rules that produce the same expected hit rates, it selects the one that makes more probabilistic predictions close to the uniform distribution over states.

There are several ways to solve this problem. Purists would still argue in favour of the *MSD*, with the difference that it should be applied to independent histories of play, that is, the state to be predicted would be the evolution of decisions for the whole of a *T*-round repeated game. The problem with this approach is that even for a small number of players, a small number of alternative strategies, little informational feedback and a moderate number of repetitions of the game the number of alternative states (that is, histories) quickly becomes computationally intractable.

Component 1: Measure

The second solution is to use different measures (component i). The *mean absolute deviation* (*MAD*), for example, does not have the above property, since deviations are treated proportionally. It may, thus, be an attractive alternative. Even more so, since it does fulfil the properties of the loss functions as derived from Selten's four axioms for scoring rules. Another way of dealing with predictions is to transform the predicted probabilities into point predictions. This has been done, for example, by Erev and Roth (1998) by using the *proportion of inaccuracy* (*POI*). The authors, thereby, deliberately ignored that by reducing probabilities to point predictions the probabilistic rules were deprived of their very nature. Furthermore, the transformation cuts off valuable information provided by the learning rules. Another alternative measure that suffers from the same deficiency is the *Kuipers Score* (*KS*). This measure was originally considered by Peirce (1884) and is nowadays widely applied in meteorological research (see, for example, Granger and Pesaran 2000). However, this rule has the advantage of normalising the value of uninformative predictions to 0 and that of perfect predictions to 1 (see, for example, Gandin and Murphy 1992). Our analysis will take all of these measures into account. We will also have a closer look at the comparison between the *MSD* and the *KS*.

Component 2: Method of Comparison

A third solution involves a different way of transforming the probabilistic statements into point predictions. This is done by looking at component 2, that is, by looking at the way predictions are formed and compared with aggregates of observations. In particular, one may expand the prediction probabilities to a large set of simulated events whose relative frequencies correspond to the predicted probabilities. The comparison would then involve realisations of the predicted probabilities and the actual realisation of the true random variable. Predictions and observations would, thus, be put on an equal footing without throwing away valuable information. We further argue that for dichotomous choice variables this method of comparison produces the same rankings for the *MSD*, the *MAD*, and the *POI* and asymptotically approaches the *MAD* between observations and probabilistic predictions.

The inconsistency problem of comparing probabilities with realisations of random variables can also be overcome by using aggregates of observations over individuals which are compared with aggregates of probabilistic predictions. The resulting method treats learning rules as predictors of average play. Whether it is useful to use disaggregated or aggregated data as the base depends on the purpose. Those researchers who are more interested in individual decision-making and the investigation of microeconomic dynamics should prefer using the disaggregated data of observations (for example Feltovich 2000). Those who are – within a given environment – interested in the general tendency of decisions over time do better taking averages over individuals (for example Erev and Roth 1998).

Component 3: Aggregation Level of Observations

A further topic concerns the way observations are recorded and, thus, relates to the way the term 'observation' is interpreted. We have already referred to the possibility of taking aggregates over individuals as observations. A different problem arises when one is dealing with repeated games, that is, with games that are repeatedly played by the same individuals. Strictly speaking, the choices of individuals of the same group are not independent, since they receive feedback which is correlated with actions taken by the other players of one's group. One way of addressing this (without falling back into the purist's view outlined above) is to take the group outcome of one period as one observation. This means that we use a different definition of what constitutes one observation within our data (component 3). Experimenters of public good games and coordination games played by cohorts of players started to incorporate this issue long ago. However, since the usual learning environment involves a random matching protocol that complicates matters a lot, this topic has been neglected in the past literature on learning. We will see that, for our data, this distinction does not have a large impact on rankings between learning rules. However, it is likely that the importance of this aspect rises as the number of players that constitute a group increases.

One Further Issue

Apart from the question of how to overcome disadvantageous properties of some methods of evaluation, we may also address another topic which has already been partly recognised in earlier literature. This topic involves the question of whether learning rules are supposed to use all information that has been gathered during play until the period for which the action has to be predicted, or whether to predict for a number of periods beforehand. The two extremes of usage of information illustrate that this question, again, is a matter of research purpose. One may use all information an agent has collected until period t in order to make a prediction for the choice in period $t + 1$. This is called the *one-period ahead* prediction. These predictions are more valuable for short-run investigations of adaptive play and are better suited to elicit the cognitive processes of players within a given environment (for example Camerer and Ho 1999). The other extreme of making predictions is to completely simulate the course of play from the first period to the last (for example Erev et al. 1999). We call this the *complete simulation*. The advantage of this approach is that it better captures whether a learning rule is able to replicate long-run dynamic trends. We incorporated this distinction between types of predictions into our component 2, the *method* of comparison.

Related Work

Some brief discussions of the impact of the choice of method of evaluation on the comparative performance of adaptive theories of behaviour can be found in the experimental investigations by Erev and Roth (1998), Camerer and Ho (1999), Feltovich (2000) and Chen and Khoroshilov (2001). However, the most closely related work to ours is that of Erev and Haruvy (2000). They show on a data set of single-person decision tasks that, depending on the way the comparison between rules is performed, either of three rules may perform best. In particular, they replicate three differing rankings between three rules by using three methods of comparison used in previous literature.

Our study differs from theirs in three respects. First, Erev and Haruvy also consider the way parameter estimations of the respective rules were determined. We simplify the comparison by taking estimations as given. Second, the data on which our comparison is based were taken from an experiment whose informational conditions do not allow for the use of the experienced weighted attraction (EWA) learning first discussed in Camerer and Ho (1999). Instead of focusing on a small set of popular learning models that have different informational properties, we prefer to investigate a large set of rules with similar informational requirements. Third, the scope of our study is not to replicate a set of diverse former results on learning rules within a single data set, but to discuss problems and pitfalls associated with the choice of method of comparison between dynamic rules.

Concern about the problem of effectively evaluating predictions generated by different models arose much earlier among meteorologists.[4] Brier (1950) is supposed to be the first thoroughly to discuss methodological issues of scoring rules. Early on, this literature recognised that predictions share various characteristics that cannot all be captured by a single evaluating function. The starting point was made by Sanders (1963) who offered a decomposition of the *MSD* (which is also known as the *Brier Score*). He thereby suggested considering various components that had previously been hidden within a single skill score. The idea of distinguishing between *resolution* and *calibration* of predictions has been developed further by Murphy (1972a; 1972b; 1973), Yates (1982) and Murphy and Winkler (1987). By now, the literature has matured to consider even more aspects of the quality of probabilistic predictions (Murphy 1996) as well as the inclusion of regression models in order effectively to reduce the dimensionality of comparisons (Murphy and Wilks 1998). We decided not to follow this literature for mainly two reasons. First, the decompositions of the skill score always assume that predictions are made independently in each period. This is in conflict with most learning models that typically assume cumulative adjustment of behaviour. Second, and somehow related to the

Table 8.1:   Overview of dimensions and levels of comparison

Component 1: Measure
- mean squared deviation   *MSD*
- mean absolute deviation   *MAD*
- proportion of inaccuracy   *POI*
- Kuipers score   *KS*

Component 2: Method of comparison
- measure of actual observations and probabilistic one-period ahead predictions $M(Y,P)$
- average measure of actual observations and simulated one-period ahead predictions $M(Y,X)$
- average measure of actual observations and completely simulated actions
  $$M(Y,\overline{Z})$$
- measure of observations aggregated over individuals or pairs and average of completely simulated probabilistic predictions $M(\overline{Y},\overline{P})$
- measure of observations aggregated over individuals and average probabilistic one-period ahead predictions $M(\overline{Y},\overline{Q})$

Component 3: Aggregation level of observations
- individual actions Y
- group outcomes Y^O

Game
- mutual fate control   MFC
- fate–control behaviour–control   FCBC
- simple coordination   CO
- matching pennies   MP
- data on all games combined   all

Rule
- Bush-Mosteller   BM
- Mookherjee–Sopher   MS
- Cross   CR
- Börgers–Sarin   BS
- Roth–Erev   RE
- Variant on RE   REL
- Karandikar et al.   KA
- Experimentation   EX
- Sarin–Vahid   SV
- Win–Stay Lose–Change   WSLC
- Win–Stay Lose–Randomise   WSLR
- Randomisation   RAND

---

first argument, we investigate learning in repeated games, which means that whenever we generate predictions for more than one period ahead, we take into account the future impact of predicted choices on opponent's choices. This is different to settings where nature is the object of prediction. However, some of the insights gained from this literature will influence our analysis.

Table 8.1 gives an overview of all dimensions and levels of comparison.

8.2 NOTATION FOR OBSERVATIONS AND PREDICTIONS

The intense discussion of various kinds of comparison of different sets of data, either generated by experiments or generated by application of theoretical models, requires a very sensitive use of notation. To this end we use a special notation that allows us to unambiguously address all issues we are dealing with. For the same reason we devote a lot of space to thoroughly introduce all elements of our notation.

Individual Observations

We denote the set of players as J and the number of repetitions of the game as T. We assume that each player can choose among a set of actions A which is finite, is the same for all players, and stays fixed over time.[5] Elements of all these sets are denoted by the corresponding lower-case letters. In each period t of the game player j plays action $a_j(t)$ and receives payoff $\pi_j(t)$. For later reference we identify the action chosen with the mixed-strategy vector $Y(j,t)$ that assigns probability 1 to the observed action, that is,

$$Y\left(j,t,a\right) = 1\!\left|a_j\left(t\right) = a\right| \tag{8.1}$$

whereby, as in Chapter 3, 1[.] denotes the indicator function.

Depending on the kind of feedback given to the players, the individual subjective history is given by the vector that subsumes all previous feedback. Since for our exemplary data set it will be the case that subjects knew only about which action they themselves had chosen and which payoff resulted for themselves, the individual history $h_j(t)$ is given by $(a_j(1), \pi_j(1), \ldots, a_j(t-1), \pi_j(t-1))$.[6] Correspondingly, the set of possible histories in period t is denoted by $H(t)$. Theories of decision-making have produced a multitude of rules that do not directly select actions but assign probabilities to actions. For this reason we also need to denote the set of mixed-strategies on the set of actions, $\Delta(A)$. For each period, a decision rule L maps the individual history into the set of mixed-strategies, that is, $L(t): H(t) \rightarrow \Delta(A)$. These constitute what has been termed *adaptive rules* or *learning rules*. Note that rules that make point predictions are simply mapping into unit-vectors.

Observations on Group Outcomes

In experiments on repeated games the J players are grouped into K groups of I players that interact T times with each other. Group $k \subset J$ is identified by its members, and the members are each assigned a position $i \in I$ by the function $pos(k,j)$. Similarly to individual actions we refer to the outcome of a group k within period t by the vector $Y^O(k,t)$ that assigns probability 1 to the outcome actually observed and probability zero to all other $A^I - 1$ possible outcomes, that is, for any $o = (a_1,...,a_I) \in A^I$

$$Y^o(k,t,o) = \prod_{j \in k} 1\left[a_j(t) = a_{pos(k,j)}\right] \qquad (8.2)$$

Comparisons in previous studies have not always measured the predictive success on single observations, but sometimes the predictive success on aggregates, particularly on the average choice probability, whereby the average was taken over all individuals. In our notation this aggregate observation over all individuals will be denoted as

$$\bar{Y}(t,a) = \frac{1}{J}\sum_{j=1}^{J} Y(j,t,a) \qquad (8.3)$$

Correspondingly, we will aggregate outcomes over groups and denote the result by

$$\bar{Y}^o(t,o) = \frac{1}{K}\sum_{k=1}^{K} Y^o(k,t,o) \qquad (8.4)$$

Probabilistic One-Period Ahead Predictions

There are several ways to make predictions. The first and widely applied rule is to use the actual observations to form the individual history $h_j(t)$ for a player j at time t and to make a probabilistic prediction $P(j,t)$ for this period via the applied learning rule, that is, $P(j,t) = L(h_j(t))$ is the prediction vector whose elements sum to one. Just as before we may also aggregate these one-period ahead predictions over players and get $\bar{P}$. Correspondingly, we may make one-period probabilistic predictions for outcomes of group interactions P^O whereby the histories of all players determine the outcome probabilities of that period. The aggregate over groups is then denoted by $\bar{P}^o$.

Simulated One-Period Ahead Predictions

An alternative way of using one-period ahead prediction probabilities is to directly carry out the so-defined random variables and to use the realisations of the random predictions instead of the probabilities.[7] Since some measures will prove not to be linear, measuring the distance between actual observations and prediction probabilities will make a difference to averaging over the identically produced distances between actual observations and simulated prediction realisations. We denote the s-th simulated one-period ahead prediction realisation of actions by X_s and the corresponding one-period ahead prediction of group outcomes by X_s^O.

Completely Simulated Predictions

Predictions may be made for more than only one period ahead. The learning rules may be applied to forecast two, three or maybe more periods beforehand. We chose to use only the two extremes of this predictive ability of the learning rules. Apart from the one-period ahead prediction mentioned above we also examine the predictive power of complete T-round predictions of subjects' play. We, hence, simulated predictions which are based on the history of simulated choices of an individual and not on the actually observed choices. For this purpose we need to simulate the complete T-period repeated interaction of all the I group members. From a single simulation of choices among group members we may either record the individual choice probabilities or the actual choices. In case of probabilities the s-th such simulation is denoted by $\overline{Q}_s$, and in case of the simulated choices we get $\overline{Z}_s$. The simulations may also be used to produce predictions for group outcomes. And again we may record either outcome probabilities $\overline{Q}_s^O$ or the simulated outcomes $\overline{Z}_s^O$. Note that when simulating a complete history of play, characteristics of the history of subjects are ignored. In order to bear this in mind the 'bar' in this notation signifies that the corresponding predictions are not indexed by individuals or groups, just as the average observations $\overline{Y}$ and $\overline{Y}^O$ are not indexed by individuals or groups.

8.3   MEASURES AND AGGREGATES

The MSD and Aggregates of Data and Predictions

In the past literature only few measures for the predictive success of probabilistic learning rules have been used. The most prominent is probably the *mean squared deviation* (*MSD*; also called the *quadratic scoring rule*) which has first been described by Brier (1950) and has extensively been discussed by Savage (1971) and Selten (1998). In broad terms the *MSD* is being defined as the mean of the squared difference between prediction and observation. However, since for experimental observations we may use different aggregates of the data and for the learning rules we may use different aggregates of predictions, the *MSD* measure may be implemented in various ways. The most common way of using it (see, for example, Tang 1998; Feltovich 2000) is to calculate the mean of the mean squared difference between actually observed actions and probabilistic one-period ahead predictions. For reasons of normalisation one should finally take the square root of the result. With our notation, using individual observations Y and individual one-period ahead predictions P, we may write this measure as:

$$MSD(Y,P) = \sqrt{\frac{1}{JTA}\sum_{j=1}^{J}\sum_{t=1}^{T}\sum_{a=1}^{A}\left(Y(j,t,a)-P(j,t,a)\right)^2} \qquad (8.5)$$

Note that within this definition the actual observations Y are represented as probability distributions that place all probability on the actually chosen action.

Instead of using the probabilistic predictions P we may use the corresponding realisation of the implicitly defined random variable X. The complete measure is then defined as the average of the *MSD*s between actual observations and the S simulated realisations of predictions.[8]

$$MSD(Y,X) = \frac{1}{S}\sum_{s=1}^{S}\sqrt{\frac{1}{JTA}\sum_{j=1}^{J}\sum_{t=1}^{T}\sum_{a=1}^{A}\left(Y(j,t,a)-X_s(j,t,a)\right)^2} \qquad (8.6)$$

We may not only compare actual observations with one-period ahead predictions but also with predictions $\overline{Z}$ which simulate the realised history of a pair in which both players use the same learning rule. The resulting measure is

$$MSD(Y,\overline{Z}) = \frac{1}{S}\sum_{s=1}^{S}\sqrt{\frac{1}{JTA}\sum_{j=1}^{J}\sum_{t=1}^{T}\sum_{a=1}^{A}\left(Y(j,t,a)-Z_s(t,a)\right)^2} \qquad (8.7)$$

Note that a complete simulation of the history of a pair $\overline{Z}_s$ is independent of the characteristics of the actually observed pairs j.

There have been some arguments as to whether predictions are meant to predict individual behaviour or aggregate behaviour. We may apply predictions to different aggregates of data, for example aggregates over pairs or aggregates over periods. Similar to using individual actions, we may compare aggregates over individuals $\overline{Y}$ with aggregates over completely simulated paths of actions. Erev et al. (1999) have already pursued this approach. However, they calculated the average of simulated actions while we use the computationally more efficient way of calculating the average of simulated choice probabilities $\overline{Q}_s$, that is,

$$MSD(\overline{Y},\overline{Q}) = \sqrt{\frac{1}{TA}\sum_{t=1}^{T}\sum_{a=1}^{A}\left(\frac{1}{J}\sum_{j=1}^{J}Y(j,t,a) - \frac{1}{S}\sum_{s=1}^{S}\overline{Q}_s(t,a)\right)^2} \qquad (8.8)$$

Finally, one might compare aggregates over individuals with aggregates over one-period ahead probabilistic predictions $\overline{P}$:

$$MSD(\overline{Y},\overline{P}) = \sqrt{\frac{1}{TA}\sum_{t=1}^{T}\sum_{a=1}^{A}\left(\frac{1}{J}\sum_{j=1}^{J}Y(j,t,a) - \frac{1}{J}\sum_{j=1}^{J}P(j,t,a)\right)^2} \qquad (8.9)$$

We may calculate the same five measures using outcomes of groups instead of individual actions. The according measures $MSD^o(Y^o,P^o)$, $MSD^o(Y^o,X^o)$, $MSD^o(Y^o,Z^o)$, $MSD^o(\overline{Y}^o,\overline{Q}^o)$, $MSD^o(\overline{Y}^o,\overline{P}^o)$ differ in two ways. First, one takes the average over outcomes $o \in O$ instead of actions $a \in A$, and second, one averages over groups $k \in K$ instead of individuals $j \in J$.

MAD, POI and the Kuipers Score

We further calculate all these measures not only using the *MSD* but also using the mean absolute deviation, *MAD*, that is, instead of using the squared difference between observation and prediction, we take the absolute difference,[9] and the proportion of inaccuracy, *POI*, which has already been applied to learning theories by Erev and Roth (1998) and Feltovich (2000). The *POI* measure transforms probabilistic predictions into point predictions by way of treating the most probable event as *the* predicted event. For our data set this means that, if one of the two possible actions is predicted with probability higher than 0.5, then this action is assigned probability 1, while the other action is assigned probability 0. In case both actions are predicted with equal probability (which is typically the case in period 1), then each action is assigned probability 0.5. When examining outcomes, the *POI* measure transforms the probability distributions over the four possible outcomes into unit vectors that assign all probability to the most probable outcome. Ties are again broken by assigning equal probability to all most probable outcomes. The measure then reports the mean number of wrong predictions, whereby the mean is taken over all observations. Note that the *POI* measure requires point predictions as well as pure strategy observations. Hence, for comparisons involving aggregates of observations, that is, $\overline{Y}$ or $\overline{Y}^o$, we transform the relative frequencies into pure strategy observations by using the threshold of 0.5, just as probabilistic predictions are rendered deterministically. The same applies to the next measure.

Meteorologists usually use a different measure for assessing the predictive power of a dynamic theory. The Kuipers Score (KS) for two events with base probability of 0.5 for each is defined as the difference between the proportion of correct predictions of an event and the proportion of false predictions when the alternative event occurred. Even though this measure has some desirable properties, it lacks applicability to more than two states of the world. For our data set this means that we can apply the KS to the prediction of individual actions, but we are unable to specify an appropriate generalisation that allows us to use this measure for the four possible group outcomes.[10] We define the Kuipers Score for observed actions and probabilistic predictions as

$$KS(Y,P) = \frac{1}{J}\sum_{j=1}^{J}\left(\frac{T_{BB}(j)}{T_{BB}(j)+T_{BA}(j)} - \frac{T_{AB}(j)}{T_{AB}(j)+T_{AA}(j)}\right)$$

(8.10)

where $T_{ab}(j) = \#\{t \in T | (a_j(t) = a) \wedge (P(j,t,b) > 0.5)\}$ [11]

Note that, as are all the other measures, the KS, too, is invariant to a relabeling of actions. For probabilistic observations it also fulfils *equitability* as defined by Gandin and Murphy (1992).

In the following, when referring to a method of comparison (say, the fit of P to Y) without specifying the measure, we will denote this by the letter M, that is, $M(Y, P)$ in the above case.

8.4   THE DATA SET AND THE GAMES

The data set is taken from the experiment under little information that has been analysed in Chapter 6. We make use of all data; in particular, we use one half of the data for the estimation of parameters and the other half of the data to perform the comparison on the predictive success.

We examine the ability of the calibrated learning rules to predict actual play for data on each game separately. Recall that, except for the strategic similarity between *MFC* and *FCBC*, all games show diametrically different characteristics. They led to more or less volatility in subject behaviour. For this reason, we may expect certain adaptive rules to perform better in some games while others perform best in other games. However, we do not refrain from checking on the predictive power of rules for the entire set of data.

In our new notation the number of rounds of one repeated game is $T = 40$. We have $A = 2$ actions available to each player, and $I = 2$ subjects constitute a pair (or group). Since in each of the 12 sessions 10 subjects were randomly assigned to pairs for four subsequent runs, we have data on 20 pairs for each session, which totals to $K = 240$ pairs over all sessions.

8.5   PARAMETER ESTIMATION

It is beyond the scope of this work to study the method of calibration of learning rules. In the following the estimation results will be taken as given, without questioning the validity or the robustness.[12] The results on the comparison of different learning rules will, however, give rise to discussions about the impact on methods of estimation.

The calibration of the learning rules was done via a maximum-likelihood estimation on the probabilistic one-period ahead predictions for half of the data set. The other half of the data set will serve as the base for predictions. Table 8.2 shows the estimation results for the nine rules that involve parameters. All parameters, except one, turned out to be highly significant (p < 0.001) according to a Wald-Test. The only parameter not being significantly different from 0 (not even to the 10 per cent level) is β^{KA}, the adjustment parameter for the aspiration level. Since the initial aspiration level α^{KA} is very close to 0.5, the resulting KA scheme is statistically indistinguishable from WSLR. This similarity is useful for detecting whether measures sufficiently discriminate between similar and dissimilar rules.

Table 8.2:   Estimation results on the nine rules involving parameters

Rule	Alpha	Beta	Log-Likelihood	Rank
BM	0.27	0.12	−4245.53	1
MS	0.22	0.23	−4338.23	2
CR	0.18	0.03	−4406.63	3
BS	0.40	0.06	−4852.49	8
RE	3.00	0.91	−4446.94	4
REL	13.76	11.22	−4618.87	7
KA	0.49	0.00	−8894.75	9
EX	8.00	0.99	−4489.30	5
SV	0.13	0.27	−4503.46	6

The log-likelihood after calibration already gives a measure of the goodness of fit and allows for a comparison between rules. However, as can easily be seen, rules that make almost point predictions do have a considerable disadvantage as compared with those rules that make predictions with moderate probabilities, since few predictions close to unit vectors that turn out to be false dramatically reduce the likelihood of the observations. Selten (1998) has pointed out this oversensitivity of the log-likelihood measure. We follow him in rejecting this measure as a means to compare different rules with each other and, thus, we will not include it in the following analysis.

8.6   HYPOTHESES AND RESULTS

Characteristics of the Classical MSD

Selten (1998) points out the desirable properties of the *MSD* measure when comparing probabilistic observations with probabilistic predictions. The method $MSD(Y,P)$ is the corresponding measure for the closeness of probabilistic predictions to probabilistic disaggregated events. Contrary to this assumption, experimental data usually consist of a number of correlated observations on events that appear to be realisations of dynamically determined random variables. As a consequence, one must admit the structural difference between predictions and observations.[13]

One way of dealing with this difference is to compare observations with realisations of probabilistic predictions. The corresponding measure is $MSD(Y,X)$. Representing Y, P, and X as column vectors one easily calculates the difference between these two measures as

$$\Delta_{MSD}^{X,P} = E[MSD(Y,X)] - MSD(Y,P)$$
$$= \sqrt{v + 1'P} - \sqrt{v + P'P} \qquad (8.11)$$
$$\geq 0$$

where $v = Y'Y - 2 \cdot Y'P$ and 1 is the vector consisting of ones. More important than the sign of Δ is its dependence on the structure of the probabilities P. The difference is substantially higher, if the predictions P mainly contain intermediate values (around 0.5 for individual actions, or around 0.25 for group outcomes) than if these predictions frequently contain almost sure predictions, that is, many entries close to 0 or close to 1. As a consequence, cautious probabilistic learning rules that mainly predict probabilities around the equal distribution may perform well under $MSD(Y,P)$ but badly under $MSD(Y,X)$. Table 8.3 shows the comparison of ranks for each rule over all measures and for the methods $MSD(Y,P)$ and $MSD(Y,X)$. We restricted the table to show only the results for the aggregation level of individual actions Y and the data set containing observations from all games.

Table 8.3 shows that, indeed, the performance of certain rules varies between $MSD(Y,P)$ and $MSD(Y,X)$. Most intriguing is the jump of the rule

WSLC within the measure *MSD* when turning from probabilistic to simulated predictions. On the other hand, most purely probabilistic rules rank worse when using simulated predictions than when using probabilistic ones. A notable exception is the Börgers–Sarin scheme BS.

Table 8.3: *Comparison of ranks for all rules over all measures and over methods M(Y,P) and M(Y,X), restricted to levels of actions Y and values on all games*

		BM	MS	CR	BS	RE	REL	KA	EX	SV	RAND	WSLC	WSLR
MSD	$M(Y,P)$	2	1	6	3	5	7	8	12	4	11	10	9
	$M(Y,X)$	5	6	9	2	8	10	4	12	7	11	1	3
MAD	$M(Y,P)$	5	6	9	2	8	10	4	12	7	11	1	3
	$M(Y,X)$	5	6	9	2	8	10	4	12	7	11	1	3
POI	$M(Y,P)$	5	3	10	1	9	8	7	12	4	11	2	6
	$M(Y,X)$	5	6	9	2	8	10	4	12	7	11	1	3
KS	$M(Y,P)$	7	3	10	1	9	8	6	11.5	4	11.5	2	5
	$M(Y,X)$	6	5	10	2	9	8	4	11	7	12	1	3

As long as we are dealing with bivariate observational data the *MAD* measure does not suffer from this deficiency. This measure produces the same results for both methods of comparison, that is,

$$\Delta_{MAD}^{X,P} = 0 \tag{8.12}$$

The measures *POI* and *KS* are not quite as stable, but also show less variance between methods than the *MSD*. As will be illustrated later, *MAD*'s independence of the method of comparison is no longer true if we switch to group outcomes as observations, that is, to data with more than two possible states.

Furthermore, if the set of events to be predicted is a finite unordered space, we have $MSD(Y,X) = MAD(Y,X) = POI(Y,X) = MAD(Y,P)$.[14] This means that the method based on simulations of one-period ahead predictions has the advantage of being invariant to whether the *MSD*, the *MAD* or the *POI* measure is being used. And, trivially, this holds even when turning to outcomes as observational data. But the prime argument in favour of using simulations is that the observations are taken as realisations of random variables, which is exactly the way they are treated by the probabilistic theories. To the contrary, the $M(Y,P)$ method, implicitly treats observations as probabilistic events.

The *MSD* versus the *KS*

In earlier literature it has been noted that the *MSD* and the *KS* differ in the way they treat the prediction that consists of a randomisation with uniform distribution over all actions available, which in our case is the RAND rule (see, for example, Gandin and Murphy 1992). While the *MSD* gives some positive value, the *KS* always normalizes the value to 0. For practitioners in applied fields of research this characteristic of the *KS* may be a valuable feature. For the testing and comparison of theories, however, what value is given to the RAND rule is not as important an issue as its rank compared with alternative rules.

Table 8.4: Ranks of the rule RAND for the aggregation level of actions Y *and for measures* MSD *and* KS

		MFC	FCBC	CO	MP	all
$M(Y,P)$	*MSD*	10	10	11	7	11
	KS	11.5	11.5	11.5	11.5	11.5
$M(Y,X)$	*MSD*	11	11	12	11	11
	KS	12	11	12	12	12
$M(Y,\overline{Z})$	*MSD*	3	6	11	1	2
	KS	1	6	10	1	2
$M(\overline{Y},\overline{Q})$	*MSD*	10	5	10	1	9
	KS	12	4		2	1
$M(\overline{Y},\overline{P})$	*MSD*	11	11	11	7	11
	KS	6.5	11.5		7	11.5

Table 8.4 shows all ranks of the RAND rule for the measures *MSD* and *KS* over all methods of comparison and over all games. We restricted the table to only show ranks for the aggregation level of actions *Y*, because for outcomes we do not have a proper definition of the *KS*. Note that, for the CO game, after aggregating observations over individuals, that is, $\overline{Y}$, and after transforming the relative frequencies into a point decision, we were left with the same observation over all 40 rounds. So, the *KS* is not well defined. Table 8.4 shows that there are only few instances of a significant difference in ranks between the *MSD* and the *KS*. Whether RAND performs rather well or rather badly depends on the method of comparison as well as on the characteristics of the data.

The three notable exceptions are implicitly or explicitly discussed below when the performance of rules is investigated for each game separately.

Disaggregated Data Y versus Aggregated Data $\overline{Y}$

Research on adaptive behaviour may serve different purposes. While some researchers may be interested in explaining and predicting individual play, others may be interested purely in aggregate numbers. Within our set of methods of comparison there are two pairs of methods that basically do the same, the only difference being the level of aggregation. In particular, $M(\overline{Y},\overline{P})$ is the same as $M(Y,P)$ on aggregated data, and $M(\overline{Y},\overline{Q})$ is the same as $M(Y,Z)$ on aggregated data. Tables 8.5 and 8.6 show these two comparisons on the ranks generated from the data of all games. The usage of data on particular games exhibits a similarly large discrepancy in ranks between levels of aggregation of observations.

Table 8.5: *Comparison of ranks for all rules over all measures and over methods $M(Y,P)$ and $M(\overline{Y},\overline{P})$, restricted to levels of actions Y and values on all games*

		BM	MS	CR	BS	RE	REL	KA	EX	SV	RAND	WSLC	WSLR
MSD	$M(Y,P)$	2	1	6	3	5	7	8	12	4	11	10	9
	$M(\overline{Y},\overline{P})$	2	1	8	5	9	4	6	12	3	11	10	7
MAD	$M(Y,P)$	5	6	9	2	8	10	4	12	7	11	1	3
	$M(\overline{Y},\overline{P})$	5	1	8	2	10	4	7	12	3	11	9	6
POI	$M(Y,P)$	5	3	10	1	9	8	7	12	4	11	2	6
	$M(\overline{Y},\overline{P})$	3.5	3.5	10.5	7.5	10.5	3.5	3.5	12	3.5	7.5	9	3.5
KS	$M(Y,P)$	7	3	10	1	9	8	6	11.5	4	11.5	2	5
	$M(\overline{Y},\overline{P})$	3.5	3.5	9.5	7	9.5	3.5	3.5	11.5	3.5	11.5	8	3.5

Tables 8.5 and 8.6 show considerable differences in rankings dependent on whether data had been aggregated over players before calculation or not. This is true for both comparisons of methods and is independent of the measure used.

We first discuss the comparison between $M(Y,P)$ and $M(\overline{Y},\overline{P})$ from Table 8.5. As noted in the first subsection, the $M(Y,P)$ method treats observations on pure strategy choices the same as probabilistic predictions. Taking the mean of all observations for each period over all players, thus, transforms data into observations of approximates on choice probabilities for a representative agent. As a result, the method $M(\overline{Y},\overline{P})$ can be viewed as the comparison between observed and predicted choice probabilities of a representative agent who is composed from agents with diverse histories. By aggregation, hence, the method regains internal consistency. The consequence for the rankings depends on the measure used. Since *MSD* punishes large deviations stronger than small deviations, rules making point predictions suffer a disadvantage under disaggregated data as compared to the application of the *MSD* after aggregation (REL, KA, WSLR). Conversely, rules that regularly predict probability distributions rather close to uniformity tend to perform worse after aggregation (CR, BS, RE). This observation is not true for the measure *MAD*, since *MAD* treats large deviations proportionally to small deviations. Still, there are differences in ranks between disaggregated data and aggregated data. Correlation coefficients for each measure on the ranks from the two methods even reveal that the *MSD* produces fewer differences ($\rho = 0.85$) than *MAD*, *POI* or the *KS* (0.43, 0.45, 0.57, respectively).

Table 8.6: Comparison of ranks for all rules over all measures and over methods $M(Y, \overline{Z})$ *and* $M(\overline{Y}, \overline{Q})$, *restricted to levels of actions* Y *and values on all games*

		BM	MS	CR	BS	RE	REL	KA	EX	SV	RAND	WSLC	WSLR
MSD	$M(Y, \overline{Z})$	8	9	2	11	3	6	4	7	12	5	10	1
	$M(\overline{Y}, \overline{Q})$	4	5	8	1	7	11	3	10	6	9	12	2
MAD	$M(Y, \overline{Z})$	8	9	2	11	3	6	4	7	12	5	10	1
	$M(\overline{Y}, \overline{Q})$	4	5	9	1	7	11	3	10	6	8	12	2
POI	$M(Y, \overline{Z})$	8	9	2	11	3	6	4	7	12	5	10	1
	$M(\overline{Y}, \overline{Q})$	6	9.5	11	6	8	6	2.5	9.5	2.5	12	2.5	2.5
KS	$M(Y, \overline{Z})$	10	4	7	9	5	3	8	1	6	2	12	11
	$M(\overline{Y}, \overline{Q})$	8	6	12	8	10	8	3.5	11	3.5	1	3.5	3.5

Discrepancies in rankings between aggregation over players are more pronounced for the comparison between methods $M(Y, \overline{Z})$ and $M(\overline{Y}, \overline{Q})$ which are based on complete simulations of 40-round play (see Table 8.6). Correlation coefficients on the differences in rankings between methods reveal that after aggregation the order of rules is significantly affected ($\rho_{MSD} = 0.03$, $\rho_{MAD} = 0.01$, $\rho_{POI} = -0.23$, $\rho_{KS} = -0.22$). This finding is confirmed by looking at the corresponding figures for specific games. As an example, Table 8.7 shows this comparison of methods for the *MSD* measure and for each game separately. Note that for $M(Y, \overline{Z})$ and $M(\overline{Y}, \overline{Q})$ the measures *MSD* and *MAD* produce the same rankings. The according correlation coefficients between methods vary a lot ($\rho_{MFC} = -0.41$, $\rho_{FCBC} = 0.81$, $\rho_{CO} =$

0.46, ρ_{PM} = 0.08) with the worst correlation between ranks for the game MFC.

Table 8.7: *Comparison of ranks over all rules, over methods* $M(Y,\overline{Z})$ *and* $M(\overline{Y},\overline{Q})$, *and over all games restricted to levels of actions* Y *and the measure* MSD

		BM	MS	CR	BS	RE	REL	KA	EX	SV	RAND	WSLC	WSLR
MFC	$M(Y,\overline{Z})$	9	11	3	10	5	6	4	8	12	7	1	2
	$M(\overline{Y},\overline{Q})$	3	2	7	11	6	9	4	8	1	10	12	5
FCBC	$M(Y,\overline{Z})$	8	9	2	10	3	4	7	6	12	5	11	1
	$M(\overline{Y},\overline{Q})$	9	10	4	12	3	7	2	6	11	5	8	1
CO	$M(Y,\overline{Z})$	8	9	2	11	3	6	4	7	12	5	10	1
	$M(\overline{Y},\overline{Q})$	5	9	1	11	2	3	6	8	4	10	12	7
MP	$M(Y,\overline{Z})$	7	10	6	2	8	5	11	9	3	4	12	1
	$M(\overline{Y},\overline{Q})$	7	9	5	12	4	6	3	8	11	1	10	2

Note that for the game CO the method $M(Y,\overline{Z})$ is not really meaningful, since observations are distributed in a bimodal way. Pairs most often eventually coordinated on either (A, A) or (B, B), with both outcomes being almost equally likely. Simulated players, hence, cannot capture the trend towards a particular action of an individual over time. This deficiency is eliminated when using the relevant method on aggregated data, that is, $M(\overline{Y},\overline{Q})$, since both observations as well as predictions are formulated independently of individuals.

Returning to Tables 8.5 and 8.6 we also note that *POI* and *KS* are better not used on aggregated data because they do not sufficiently discriminate among rules. In our case, after aggregation there are only 40 data points left for comparison. Since aggregated data as well as aggregated predictions are internally highly correlated, these measures by transforming into point predictions and pure strategy observations eliminate too much information.

One-Period Ahead Predictions *P* versus Complete Simulations $\overline{Z}$, $\overline{Q}$

When forecasting economic indicators or indices from stock markets, it is naturally an important issue for which time horizon predictions are formed. Apart from seasonal influences that have to be taken into account, there is a trade-off between the size of the prediction period and accuracy. When experimentalists use models of adaptive decision-making, then the same decision upon the size of the prediction interval involves more methodological considerations. While the forecasting of stocks and bonds or economic indicators serves the sole purpose of making the optimal decision on investment or policy, experimental economics has an additional interest in finding a good model of the underlying cognitive processes. As a consequence, different methods of evaluation may serve different aspects of research in learning. If models are supposed to fit as closely as possible to the actual process of decision-making of subjects, then it is best to compare the performance of a decision rule by measuring its efficacy in predicting the immediately following decision, given the history of decisions before. This is represented by our set of one-period ahead predictions P. The design of market institutions, however, requires the anticipation of general dynamic trends. This is better captured by predictions of long sequences of dynamic play. For this purpose we also chose to simulate complete 40-round sequences of repeated play with artificial agents. We denote one such sequence as $\overline{Z}_s$ and the average of a number of such sequences as $\overline{Q}$.

We, first, stay at the disaggregated level of data and look at the difference in ranks among rules between using realisations of the probabilistic predictions $M(Y,X)$ and the completely simulated predictions $M(Y,\overline{Z})$. Table 8.8 shows the corresponding figures.

Note, first, that for simulated disaggregated data the *MSD* produces the same ranks as *MAD* and the *POI*. Note further that for the reasons mentioned in the preceding subsection we do not present figures for the game CO.

It is fairly obvious that the method employed has a larger impact on the rank of a rule than the game. Most striking is the good performance of the simple model WSLC over all games, if one-period ahead predictions are considered. For the game MFC performance stays good even when turning to simulated predictions. But for the other games, WSLC rather badly predicts the long-run trend of pairs. The more appropriate rule WSLR performs well independently of the game and independently of the way predictions are being generated. A further striking observation concerns the rule RAND. The bad result of the purely randomising decision rule when predicting individual decisions had to be expected. Also, no surprise causes the good performance of RAND for the game MP, since, by the dynamics of the game, subjects can be expected to be driven to randomising behaviour. However, the intermediate ranks for the two other games show that more sophisticated rules have difficulties in capturing coordination by pairs.

We now have a look at the same figures for the comparison of rules based on aggregated data. Table 8.9 shows the ranks of rules once for the comparison between aggregate one-period ahead predictions and aggregated data, that is, $M(\overline{Y},\overline{P})$, and once for the comparison between completely simulated predictions and aggregated data, $M(\overline{Y},\overline{Q})$.

Table 8.8: *Comparison of ranks over all rules, over methods* $M(Y,X)$ *and* $M(Y,\overline{Z})$, *and for each game separately restricted to levels of actions* Y *and the measure* MSD

		BM	MS	CR	BS	RE	REL	KA	EX	SV	RAND	WSLC	WSLR
MFC	$M(Y,X)$	5	6	9	1	7	10	4	12	8	11	3	2
	$M(Y,\overline{Z})$	9	11	3	10	5	6	4	8	12	7	1	2
FCBC	$M(Y,X)$	5	6	7	4	8	10	2	12	9	11	1	3
	$M(Y,\overline{Z})$	8	9	2	10	3	4	7	6	12	5	11	1
MP	$M(Y,X)$	7	5	10	2	9	8	4	12	6	11	1	3
	$M(Y,\overline{Z})$	7	10	6	2	8	5	11	9	3	4	12	1

Table 8.9: *Comparison of ranks over all rules, over methods* $M(\overline{Y},\overline{P})$ *and* $M(\overline{Y},\overline{Q})$, *and for each game separately restricted to levels of actions* Y *and the measure* MSD

		BM	MS	CR	BS	RE	REL	KA	EX	SV	RAND	WSLC	WSLR
MFC	$M(\overline{Y},\overline{P})$	5	3	7	1	10	8	2	12	6	11	9	4
	$M(\overline{Y},\overline{Q})$	3	2	7	11	6	9	4	8	1	10	12	5
FCBC	$M(\overline{Y},\overline{P})$	5	2	9	1	10	8	3	12	6	11	7	4
	$M(\overline{Y},\overline{Q})$	9	10	4	12	3	7	2	6	11	5	8	1
MP	$M(\overline{Y},\overline{P})$	2	1	6	4	5	10	8	12	3	7	11	9
	$M(\overline{Y},\overline{Q})$	7	9	5	12	4	6	3	8	11	1	10	2

Comparing Tables 8.8 and 8.9 with each other we see that after turning to aggregated data the rules that require little sophistication do not perform as extremely as for the disaggregated data. For one-period ahead predictions of aggregated data the BS rule performs particularly well. However, the same rule performs worst when turning to complete simulations. It appears that data on the MFC game produce less differences in ranks ($\rho_{\text{MFC}} = 0.38$) than the data for the other two games for which correlations of ranks even tend to be negative ($\rho_{\text{FCBC}} = -0.34$, $\rho_{\text{MFC}} = -0.27$). We, hence, find that when looking at aggregated data, the incentives of the games are as important a factor for the rankings as is the way predictions are generated.

Individual Actions Y versus Group Outcomes Y^o

Up to now, in order to assess the predictive power of a learning rule, we always used individual actions as the underlying observations. This is in line with general practice in experimental learning literature. However, without loss of information we may also use the group outcome as the observed variable. Similar to the comparison of methods $M(Y,P)$ and $M(Y,X)$ from the first subsection, we obtain that the $MSD^o(Y^o,P^o)$, as compared with $MSD^o(Y^o,X^o)$, favours predictions close to uniform distributions over predictions close to unit vectors. We have seen that the MAD measure did not discriminate between probabilistic rules and learning rules that make point predictions as long as the expected number of hits is the same. However, MAD suffers from the same deficiency as the MSD measure when turning to outcomes as observational data. That is, $MAD^o(Y^o,P^o)$ will favour probabilistic over point predicting rules as compared with the usage of simulations, that is, $MAD^o(Y^o,X^o)$. A set of stylised data illustrates this point. We use the simplest possible observation, namely that both players use the same action (action B) over all four periods. Observations and predictions are displayed in Table 8.10.

Table 8.10: Exemplary data for observations, point predictions and probabilistic predictions

			Prediction			
			Point predicting rule		Probabilistic rule	
	Observation					
Period	Player 1	Player 2	Player 1	Player 2	Player 1	Player 2
1	B	B	A	B	0.5	0.5
2	B	B	B	A	0.5	0.5
3	B	B	A	B	0.5	0.5
4	B	B	B	A	0.5	0.5

The resulting values for the two rules over aggregation levels and over measures for the method $M(Y,P)$ are depicted in Table 8.11.

The result is that, among those learning rules that produce the same number of correct predictions on group outcomes, the $MSD(Y,P)$ favours those that make predictions close to the uniform distribution. It does even more so when using the observational level of group outcomes rather than individual actions. $MAD(Y,P)$ does not discriminate between types of rules as long as we deal with individual actions as observations. However, probabilistic rules perform better when applied to the group outcomes. The intuition behind it is that on the level of outcomes the probabilistic prediction scatters probability mass over several possible outcomes and thus reduces the expected penalty of a wrong prediction.

Table 8.11: Values of predictive power for the exemplary data

		Point predicting rule	Probabilistic rule
MSD	Actions	0.707	0.500
	Outcomes	0.707	0.433
MAD	Actions	0.500	0.500
	Outcomes	0.500	0.375

Table 8.12: Comparison of ranks over all rules, over methods $M(Y,P)$ and $M(Y,X)$, over measures MSD, MAD and POI and over aggregation levels, restricted to data from all games

			BM	MS	CR	BS	RE	REL	KA	EX	SV	RAND	WSLC	WSLR
MSD	$M(Y,P)$	Actions	2	1	6	3	5	7	8	12	4	11	10	9
		Outcomes	1	2	4	5	6	7	8	12	3	10	11	9
	$M(Y,X)$	Actions	5	6	9	2	8	10	4	12	7	11	1	3
		Outcomes	5	6	7	4	8	10	3	11	9	12	1	2
MAD	$M(Y,P)$	Actions	5	6	9	2	8	10	4	12	7	11	1	3
		Outcomes	5	6	7	4	8	10	3	12	9	11	1	2
	$M(Y,X)$	Actions	5	6	9	2	8	10	4	12	7	11	1	3
		Outcomes	5	6	7	4	8	10	3	11	9	12	1	2
POI	$M(Y,P)$	Actions	5	3	10	1	9	8	7	12	4	11	2	6
		Outcomes	5	3	10	1	9	7	8	11	4	12	2	6
	$M(Y,X)$	Actions	5	6	9	2	8	10	4	12	7	11	1	3
		Outcomes	5	6	7	4	8	10	3	11	9	12	1	2

Table 8.12 shows the corresponding values for the actual data. It is plain to see that the above result for extreme learning rules and extreme data does not carry over to the analysis of our data. The method and the measure do have a larger impact on rankings than whether we use individual actions or group outcomes.

Still, the problems described above again lead us to support the usage of simulated predictions, which do not suffer from similar problems of inconsistency. We suspect, that the larger the number of the group members and the larger the number of alternative actions, the stronger is the impact of the representation of the data as actions or as outcomes. The idea behind our conjecture is that this would quickly lead to outcome spaces that are much larger and allow probabilistic rules to scatter probability mass even more.

8.7   SUMMARY

This chapter was devoted to eliciting the impact of the choice of the method of comparison on the resulting ranking between learning rules. We found that the choice of method can have a significant impact on the ranking. The analysis of this chapter helps to clarify the characteristics of the various methods of evaluation and offers ways of how to produce robust results. Where methods differ from each other in fundamental ways we argue that each method may be conceived of as serving different purposes. Furthermore, we find some applications in earlier literature suffer from lack of consistency. As a result, we suggest that future research on learning should be more sensitive to methodological issues. Either researchers support their choice of method of comparison by arguments related to the purpose of their study, or they support the robustness of their results by checking on a wide range of alternative methods.

In particular we find that the popular *MSD* measure suffers from some deficiencies and should better not be used in conjunction with a comparison between observational data on individual actions and probabilistic predictions. The classical way around this problem is to use measures that transform probabilistic predictions into point predictions by using a cut-off prediction probability (in our case 0.5). This is done in the *POI* and *KS* measures. This procedure, however, is accompanied by a severe loss of information. Instead, we suggest to use simulations of probabilistic predictions. So, a mean of measures of predictive power between actual observations and simulated predictions can be calculated.

We further find that the method of comparison is crucial for the resulting ranking between rules. It does matter whether one uses disaggregated data or mean values averaged over individuals. It also does matter whether one chooses one-period ahead predictions or complete simulations of play. Experimentalists analysing their data may justify their decision on these two dimensions by pointing to their research purpose. Disaggregated data and one-period ahead predictions are better suited to studying individual cognitive processes, while aggregated data and long-run predictions better elicit the ability to forecast general dynamic trends. In any case, the purpose of the study should be made clear.

For our data, which are generated by repeated interaction of groups consisting of only two players, the question of whether predictions are made for individual actions or for group outcomes seems not to matter much.

However, the analysis on exemplary data shows that its importance may be expected to rise when groups consist of more players.

The scope of this work is not limited to repeated games. The insights gained into the use of measures for the predictive power of dynamic theories carry over to the literature on econometrics and meteorological forecasting. Considering that measures may as well be used for estimation purposes, our conclusion is that the estimation of learning theories of the kind used in this study involves a lot of sensitivity towards the employed method of estimation. For example, the maximum-likelihood estimation procedure has long been criticised (see, for example, Friedman 1983). Modern econometric approaches further investigate the variance of predictions based on the variance of parameter estimations, given the probabilistic nature of the observations. The usual approach is to use bootstrapping techniques, such as, for example, in Pascual et al. (2001) or Bracht (2001). At this stage, due to the large number of candidates as methods of evaluation and the large number of conceivable learning rules, we deem it not promising to follow this approach. Future research on the theory of learning may successfully single out a small set of reasonable learning rules. Then, the usage of bootstrapping or similar statistical methods may well be reconsidered.

NOTES

1. This chapter is based on Mitropoulos (2001c).
2. Indeed, simple adaptive rules have most often been studied in conjunction with either decision-making under risk (see Erev et al. 1999 and references therein) or games with unique mixed-strategy equilibrium (see Erev and Roth 1998 and references therein). Behaviour in such environments has been shown to change rather smoothly over time (at least on aggregate).
3. This component is equivalent to the scoring rule, if that exists.
4. Murphy (1998) surveys the early development of probabilistic weather forecasting.
5. We may easily generalise to player-specific and time-varying action spaces.
6. Again we may easily generalise to accustom different informational settings.
7. In the terminology of Selten (1991) probabilistic learning rules are distribution theories while predictions of single events are point theories. Hence, we transfer predictions of distributions into sets of correlated point predictions. Selten, however, focuses on area theories, which we do not consider in this work.
8. We used $S = 10\ 000$.
9. Of course, the normalisation by way of taking the square root has to be dropped.
10. Gandin and Murphy (1992) show that the KS is the only equitable rule for two-state predictions. They show that equitability imposes necessary constraints on the scoring rule that for predictions on more than two states do not suffice to characterise the rule. Thus, we could have generated a scoring rule that shares the equitability properties and can be applied to predictions of four states. Since

      this literature is not well developed yet, we refrain from determining our own generalisation of the KS.

11.   Within the computations, ties in prediction probabilities, that is, $p = 0.5$ for either strategy, are broken in favour of action B.

12.   A similar study on the impact of various methods of estimation of one adaptive learning rule on the resulting estimation parameters has been done independently by Bracht (2001).

13.   The problem that predictions and observations are of different type has already been discussed by Bossuyt and Roskam (1987). However, their analysis is limited to static probabilistic choice models.

14.   Except for the normalisation, which however does not affect ranks.

9.   Discussion and Outlook

There are three ways to act wisely:
The first way, by cogitation, is the noblest.
The second way, by imitation, is the easiest.
The third way, through experience, is the hardest.
(Confucius)

It is intriguing to observe that current models of decision-making are based on the same principles that were identified thousands of years ago. Still, we have good reason to believe that research in decision-making has made considerable progress. We are now able to state *exact* models of cogitation, *exact* models of imitation and *exact* models of how to process experience. This state allows us to rigorously compare models with each other and to select those that serve one's goal best. By now, research has made some progress in selecting among models, though much is still in the making. The present work adds quantitative as well as qualitative results to the existing set of comparisons and makes suggestions as to how to make progress in the way comparisons are carried out.

9.1   SUMMARY OF RESULTS

Our work focuses on the 'hard' way of acting wisely. We examine properties of adaptive learning theories, that is, theories of how experience is mapped into actions. We do not consider the noble way, which we take to be the rationalistic approach of classical economic methodology. Nor do we consider imitation, which, in economics, has most often been studied in conjunction with evolutionary models. The reason for our restrictive approach stems from recent developments in the economics literature.

Currently, there is a hot debate going on about the performance of different learning theories in different environments. During the last few years many learning rules have been proposed to account for actual human behaviour and have been applied econometrically to data from various experiments. Most of the recently proposed learning rules draw on concepts developed by psychologists and challenge the traditional economic methodology. In particular, many models have been reported to be quite successful in accounting for adaptive behaviour in situations where much more information was available than the learning rules assumed to be used (for example, Roth and Erev 1995; Erev and Roth 1998; Camerer and Ho 1999; Feltovich 2000). The multitude of different set-ups and ways of comparison led us to downscale – from an informational point of view – the setting in which comparisons between learning rules are made. Most of the earlier studies ask whether simple rules, which rely solely on the processing of feedback about one's own payoff, are better at accounting for behaviour in complex environments than complex rules, which make use of much more of the available information. We depart from this approach in that we assess the explanatory power of simple learning rules in situations in which there is hardly any other information available than is used by these theories. We restricted the feedback from play to the own payoff that resulted from the last interaction and called this setting the 'little-information environment'. This setting thus excludes models of 'easy' imitation and 'noble' best reply, and limits comparisons among rules to those processing 'hard' experience.

The formulation of *exact* models of behaviour bears several advantages over vague ones. First, differences in properties between models may be specified and discussed in much more detail. Second, quantitative comparisons can be carried out and statistical methods can be applied in order to single out the best-performing model. Third, models can be compared to data, in particular to carefully collected experimental data. The last property allows researchers to select the ability to explain and predict actual human behaviour as the objective according to which models are formed. In the past, much experimental work was devoted to show the limitations of existing models of behaviour. By investigating the resulting discrepancies between model and actual behaviour theories have been improved. As regards learning, earlier experimental investigations were thus meant to make suggestions for theoretical work on learning. For most of our work, we go back one step and question the stability of past results along informational and technical dimensions. However, on a meta-level the study of the stability of results serves to improve the process of selecting among descriptive rules of adaptive behaviour and, thus, indirectly affects the theory of learning. In some instances, we are even able to formulate concrete suggestions for future research.

In Chapter 3 we studied the dynamics of a number of learning rules on a set of four games. The games were selected to be part of a global game that was later implemented in the laboratory. We found that some, from an analytic point of view, similar rules show different dynamic paths, while other dissimilar looking rules show similar dynamics. In a preliminary experiment (Chapter 5) on the game mutual fate control we then selected two learning rules that make qualitatively different predictions on long-run behaviour and compared them on various grounds. We found that each of the two rules captures certain features of observed behaviour, but none satisfactorily accounts for all qualitative findings. In a larger experiment (Chapter 6) we investigated the ability of subjects to coordinate in a controlled global-game environment in which there is uncertainty about the strategic situation. We found that the repetition of the task clearly had an impact on the coordination speed. However, none of the learning rules was able to capture the change in behaviour, neither qualitatively nor via estimated parameters. Instead, we found evidence in favour of the hypothesis that subjects make use of sequences of actions that serve them to explore the environment. Adaptive learning rules do not capture such behaviour. The small experiment we report in Chapter 7 was then aimed at testing whether subjects are more successful in coordinating in the mutual fate control game when there is no uncertainty about the strategic situation. We found that subjects are indeed able effectively to use the additional information. Subjects exhibit larger rates of the almost optimal win–stay lose–change strategy (a strategy that quickly leads to coordination, if applied by both players) than under strategic uncertainty. Furthermore, the questionnaires reveal that subjects had similar strategies in mind when applying their otherwise more complex and diffuse individual rules. This predisposition to accord to something similar as win–stay lose–change suffices to let subjects coordinate in most of the cases. Finally, Chapter 8 is devoted to elicit problems and fallacies when trying to compare calibrated learning rules on the grounds of their predictive success. The quintessence of that chapter is that there is a multitude of ways comparisons may be carried out. Researchers, here, face a trade-off: either they check on the robustness of their ordering of rules by using a large number of different methods of comparison, or they restrict the comparison to a certain research purpose. In any case, contrary to most studies so far, we suggest that individual predictions of actual behaviour should be compared via their simulated realisations, instead of their predicted probabilities.

9.2   ON INFORMATION

Our work is mostly critical of current developments in the experimental analysis of learning. We find that learning rules are not readily applicable to any environment. Those learning rules that have been reported to predict best in richer informational environments are found to perform rather poorly in a little-information setting. This is so even though their restricted use of information renders them particularly salient for such environments. The lesson to be learned from this result is that the level and structure of information that is provided to the players is a crucial element for actual behaviour. As we have laid out briefly in Chapter 2, this topic is hotly discussed in the literature on static rules of decision-making. Our analysis shows that the problems carry over to dynamical behavioural rules. In particular, as we have shown in Chapter 7, it is not only the amount of feedback that matters. Information provided to the players prior to playing a repeated game seems to be of as much importance. Such considerations have rarely been dealt with in the economic literature on learning.[1]

What are the implications for economic theorising and its empirical analysis? Economics (in contrast to psychology) has always been led by the trial to find universal truths. Therein, the rationality paradigm served as a benchmark that gave insights into the general incentives of economic settings. The profession currently seems to have reached a turning point. Experimental evidence casts doubt on the usefulness of the rationality assumption. Experimentalists as well as theorists are intensively discussing framing effects, that is, differences in behaviour that cannot be accounted for by standard assumptions, including the rationality postulate (see, for example, Camerer 1995). Different framing effects suggest different modifications of the standard assumptions, and one is inclined to believe that there is no other way out than to drop the aspiration of universal applicability of economic theories. The development of special theories whose scope is limited to special settings may enhance the predictive power of economic theory. On the other hand, the case of psychology shows that such a separation into narrow research areas may come at a severe cost. Economists often complain about psychology that theories as well as experimental evidence is so abundant that no single person will ever be able to reconcile all related studies of any one topic. Furthermore, economists express the fear that publication incentives are such that, once separation into narrowly defined research areas has set in, further studies that deal with topics of very limited scope are strongly encouraged (see, for example, Rubinstein 2001).

In the past economic literature on learning some utterances have been made that sound like appeals to such a separation. Arthur (1991), for example, states:

> It is unlikely there exists some yet-to-be-defined decision algorithm, some 'model of man,' that would represent human behavior in all economic problems – an algorithm whose parameters would constitute universal constants of human behavior. Different contexts of decision making in the economy call for different actions; and an algorithm calibrated to reproduce in a search problem might differ from one that reproduces strategic-choice behavior. We would likely need a repertoire of calibrated algorithms to cover the various contexts that might arise. (Arthur 1991, p. 353)

However, Roth and Erev (1995) successfully reinterpret Arthur's approach along the lines of standard economic methodology. They try to find the best-fitting learning rule, given that parameters have to be fit for each experimental setting separately. In Erev and Roth (1998) they even try to find the universally optimal parameters for their learning rule; a goal that Arthur deemed impossible to reach. Indeed, their results are challenged by more recent evidence (Sarin and Vahid 2001). Another, and more determined, trial to establish a methodology of 'scattered' research areas is Slembeck's (1998) call for 'contingent learning theories': 'It is argued that the introduction of the main determinants of learning behavior as situational restrictions into the standard economic model may be a fruitful way to capture some important aspects of human behavior that have often been omitted in economic theory' (Slembeck 1998, abstract).

At this point we content ourselves with presenting the current state of discussion, since we neither feel confident enough in making predictions about the fate of a whole branch of science, nor do the results of the present work allow for a definitive judgement. We only believe that they may be of relevance for future discussions on the methodology of economic thought. The special shape of information that is provided to the players prior to playing a repeated game may turn out to be of such relevance that any predictive learning rule must be made contingent on this information. On the other hand, modelling techniques may advance in such a way that the crucial parts of prior information can be fed into good learning rules via special parameters. We do not dare to predict what future research will look like.

9.3   ON LEARNING TO LEARN

Economists have been reluctant to touch upon the topic of meta-learning. The only theoretical work in this area that we know of is Sonsino's (1997) study on the impact of pattern recognition on equilibrium selection.[2] Psychologists, on the other hand, have dealt with this topic for many decades, with the peak of interest having been during the 1950s and 1960s (see Walker 1996, pp. 78–80, for a brief introduction). Almost all studies, however, deal with this topic in conjunction with tasks on problem-solving. That is, several stages of repeatedly encountered single-person decision tasks are linked by common characteristics which have to be recognised by the subjects. Lately, the topic of learning to learn has been almost exclusively applied to educational studies. To our knowledge, economic issues, such as efficiency, have never been touched upon.

By now, some experimental economists have tried to incorporate meta-learning by extending their models to allow for the ability to change learning rules over time (Camerer et al. 1999; Stahl 2000; 2001). However, Salmon (1999b) criticises these studies because they continue to suffer from their inability to prove the improvement in explanatory power, since more involved models that incorporate more generality imply a better fit, possibly without being closer to the true generating process. Salmon resorts to interview data in order to get more reliable information about the actual processes that govern subjects' choices. Still, as laid out in Chapter 6, we criticise his method of revealing information about the change in learning rules.

Our study on the repeatedly played repeated global game shows that, in the present context, subjects are able to improve their skills in dynamic decision-making. Hence, the difficulties in coordinating without having much information can, at least partly, be overcome with experience. However, our trial to account for improved coordination abilities via adaptive learning models failed. Estimated parameters gave no hint at any systematic change of a disposition towards a particular dynamic process. We think that more research on subjects' ability to learn about effective learning behaviour may enhance greatly our understanding of human cognition and, thus, promises to improve on current models of adaptive behaviour.

9.4   UNTOUCHED TOPICS

Strategy Space

Recall our discussion of Van Huyck et al.'s (2001) analysis from Chapter 4. In their experiment, subjects had the choice of 101 alternative strategies. They tried to analyse behaviour based on the standard reinforcement and fictitious play dynamics and came to the counter-intuitive result that fictitious play accounts for behaviour better than does reinforcement, even though subjects had not sufficient information to actually perform the calculations needed for fictitious play. Our suspicion is that the use of the original versions of the learning rules was unjustified here, since these rules have been developed for small strategy spaces of no more than six or seven strategies. Roth and Erev (1995) already suggested a modification of their reinforcement learning rule so that it better accounts for behaviour in large strategy spaces with ordered alternatives. Their idea is to define a metric on the strategy space and to reinforce all strategies that lie within an interval around the previously successful strategy. Chen and Khoroshilov (2001) implemented this and were, thus, able to estimate a best-fitting length of the reinforcement interval.

This line of research may easily be complemented with ideas that have recently developed in computer science. Reinforcement models that can be applied to continuous strategy spaces have already been discussed in the literature on neural networks.[3] Within the field of control theory a promising looking extension to neural nets has been the combination with fuzzy systems. The resulting *fuzzy-neural* models overcome the problem of lack of interpretability of pure neural nets. Neural nodes are now linked via linguistic rules that are formulated with fuzzy logic. In terms of adaptive learning theories, fuzzy sets represent the topology of the strategy space on which the activation of rules is defined. The more payoff a strategy generates, the more those fuzzy sets are activated to which the strategy belongs. And, the more a fuzzy set is activated, the likelier is it that one of its strategies will be the next action the system will choose. A function that maps the activation level of the fuzzy sets onto the strategy space determines the next action to take.

A common problem with all connectionist models is that there are many free parameters that may be adjusted. For that reason, fitting such models to data may result in overfitting and comparisons to simpler adaptive rules may be difficult. Still, due to their difference to conventional approaches, a thorough investigation into the characteristics of such models may trigger new ideas on theories of learning.

Transfer

The transfer of learned concepts from one environment into another is also a topic much neglected in economic literature. While psychologists, again, have marked the lead, it is only recently that economists have attempted to investigate the transfer of skills. Slonim (1999) conducted an experiment on several successively played sets of differently shaped single-person decision tasks and was thus able to distinguish those subjects who learn via focusing on rules of thumb from those subjects who learn via gaining insight into the incentives. His results are favourable of the hypothesis that subjects are able to learn rationally.

A different approach was chosen by Stahl (1999). He estimated learning rules on two series of games, the series being distinguished by characteristics of the games. Stahl included a parameter that captured the degree to which subjects transferred the rule they were using in the last round of the first series to the first round of the second series. The estimation result indicates that subjects completely carry over the rule they had learned before, even though a regime shift in the type of game occurred.

Changes in the way people adapt to collected information may not only be caused by changes in the incentive structure. Framing effects, as have been investigated extensively in single-person decision-making[4] and behaviour in games,[5] will also have to be investigated with respect to learning behaviour. We would not be surprised to find regime shifts in the way people learn when placed in a different context without changing the basic characteristics of the interaction.

Payment Scheme

A recent study by Merlo and Schotter (1999) revealed that the way people are payed according to their decisions may significantly affect incentives, and thus the way people learn in experiments. They used two settings in order to check a treatment effect which turned out to be highly significant. In the first treatment ('learn while you earn') subjects received a small payoff after each round. This is essentially the method we used to pay out subjects in all of our experiments. The second treatment ('learn before you earn') had subjects play (almost) the same amount of repetitions but did not pay subjects except for the last round. The last round was then paid out with high stakes. The study compares subject behaviour between the last round of the second treatment and a high-stakes round in the first treatment that was added at the end of the experiment without having been announced prior to finishing the low-stakes rounds.

The results show that low regular payments foster myopic adaptive play while subjects in the learn-before-you-earn treatment are able to make choices much closer to optimality. This result supports our choice of choosing low payments on a regular basis, since our goal was to detect properties and modifications of adaptive play. Our finding that adaptive learning rules ignore important aspects of actual behaviour has, thus, been derived within a setting particularly favorable for the applicability of adapting learning rules.

However, the study of Merlo and Schotter was based on a single-person decision task. In such a setting, experimentation behaviour is sure to improve the informational state of the subject. Small payoffs on a regular basis, thus, impose an opportunity cost on experimentation, while there is no such opportunity cost in the learn-before-you-earn treatment. Considering this, it is not surprising to observe subjects in the learn-before-you-earn treatment to choose closer to optimal play than the subjects in the learn-while-you-earn treatment. Things are different in games, however. There, as argued in more detail in Chapter 6, experimentation may cause a lack of interpretability of his action by the other player. It is an open question which of the two treatments leads to more adaptive play and, thus, may worsen his or her informational state, especially in games requiring coordination-like play, and which leads to improved results in games under little information.

Relation to Static Models of Decision-Making

Some recent studies try to bridge the gap between descriptive models of adaptive play and static models of boundedly rational decision-making. In particular, Erev and Barron (2001) and Barron and Erev (2002) examine in a series of experiments whether systematic deviations from maximising behaviour, which are well known from one-shot probabilistic-choice tasks, continue to hold in an environment with repeated decisions and feedback. The results indicate that certain phenomena are counteracted by experience. For example, the inclination by subjects to prefer certain safe alternatives over similarly profitable, but slightly risky outcomes can be reversed through adaptive learning. Likewise, risk aversion in the gain domain and risk-seeking in the loss domain can be reversed, if subjects have to repeat the same choice for a large number of times and feedback is provided to them after each round. Also, in repeated choice tasks small probabilities may end up being underweighted by the decision-maker, contrary to what was found in one-shot probabilistic choice. The only phenomenon that has been found to resist repetition is loss aversion.

Insights gained from previous studies on learning tasks may help interpret the results. Barron and Erev show that typical features of adaptive learning models are consistent with the observed phenomena. In particular, risky choices that are sufficiently probable may reinforce probabilistic outcomes stronger than certain alternatives with the same expected outcome. For the same reason, risk aversion in the gain domain may vanish or even reverse after repeating the task many times. Small probabilities are reinforced very rarely and may quickly be neglected, if subjects repeatedly facing the choice task weigh recent feedback more than experience that lies further in the past.

Up to now, these studies are limited to the investigation of behaviour in single-person probabilistic choice tasks. One may extend these analyses to games with stochastic outcomes.

9.5 CONCLUSION

Even though some of our results seem to run counter to many recent developments in the theory and experimental investigation of learning, we believe that we contribute to this field in a constructive way. The basic insight of our studies is that more attention should be paid to the informational setting in which learning occurs. Current theories seem inadequate to capture basic behavioural features in very basic experimental settings. In addition, we show ways of how to improve on the way little information can be implemented in the laboratory, especially focusing on the control of initial beliefs. Finally, we hint at rarely discussed methodological problems of model comparison and make suggestions for an improved choice among objective functions.

Our study of learning in experiments led us to conclude that research on descriptive models of learning is still in its infancy. There are many basic issues that are awaiting exploration, and so we believe that the best and most efficient way of improving the insight into learning behaviour is to check on the robustness of phenomena in various ways. To this end, the list of topics we did not deal with in the present work might serve as a starting point. Our conclusion is that the most important virtue of a researcher who is studying learning behaviour will probably be his or her openness to learning. So, we conclude with the following humorous quotation which we take as philanthropic plea to continue to learn, especially to continue to learn about learning.

> Also lautet ein Beschluss,
> Dass der Mensch 'was lernen muss.
> Lernen kann er, Gott sei Dank,
> Aber auch sein Leben lang.
> (Wilhelm Busch)[6]

NOTES

1. One exception is Experiment 5 in Barron and Erev (2002) which, however, focuses on choice among probabilistic gambles.
2. Sonsino (1997) shows that the recognition of repeated sequences of play leads players to select only pure-strategy Nash-equilibrium profiles, if those exist.
3. Nauck et al. (1996) give an introduction into neural networks in general as well as an overview of reinforcement learning models in soft computing.
4. For a survey, see, for example, Camerer 1995.
5. For a survey, see, for example, Cookson 2000.
6. A translation might sound like this: 'So, there is a decision that people have to learn things. Thank goodness, one can learn one's whole life long.'

Appendix A: Instructions for the Experiment on Mutual Fate Control (Translated from German)

PRELIMINARIES

You are participating in a study on decision-making within the framework of experimental economics. After you have read these instructions we will come to you in order to clarify open questions. If you encounter any further questions during play please raise your hand, so a member of the staff can come to you.

Please do not touch the computer until you are asked to start the game. Tips on the use of the computer are given on the back page.

During the session you will face a sequence of decision tasks. At each decision you may earn money. How much money you will get depends on your decisions. The aggregated payoff will be paid to you in cash at the end of the experiment. Your decisions as well as your payoff is known only to you, that is we take care that no other participant will get any information on your decisions or payoffs.

DECISION TASK

You are one of eight (ten) persons. All persons are faced with the same task, that is, they have all got identical instruction sheets and sit, separated from each other, in front of a computer terminal.

Before the start of the first round, all eight (ten) persons are matched randomly into four (five) pairs. The pairs remain fixed throughout the whole session, that is, the person you are playing with will be the same throughout the whole session. You will never be told whom you are paired with.

Soon, you will be required to make the following identical decision in 100 successive rounds.

In each round you have the choice between two alternatives: action A and action B. After you and the person you are paired with have entered the decisions upon your choice the computer will calculate your payoff according to a predetermined scheme and subsequently inform you of your payoff.

PAYOFF SCHEME:

The payoff scheme will not be made public. What is known is that the payoffs within your pair solely depend on your decision and the decision of your opponent of that round. Particularly, no random process will be used to calculate payoffs. Furthermore, it is known that payoffs can take either of the values, 0 or 1, where 0 is equivalent to 0 Deutschmark and 1 is equivalent to 0.30 Deutschmark.

Your MaxLab team

TIPS FOR USE OF COMPUTER:

1. Please do not touch the computer until you are asked to start the play.
2. Please do not start any other programs during the experimental session.
3. You can enter your decision by clicking with your mouse on one of the two buttons, A or B. After that, a window appears that asks you to confirm your choice.
4. After confirming your choice, please wait until the information on the last round appears before you go on with the next round.
5. In case there are any technical problems with the use of the program, please immediately inform a member of the staff by raising your hand.

Appendix B: Data of the Experiment on Mutual Fate Control

Round Player	Pair 1 1	2	Pair 2 3	4	Pair 3 5	6	Pair 4 7	8	Pair 5 9	10	Pair 6 11	12	Pair 7 13	14	Pair 8 15	16	Pair 9 17	18
1	A	A	A	A	A	B	B	A	B	A	B	B	A	A	B	A	A	A
2	A	B	B	B	A	A	A	A	A	B	B	B	B	A	B	A	A	A
3	A	B	B	B	A	A	A	A	A	B	A	B	B	A	B	A	A	A
4	A	A	B	B	B	B	A	B	B	A	B	B	B	A	A	A	B	B
5	A	A	B	B	A	B	A	B	B	A	B	B	A	A	B	B	B	B
6	A	A	B	B	B	B	A	A	A	A	B	B	A	A	B	B	B	B
7	B	B	B	B	A	B	B	A	B	B	B	A	A	A	B	A	B	B
8	A	B	B	B	B	A	B	A	A	A	B	A	A	B	A	A	B	B
9	A	A	B	B	B	B	A	A	B	A	A	A	A	B	A	B	B	B
10	B	B	B	B	A	A	A	A	A	A	A	A	A	A	A	B	B	B
11	B	B	B	B	A	B	A	A	A	B	B	A	A	A	A	A	B	B
12	A	B	B	B	A	B	B	A	B	B	B	A	A	A	B	A	B	B
13	B	B	B	B	A	A	B	A	A	A	B	A	A	A	B	B	B	B
14	A	B	B	B	B	A	B	A	A	A	A	B	B	A	B	A	B	B
15	B	B	B	B	B	A	A	A	A	A	A	B	B	A	A	B	B	B
16	A	B	B	B	A	A	A	A	B	B	A	B	B	A	A	A	B	B
17	B	B	B	B	B	B	A	A	A	B	A	A	B	A	A	A	B	B
18	A	B	B	B	A	A	A	A	B	A	A	B	B	A	A	A	B	B
19	B	B	B	B	A	A	B	A	A	A	B	A	A	A	B	B	B	B
20	A	A	B	B	B	A	B	A	B	B	A	A	B	B	A	B	B	B
21	B	B	B	B	B	B	B	A	A	B	A	A	A	B	B	A	B	B
22	A	B	B	B	B	B	B	A	A	A	B	A	B	A	A	B	B	B
23	B	B	B	B	B	A	B	A	A	A	B	A	A	A	A	A	B	B
24	A	B	B	B	A	A	B	A	B	B	B	B	B	B	A	B	B	B
25	B	B	B	B	A	A	B	A	A	A	B	B	A	A	A	A	B	B
26	A	A	B	B	A	B	B	A	B	B	B	B	B	A	A	A	B	B
27	B	B	B	B	A	A	A	A	B	A	B	A	A	A	B	B	B	B
28	A	B	B	B	A	A	A	A	A	B	B	A	B	B	B	B	B	B
29	B	A	B	B	B	A	A	A	A	A	A	A	A	B	B	A	B	B
30	A	B	B	B	A	A	A	A	B	A	A	B	B	A	A	A	B	B
31	B	A	B	B	A	B	A	B	B	B	A	A	A	B	B	B	B	B
32	A	A	B	B	B	B	A	B	B	B	A	A	B	B	B	B	B	B
33	B	B	B	B	A	B	A	A	B	A	B	B	A	A	B	B	B	B
34	A	B	B	B	B	A	A	B	A	B	B	A	B	A	A	B	B	B
35	B	B	B	B	A	B	A	B	B	B	B	A	A	A	A	B	B	B
36	A	B	B	B	A	A	A	A	A	B	A	B	B	A	B	A	B	B
37	B	B	B	B	A	A	A	A	A	A	B	B	A	A	B	A	B	B
38	A	B	B	B	B	B	A	A	A	B	A	B	B	A	B	A	B	B
39	B	B	B	B	A	B	B	A	B	A	B	A	A	A	B	B	B	B

Round	Pair 1		Pair 2		Pair 3		Pair 4		Pair 5		Pair 6		Pair 7		Pair 8		Pair 9	
Player	1	2	3	4	5	6	7	8	9	10	11	12	13	14	15	16	17	18
40	A	A	B	B	B	A	A	A	B	A	B	A	B	A	B	B	B	B
41	B	A	B	B	A	B	A	B	B	B	A	A	B	A	B	B	B	B
42	A	A	B	B	B	B	A	B	B	A	A	A	A	A	A	B	B	B
43	B	A	B	B	A	B	A	A	A	B	A	B	A	A	A	A	B	B
44	A	A	B	B	B	A	A	A	A	B	B	B	B	A	B	A	B	B
45	B	A	B	B	A	A	A	A	B	A	B	B	B	A	B	A	B	B
46	B	B	B	B	A	B	A	A	A	A	A	A	A	A	A	A	B	B
47	A	B	B	B	B	A	B	B	B	B	A	B	A	A	B	B	B	B
48	B	A	B	B	B	A	A	A	A	A	B	B	B	A	B	A	B	B
49	B	B	B	B	A	B	B	B	A	B	A	B	A	A	A	B	B	B
50	B	A	B	B	B	A	B	A	B	A	B	B	B	A	A	B	B	B
51	A	A	B	B	B	A	B	B	B	A	A	B	A	A	A	B	B	B
52	B	B	B	B	A	A	A	A	B	A	B	A	A	A	B	A	B	B
53	A	A	B	B	B	B	B	B	B	A	A	B	A	A	B	A	B	B
54	B	A	B	B	A	B	B	A	B	B	B	B	A	A	A	B	B	B
55	A	B	B	B	B	A	B	B	B	B	A	B	A	A	A	A	B	B
56	B	A	B	B	B	A	B	A	A	B	B	B	A	A	B	B	B	B
57	A	B	B	B	B	B	B	B	A	A	A	A	A	B	B	B	B	B
58	B	B	B	B	B	A	B	A	A	B	B	B	A	B	B	B	B	B
59	A	A	B	B	A	A	B	B	B	A	A	A	A	B	A	B	B	B
60	B	B	B	B	A	A	A	A	A	A	B	A	A	B	A	B	B	B
61	A	B	B	B	B	B	B	B	B	B	B	A	A	B	A	A	B	B
62	B	A	B	B	A	A	A	A	B	B	B	A	A	B	B	A	B	B
63	A	B	B	B	B	B	B	B	A	B	A	A	A	A	A	B	B	B
64	B	B	B	B	A	A	B	A	B	A	A	B	A	A	A	A	B	B
65	A	B	B	B	B	B	B	B	A	A	A	A	A	A	A	A	B	B
66	B	A	B	B	B	B	B	A	A	B	A	A	A	A	A	A	B	B
67	A	B	B	B	B	B	B	B	B	A	B	A	A	A	A	B	B	B
68	B	B	B	B	B	B	A	A	B	A	A	A	A	A	A	B	B	B
69	A	B	B	B	B	B	B	B	A	A	A	B	A	B	A	A	B	B
70	B	B	B	B	B	B	B	B	A	A	A	B	B	A	B	A	B	B
71	A	A	B	B	B	B	B	B	B	A	A	B	A	B	B	B	B	B
72	B	A	B	B	B	B	A	A	B	A	A	B	A	B	B	B	B	B
73	A	A	B	B	B	B	B	B	A	A	A	B	A	B	B	B	B	B
74	A	B	B	B	B	B	B	A	B	B	A	A	A	B	A	A	B	B
75	A	B	B	B	B	B	B	B	B	B	A	B	B	A	A	B	B	B
76	B	A	B	B	B	B	B	A	A	A	A	B	B	A	B	A	B	B
77	B	A	B	B	B	B	B	B	B	A	A	A	B	A	A	B	B	B
78	B	A	B	B	B	B	A	A	A	A	A	A	A	A	B	B	B	B
79	A	A	B	B	B	B	B	B	A	B	B	B	A	A	A	B	B	B
80	B	B	B	B	B	B	B	A	B	A	B	B	A	A	B	A	B	B
81	A	B	B	B	B	B	B	B	B	A	B	B	A	A	A	A	B	B
82	B	B	B	B	B	B	B	A	A	B	B	A	A	A	A	A	B	B
83	A	A	B	B	B	B	B	B	B	B	A	B	A	A	A	A	B	B
84	B	A	B	B	B	B	B	A	B	B	A	B	A	B	A	B	B	B
85	B	B	B	B	B	B	B	B	B	A	A	A	A	B	A	B	B	B
86	B	B	B	B	B	B	A	A	B	B	B	B	A	B	A	A	B	B
87	B	A	B	B	B	B	B	B	A	A	B	B	A	B	A	A	B	B
88	A	A	B	B	B	B	B	A	A	B	B	A	A	B	A	A	B	B
89	B	B	B	B	B	B	B	B	A	A	A	A	A	B	A	A	B	B
90	A	A	B	B	B	A	A	A	A	B	A	B	A	A	A	A	B	B
91	A	B	B	B	B	B	B	B	A	A	A	A	A	A	A	A	B	B
92	B	B	B	B	B	B	B	A	A	B	B	A	A	A	B	A	B	B

Round Player	Pair 1 1	2	Pair 2 3	4	Pair 3 5	6	Pair 4 7	8	Pair 5 9	10	Pair 6 11	12	Pair 7 13	14	Pair 8 15	16	Pair 9 17	18
93	B	B	B	B	B	B	B	B	B	B	B	B	A	A	A	A	B	B
94	A	A	B	B	B	B	B	A	A	A	A	A	A	A	B	A	B	B
95	B	A	B	B	B	B	B	B	A	B	B	A	A	A	B	A	B	B
96	B	B	B	B	B	B	A	A	B	B	B	A	A	B	A	A	B	B
97	B	B	B	B	B	B	B	B	B	B	B	B	A	B	A	A	B	B
98	B	A	B	B	B	B	B	A	B	B	B	B	A	B	B	A	B	B
99	A	B	B	B	B	B	B	B	B	A	B	A	A	B	A	B	B	B
100	A	B	B	B	B	B	B	A	B	A	B	A	A	B	A	B	B	B

Round Player	Pair 10 19	20	Pair 11 21	22	Pair 12 23	24	Pair 13 25	26	Pair 14 27	28	Pair 15 29	30	Pair 16 31	32	Pair 17 33	34
1	A	A	A	A	A	A	A	A	B	A	B	A	A	B	A	B
2	B	B	B	A	A	B	B	B	B	B	A	A	B	B	A	B
3	B	B	A	B	A	B	B	B	B	B	A	A	B	B	A	B
4	B	B	A	B	A	A	B	B	B	A	A	B	B	B	A	B
5	B	B	B	A	A	B	B	B	B	A	B	B	A	B	A	B
6	B	B	A	A	A	B	B	B	B	B	A	B	B	A	A	B
7	B	B	A	B	A	B	B	B	B	B	A	B	A	A	A	A
8	B	B	A	B	A	B	B	B	B	A	A	B	A	A	A	A
9	B	B	A	B	A	A	B	B	B	A	A	A	B	B	B	B
10	B	B	A	A	A	A	B	B	B	B	A	A	A	B	B	B
11	B	B	B	B	A	B	B	B	B	B	A	B	A	A	B	B
12	B	B	B	B	A	B	B	B	A	A	B	A	B	B	B	B
13	B	B	A	A	A	B	B	B	A	A	B	B	A	B	B	B
14	B	B	A	B	A	A	B	B	A	A	B	A	B	A	B	B
15	B	B	B	A	A	A	B	B	A	B	A	A	A	B	B	B
16	B	B	A	B	A	A	B	B	A	A	A	A	B	B	B	B
17	B	B	A	B	A	A	B	B	A	A	B	A	A	A	B	B
18	B	B	A	A	A	B	B	B	A	A	B	B	B	A	B	B
19	B	B	B	A	A	B	B	B	A	A	A	B	B	A	B	B
20	B	B	A	A	A	B	B	B	A	B	B	B	B	A	B	B
21	B	B	A	A	A	B	B	B	A	A	A	A	A	A	B	B
22	B	B	A	B	A	B	B	B	B	A	B	B	B	B	B	B
23	B	B	B	A	A	A	B	B	B	A	B	B	A	B	B	B
24	B	B	B	A	A	B	B	B	B	A	B	A	A	B	B	B
25	B	B	A	A	A	B	B	B	B	A	A	B	B	A	B	B
26	B	B	A	A	A	A	B	B	B	A	A	B	A	A	B	B
27	B	B	A	A	A	A	B	B	B	A	A	A	A	B	B	B
28	B	B	A	B	A	B	B	B	B	A	A	A	A	B	B	B
29	B	B	A	B	A	B	B	B	A	A	A	B	B	A	B	B
30	B	B	B	A	A	B	B	B	A	B	A	A	A	A	B	B
31	B	B	B	B	A	A	B	B	B	A	A	B	B	B	B	B
32	B	B	A	A	A	B	B	B	B	A	A	B	B	B	B	B
33	B	B	A	B	A	A	B	B	A	A	A	A	A	B	B	B
34	B	B	A	B	A	A	B	B	A	B	B	A	A	B	B	B
35	B	B	B	A	B	A	B	B	B	B	B	B	B	A	B	B
36	B	B	B	A	B	A	B	B	A	B	B	A	A	A	B	B
37	B	B	B	B	A	A	B	B	B	A	B	B	A	B	B	B
38	B	B	B	B	A	B	B	B	B	A	B	B	A	B	B	B
39	B	B	A	A	A	A	B	B	B	A	A	B	A	A	B	B
40	B	B	A	A	A	A	B	B	A	A	B	A	B	A	B	B
41	B	B	A	B	A	B	B	B	A	B	B	B	B	A	B	B

Round Player	Pair 10		Pair 11		Pair 12		Pair 13		Pair 14		Pair 15		Pair 16		Pair 17	
	19	20	21	22	23	24	25	26	27	28	29	30	31	32	33	34
42	B	B	A	B	A	B	B	B	A	B	B	B	B	A	B	B
43	B	B	A	B	A	B	B	B	A	A	A	A	A	A	B	B
44	B	B	A	B	A	B	B	B	A	B	A	B	A	B	B	B
45	B	B	B	A	A	A	B	B	A	A	A	B	A	B	B	B
46	B	B	B	B	A	A	B	B	A	A	A	A	A	A	B	B
47	B	B	B	A	A	A	B	B	B	A	A	A	A	A	B	B
48	B	B	B	B	A	A	B	B	B	A	B	A	A	B	B	B
49	B	B	A	B	A	A	B	B	A	A	B	B	A	A	B	B
50	B	B	A	B	A	A	B	B	A	B	B	B	B	A	B	B
51	B	B	A	B	A	A	B	B	B	A	B	A	A	A	B	B
52	B	B	A	A	A	B	B	B	A	A	A	A	A	A	B	B
53	B	B	B	B	A	B	B	B	A	B	A	B	B	B	B	B
54	B	B	B	A	A	B	B	B	A	A	A	A	B	B	B	B
55	B	B	B	B	A	B	B	B	A	A	B	A	A	A	B	B
56	B	B	B	A	A	B	B	B	B	A	B	B	B	B	B	B
57	B	B	B	A	A	B	B	B	B	A	B	B	B	B	B	B
58	B	B	B	B	A	A	B	B	B	A	A	B	B	B	B	B
59	B	B	A	A	A	B	B	B	B	A	A	B	B	B	B	B
60	B	B	A	A	A	A	B	B	B	A	B	B	A	B	B	B
61	B	B	A	B	A	A	B	B	B	A	B	B	A	A	B	B
62	B	B	A	A	A	B	B	B	A	A	A	B	B	B	B	B
63	B	B	B	B	A	B	B	B	A	B	A	B	B	B	B	B
64	B	B	B	B	A	B	B	B	B	B	A	B	B	B	B	B
65	B	B	B	A	A	B	B	B	A	B	B	B	B	B	B	B
66	B	B	A	A	A	A	B	B	B	B	B	B	B	B	B	B
67	B	B	A	B	A	A	B	B	A	B	B	B	B	B	B	B
68	B	B	A	B	A	A	B	B	B	A	A	B	B	B	B	B
69	B	B	B	A	A	B	B	B	B	A	A	B	B	B	B	B
70	B	B	B	B	A	B	B	B	A	A	B	B	A	B	B	B
71	B	B	B	A	A	B	B	B	A	B	B	B	B	A	B	B
72	B	B	B	B	A	B	B	B	B	B	A	B	A	A	B	B
73	B	B	A	A	A	B	B	B	A	B	A	A	B	B	B	B
74	B	B	A	A	A	B	B	B	B	B	A	B	B	B	B	B
75	B	B	A	A	A	B	B	B	A	B	B	B	B	B	B	B
76	B	B	A	B	A	B	B	B	B	B	B	B	B	B	B	B
77	B	B	A	A	A	A	B	B	A	B	B	B	B	B	B	B
78	B	B	A	B	A	A	B	B	B	B	A	A	B	B	B	B
79	B	B	B	B	A	A	B	B	A	A	A	B	B	B	B	B
80	B	B	A	A	A	A	B	B	A	A	A	B	A	B	B	B
81	B	B	A	A	A	A	B	B	B	A	B	B	A	A	B	B
82	B	B	A	B	A	A	B	B	B	A	B	B	B	B	B	B
83	B	B	B	B	B	A	B	B	B	A	B	B	B	B	B	B
84	B	B	B	B	B	A	B	B	B	A	B	A	B	B	B	B
85	B	B	A	A	A	A	B	B	A	A	A	A	B	B	B	B
86	B	B	A	B	A	A	B	B	A	B	B	A	B	B	B	B
87	B	B	A	A	A	A	B	B	A	B	B	B	B	B	B	B
88	B	B	B	A	A	B	B	B	A	A	B	B	B	B	B	B
89	B	B	B	B	A	B	B	B	B	A	B	B	B	B	B	B
90	B	B	B	A	A	A	B	B	A	A	B	A	A	B	B	B
91	B	B	A	B	A	A	B	B	B	A	A	A	A	B	B	B
92	B	B	B	B	A	B	B	B	B	A	A	A	B	A	B	B
93	B	B	B	A	A	A	B	B	A	A	A	B	B	A	B	B
94	B	B	A	B	A	A	B	B	B	A	A	B	A	A	B	B

Round Player	Pair 10 19	20	Pair 11 21	22	Pair 12 23	24	Pair 13 25	26	Pair 14 27	28	Pair 15 29	30	Pair 16 31	32	Pair 17 33	34
95	B	B	B	B	A	A	B	B	B	A	A	B	B	B	B	B
96	B	B	B	A	A	A	B	B	A	A	A	B	B	B	B	B
97	B	B	A	B	A	A	B	B	A	A	B	B	B	B	B	B
98	B	B	B	B	A	B	B	B	B	A	B	B	B	B	B	B
99	B	A	A	A	A	B	B	B	A	A	B	B	A	B	B	B
100	B	A	A	A	A	A	B	B	B	B	B	B	A	B	B	B

Appendix C: Accordance with Experimentation Learning in the Mutual Fate Control Game

m=1

Player	FSA	FA	FSArate	FSB	FB	FSBrate	FS	F	FSrate	ACA	AA	ACArate	ACB	AB	ACBrate	AC	A	ACrate
1	5	27	0.19	7	32	0.22	12	59	0.20	16	21	0.76	13	19	0.68	29	40	0.73
2	9	19	0.47	20	32	0.63	29	51	0.57	12	21	0.57	9	27	0.33	21	48	0.44
7	8	8	1.00	17	27	0.63	25	35	0.71	15	34	0.44	5	30	0.17	20	64	0.31
8	14	30	0.47	0	27	0.00	14	57	0.25	15	34	0.44	4	8	0.50	19	42	0.45
9	10	23	0.43	11	24	0.46	21	47	0.45	12	25	0.48	12	27	0.44	24	52	0.46
10	16	27	0.59	13	24	0.54	29	51	0.57	16	25	0.64	16	23	0.70	32	48	0.67
11	17	25	0.68	18	25	0.72	35	50	0.70	10	23	0.43	11	26	0.42	21	49	0.43
12	17	26	0.65	14	25	0.56	31	51	0.61	11	23	0.48	10	25	0.40	21	48	0.44
13	23	27	0.85	0	4	0.00	23	31	0.74	13	45	0.29	13	23	0.57	26	68	0.38
14	22	23	0.96	2	4	0.50	24	27	0.89	8	45	0.18	6	27	0.22	14	72	0.19
15	19	25	0.76	13	17	0.76	32	42	0.76	13	30	0.43	16	27	0.59	29	57	0.51
16	16	27	0.59	12	17	0.71	28	44	0.64	10	30	0.33	15	25	0.60	25	55	0.45
21	18	30	0.60	13	21	0.62	31	51	0.61	6	26	0.23	10	22	0.45	16	48	0.33
22	7	22	0.32	5	21	0.24	12	43	0.28	14	26	0.54	13	30	0.43	27	56	0.48
23	49	49	1.00	0	0		49	49	1.00	2	46	0.04	2	4	0.50	4	50	0.08
24	4	4	1.00	0	0		4	4	1.00	16	46	0.35	16	49	0.33	32	95	0.34
27	8	18	0.44	5	13	0.38	13	31	0.42	10	29	0.34	12	39	0.31	22	68	0.32
28	36	39	0.92	9	13	0.69	45	52	0.87	12	29	0.41	10	18	0.56	22	47	0.47
29	18	29	0.62	26	37	0.70	44	66	0.67	6	19	0.32	6	14	0.43	12	33	0.36
30	5	14	0.36	27	37	0.73	32	51	0.63	12	19	0.63	10	29	0.34	22	48	0.46
Mean	16.05	24.60	0.65	10.60	20.00	0.47	26.65	44.60	0.63	11.45	29.80	0.42	10.45	24.60	0.45	21.90	54.40	0.42

174

m=2

Player	FSA	FA	FSArate	FSB	FB	FSBrate	FS	F	FSrate	ACA	AA	ACArate	ACB	AB	ACBrate	AC	A	ACrate
1	1	14	0.07	4	20	0.20	5	34	0.15	25	34	0.74	22	31	0.71	47	65	0.72
2	5	9	0.56	7	12	0.58	12	21	0.57	18	31	0.58	16	47	0.34	34	78	0.44
7	4	4	1.00	9	10	0.90	13	14	0.93	15	38	0.39	14	47	0.30	29	85	0.34
8	9	16	0.56	0	26	0.00	9	42	0.21	24	48	0.50	5	9	0.56	29	57	0.51
9	4	8	0.50	5	12	0.42	9	20	0.45	21	40	0.53	18	39	0.46	39	79	0.49
10	8	15	0.53	5	10	0.50	13	25	0.52	20	37	0.54	22	37	0.59	42	74	0.57
11	9	15	0.60	10	13	0.77	19	28	0.68	12	33	0.36	15	38	0.39	27	71	0.38
12	10	15	0.67	5	13	0.38	15	28	0.54	15	34	0.44	13	37	0.35	28	71	0.39
13	18	20	0.90	0	0		18	20	0.90	15	52	0.29	17	27	0.63	32	79	0.41
14	10	10	1.00	1	1	1.00	11	11	1.00	9	58	0.16	8	30	0.27	17	88	0.19
15	8	13	0.62	5	8	0.63	13	21	0.62	14	42	0.33	17	36	0.47	31	78	0.40
16	9	12	0.75	7	9	0.78	16	21	0.76	18	45	0.40	18	33	0.55	36	78	0.46
21	10	17	0.59	4	8	0.50	14	25	0.56	11	39	0.28	14	35	0.40	25	74	0.34
22	4	12	0.33	1	8	0.13	5	20	0.25	21	36	0.58	22	43	0.51	43	79	0.54
23	33	33	1.00	0	0		33	33	1.00	2	62	0.03	2	4	0.50	4	66	0.06
24	2	2	1.00	0	0		2	2	1.00	16	48	0.33	16	49	0.33	32	97	0.33
27	2	7	0.29	2	7	0.29	4	14	0.29	15	40	0.38	15	45	0.33	30	85	0.35
28	24	26	0.92	2	5	0.40	26	31	0.84	13	42	0.31	11	26	0.42	24	68	0.35
29	10	16	0.63	18	26	0.69	28	42	0.67	11	32	0.34	9	25	0.36	20	57	0.35
30	2	5	0.40	15	22	0.68	17	27	0.63	18	28	0.64	13	44	0.30	31	72	0.43
Mean	9.10	13.45	0.65	5.00	10.50	0.52	14.10	23.95	0.63	15.65	40.95	0.41	14.35	34.10	0.44	30.00	75.05	0.40

m=3

Player	FSA	FA	FSArate	FSB	FB	FSBrate	FS	F	FSrate	ACA	AA	ACArate	ACB	AB	ACBrate	AC	A	ACrate
1	0	6	0.00	0	12	0.00	0	18	0.00	32	42	0.76	26	39	0.67	58	81	0.72
2	2	2	1.00	1	4	0.25	3	6	0.50	22	38	0.58	18	55	0.33	40	93	0.43
7	0	0		1	1	1.00	1	1	1.00	15	42	0.36	15	56	0.27	30	98	0.31
8	6	8	0.75	0	25	0.00	6	33	0.18	29	56	0.52	6	10	0.60	35	66	0.53
9	0	2	0.00	3	4	0.75	3	6	0.50	23	46	0.50	24	47	0.51	47	93	0.51
10	3	7	0.43	1	2	0.50	4	9	0.44	23	45	0.51	26	45	0.58	49	90	0.54
11	4	8	0.50	3	4	0.75	7	12	0.58	14	40	0.35	17	47	0.36	31	87	0.36
12	7	8	0.88	2	6	0.33	9	14	0.64	19	41	0.46	17	44	0.39	36	85	0.42
13	13	14	0.93	0	0		13	14	0.93	16	58	0.28	17	27	0.63	33	85	0.39
14	5	5	1.00	0	0		5	5	1.00	9	63	0.14	8	31	0.26	17	94	0.18
15	3	6	0.50	0	3	0.00	3	9	0.33	16	49	0.33	17	41	0.41	33	90	0.37
16	2	4	0.50	5	5	1.00	7	9	0.78	19	53	0.36	20	37	0.54	39	90	0.43
21	7	10	0.70	2	3	0.67	9	13	0.69	15	46	0.33	17	40	0.43	32	86	0.37
22	1	5	0.20	0	1	0.00	1	6	0.17	25	43	0.58	28	50	0.56	53	93	0.57
23	21	21	1.00	0	0		21	21	1.00	2	74	0.03	2	4	0.50	4	78	0.05
24	0	0		0	0		0	0		16	50	0.32	16	49	0.33	32	99	0.32
27	0	3	0.00	0	2	0.00	0	5	0.00	17	44	0.39	18	50	0.36	35	94	0.37
28	14	16	0.88	2	4	0.50	16	20	0.80	13	52	0.25	12	27	0.44	25	79	0.32
29	5	8	0.63	13	18	0.72	18	26	0.69	14	40	0.35	12	33	0.36	26	73	0.36
30	1	1	1.00	7	11	0.64	8	12	0.67	21	32	0.66	16	55	0.29	37	87	0.43
Mean	4.70	6.70	0.60	2.00	5.25	0.64	6.70	11.95	0.57	18.00	47.70	0.40	16.60	39.35	0.44	34.60	87.05	0.40

176

m=4

Player	FSA	FA	FSArate	FSB	FB	FSBrate	FS	F	FSrate	ACA	AA	ACArate	ACB	AB	ACBrate	AC	A	ACrate
1	0	3	0.00	0	9	0.00	0	12	0.00	35	45	0.78	29	42	0.69	64	87	0.74
2	0	0		0	2		0	0	0.00	22	40	0.55	19	57	0.33	41	97	0.42
7	0	0		0	0		0	0		15	42	0.36	15	57	0.26	30	99	0.30
8	4	4	1.00	0	24	0.00	4	28	0.14	31	60	0.52	7	11	0.64	38	71	0.54
9	0	0		1	2	0.50	1	2	0.50	25	48	0.52	24	49	0.49	49	97	0.51
10	1	3	0.33	0	0		1	3	0.33	25	49	0.51	27	47	0.57	52	96	0.54
11	2	5	0.40	0	0		2	5	0.40	15	43	0.35	18	51	0.35	33	94	0.35
12	2	2	1.00	1	2	0.50	3	4	0.75	20	47	0.43	20	48	0.42	40	95	0.42
13	9	10	0.90	0	0		9	10	0.90	16	62	0.26	17	27	0.63	33	89	0.37
14	2	2	1.00	0	0		2	2	1.00	9	66	0.14	8	31	0.26	17	97	0.18
15	2	2	1.00	0	0		2	2	1.00	19	53	0.36	20	44	0.45	39	97	0.40
16	0	0		2	2	1.00	2	2	1.00	21	57	0.37	20	40	0.50	41	97	0.42
21	3	5	0.60	0	1	0.00	3	6	0.50	16	51	0.31	17	42	0.40	33	93	0.35
22	0	2	0.00	0	0		0	2	0.00	27	46	0.59	29	51	0.57	56	97	0.58
23	13	13	1.00	0	0		13	13	1.00	2	82	0.02	2	4	0.50	4	86	0.05
24	0	0		0	0		0	0		16	50	0.32	16	49	0.33	32	99	0.32
27	0	1	0.00	1	1	0.00	0	2	0.00	19	46	0.41	19	51	0.37	38	97	0.39
28	10	11	0.91	1	3	0.33	11	14	0.79	14	57	0.25	12	28	0.43	26	85	0.31
29	3	6	0.50	10	14	0.71	13	20	0.65	14	42	0.33	13	37	0.35	27	79	0.34
30	0	0		3	4	0.75	3	4	0.75	21	33	0.64	19	62	0.31	40	95	0.42
Mean	2.5	3.45	0.62	0.90	3.20	0.29	3.45	6.65	0.54	19.10	50.95	0.40	17.55	41.40	0.44	36.65	92.35	0.40

Notes:

F denotes 'full record'.

A denotes 'ambiguous record'.

S denotes 'stay'.

C denotes 'change'.

A, B danote strategy A and strategy B, respectively.

177

Appendix D: Instructions for the Global-Game Experiment (Translated from German)

GENERAL INSTRUCTIONS

Welcome to today's experiment of the Magdeburg Experimental Laboratory (MaxLab). The experiment in which you are participating is part of a research project on experimental economics and is being financially supported by public institutions.

The experiment is going to be performed using the computers in this laboratory. The computer program is easy to handle, so that no prior knowledge or practice is required in order to use it. All actions can be performed using the mouse. During the whole experiment complete anonymity among participants will be ensured. That is, no player will ever get to know the actions of any other player. In order to make sure of this, we urge you to remain quiet and not to try to contact any other participant. Any kind of communication between participants is forbidden.

Some players were led to cabins while others are separated only by cardboard walls. This arrangement has no consequences for the present experiment. The cabins do have importance in other experiments. In the present experiment, however, all players are treated in the same way. All players are handed out identical instructions and all players use the same computer program with which he/she can submit his/her decision.

The whole experiment will probably last for less than two hours. It is divided into three phases. You are already in the first phase in which the instructions are read aloud by the experimenter. After that, you will have the opportunity to ask questions and to clarify possible misunderstandings. Please do not speak aloud. Please do not speak to any of the other participants, either. Instead, please raise your hand, so that a member of our team can approach you and privately answer your question.

In the second phase you will play a fixed number of trial rounds, within which the partner is simulated by the computer. These trial rounds are intended to make you, first, accustomed to the computer program, and second, get to know the payoff schemes that will also be relevant in the third phase. These decisions serve only as trials and are not paid out. More details on the trial rounds are given below. After the trial rounds you will again have the opportunity to ask questions. As before, we urge you to raise your hand, so that a member of our team can approach you.

Finally, in the third phase for a fixed number of rounds you will face the same decision task as has been shown to you in the trial rounds. Please note two important differences to the trial rounds: first, now you will not play together with a player simulated by the computer, instead your partner is a real player chosen among the other participants within this room. Second, each round is payoff relevant, that is, the points from each round that are assigned to you as a result of the payoff scheme, your decision and the decision of your partner, determine how much money you will get at the end of the experiment. More details concerning the rounds of this third phase follow later on.

At the end of this payoff relevant third phase each player will be paid out in cash. For this purpose each player is separately called to the experimenter's desk. There, he/she will get the money in exchange for a signature.

THE PAYOFF SCHEMES

In each round two persons play with each other. Each of the two persons has a choice between two actions, A or B. The actions of the two players determine the payoff of the two players. For this purpose various payoff schemes are being used. Altogether, there are four payoff schemes. In each round one of the payoff schemes is actually being used. In general a payoff scheme looks as follows:

Figure D.1: General payoff scheme

This payoff scheme shows for all possible combinations of actions how many points the two players get. Points for player 1 are given in the upper left corner of each cell (a, b, c and d), while points for player 2 are given in the lower right corner of each cell (w, x, y and z). For example: in case player 1 chooses action A and player 2 chooses action B, then player 1 gets exactly b points and player 2 gets x points.

The four payoff schemes actually used are the following. In each row one of these payoff schemes is given. The corresponding payoff matrices within a row are generated by exchange of actions. All matrices within a row thus share the same structure. What changes is only the meaning of actions A and B. For each game the structure is briefly explained in words.

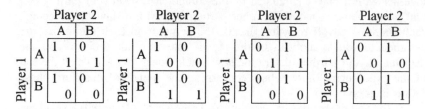

Figure D.2: Game 1

Each player has one action with which he/she can give a point to the other player. Using the other action will result in zero points for the other player.

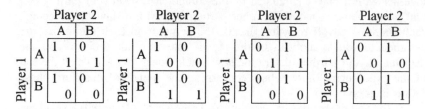

Figure D.3: Game 2

Player 1: One action gives one point to player 2. The other action gives zero points to player 2.
Player 2: Depending on which action player 1 chooses, one action by player 2 gives one point to player 1 and the other action gives zero points to player 1.

Example: given the payoff matrix at the far left, player 1 gives a point to player 2 by choosing action A, while player 1 gives zero points to player 2 by choosing action B. In case player 1 chooses action A, player 2 gives a point to player 1 by choosing action A. If player 1 chooses action B then player 2 gives a point to player 1 by choosing action B.

	Player 2	
	A	B
A	1 / 1	0 / 0
B	0 / 0	1 / 1

	Player 2	
	A	B
A	0 / 0	1 / 1
B	1 / 1	0 / 0

Figure D.4: Game 3

One combination of actions yields one point for each player. In case both players choose the alternative action they again get one point each. If, however, their actions do not 'match' with each other, then none gets any point.

	Player 2	
	A	B
A	1 / 0	0 / 1
B	0 / 1	1 / 0

Figure D.5: Game 4

There is always only one player who gets a point. Player 1 gets the point, if both players choose the same action. Player 2 gets the point, if the players choose differing actions.

THE TRIAL ROUNDS

You will be given the opportunity to get accustomed to the computer program and the payoff schemes. In more detail this trial phase is divided into four parts. Within the first part you will face game 1. In the second part game 2 will be the underlying game. In the third part will be game 3, and in the fourth part will be game 4. Within each part you will play exactly four rounds of the corresponding game. Only the first of the alternative matrices will be relevant, that is, within the trial rounds only the matrices at the far left of each row will be used. You will always take the role of player 2. Your partner will be simulated by the computer. The computer, thus, in each part will always be player 1 and will play the sequence (A, A, B, B).

Using the mouse pointer you submit your choice by clicking on one of the two buttons, A or B. After that, the choice of your partner, who is simulated by the computer, and your payoff will be shown to you.

Please note that the trial rounds are not going to be paid out, that is, your actions in this phase do not yield actual payoffs. This trial phase only serves the purpose to make you accustomed to the computer programme and the payoff schemes.

THE EXPERIMENT

The actual experiment is also divided into four parts. Each part now consists of 40 rounds. Hence, you will play 160 rounds altogether. In each part your partner will be a fixed person. This person will be randomly assigned to you at the beginning of each part and will then stay the same person throughout the 40 rounds. We will make sure that you will face a different person in each of the four parts. You will never get to know who this person is.

In each part the payoff matrix also remains fixed. The payoff matrix will be randomly assigned to you at the beginning of each part and will remain the same throughout the 40 rounds. Each game can occur with equal probability. According to the same random process it will be determined which of the possible matrices will be used. Furthermore, it is equally randomly determined whether you will be player 1 or player 2. Finally, each round is payoff relevant, that is for each point you gain you will get exactly 0.30 Deutschmark.

In comparison to the trial rounds you will get less information. In more detail you will not be told:

- who your partner is,
- which of the payoff schemes is being used,
- whether you are player 1 or player 2 within the payoff scheme, and
- which actions your partner has chosen in the last rounds.

You will get to know:

- your payoff from the last round, and
- your total payoff.

All information you gather within a part is shown to you in a separate window on the computer screen. At the end of each part this window will be cleared.

CASH PAYOFF

After the 160 payoff relevant rounds of the third phase you will be separately called to the experimenter's desk. The experimenter will pay you out according to your total payoff. Specifically, you will get a fixed amount of 5 Deutschmarks for your participation plus 0.30 Deutschmark times your total payoff. We will round the amount up to the next integer value. Please sign the receipt before you leave the room.

FINAL REMARKS

- Please do not start any programs, except of those named by the experimenter.
- In case of any kind of problems during the experiment, please contact a member of our team by raising your hand.
- After the experiment, please do not talk to anybody about the content of this experiment, so that future groups start their experiment with the same informational status as you did.

Thank you for your participation. Good luck.

Your MaxLab-Team

Appendix E: Definition of the Starting Round of Coordination

In order to give a formal definition of the starting round of coordination, we first have to introduce some notation. Let the set of possible outcomes of the stage game be denoted by

$$C = \{c_{AA}, c_{AB}, c_{BA}, c_{BB}\} \tag{E.1}$$

Then the history of outcomes of 40 rounds of play by a pair i is denoted by the vector

$$o_i = \left(o_i^1, \ldots, o_i^{40}\right) \tag{E.2}$$

whereby each $o_i^j \in C$.

Distinguishing only between sequences of successive play of the coordination cell (c_{BB}) and sequences of successive non-coordination we can rewrite the history of outcomes in a vector of sequence lengths,

$$s_i = \left(s_i^0, \ldots, s_i^{T_i}\right) \tag{E.3}$$

whereby for all j even all s_i^j denote the length of the corresponding sequence of successive non-coordinations, and for all j odd all s_i^j denote the length of the corresponding sequence of successive coordinations. Note, that only s_i^0 (the first non-coordination sequence) is allowed to have length 0, all other sequences necessarily having length greater than zero. Note also that T_i denotes the number of sequences in the history of pair i (including the possibly empty initial sequence of non-coordinations).

The central definition is the first coordination sequence of a coordinating pair i:

$$j_i^* = \arg\min_{j\in\{1,...,T_i\}}\left\{ s_i^j \left| \begin{array}{l} (j \ even) \\ \wedge\left(\forall\gamma > j, \gamma \ even : s_i^j > s_i^\gamma\right) \\ \wedge\left(s_i^j > 3s_i^{j+1}\right) \\ \wedge\left(s_i^j \geq 3\right) \end{array}\right. \right\}$$ (E.4)

The starting round of coordination (SRC) of a pair i is then given by

$$SRC_i = \sum_{j=0}^{j_i^*-1} s_i^j + 1$$ (E.5)

References

Arickx, M. and E. Van Avermaet (1981), 'Interdependent Learning in a Minimal Social Situation', *Behavioral Science*, **26**, 229–42.

Arthur, W. Brian (1991), 'Designing Economic Agents that Act Like Human Agents: A Behavioral Approach to Bounded Rationality', *AEA Papers and Proceedings*, **81**, 353–9.

Arthur, W. Brian (1993), 'On Designing Economic Agents that Behave Like Human Agents', *Journal of Evolutionary Economics*, **3**, 1–22.

Aumann, Robert J. (1976), 'Agreeing to Disagree', *Annals of Statistics*, **4**, 1236–9.

Aumann, Robert J. and Sylvain Sorin (1989), 'Cooperation and Bounded Recall', *Games and Economic Behavior*, **1**, 5–39.

Bachrach, A.J. (1981), *Psychological Research: An Introduction*, 4th edition, New York: Random House.

Barron, Greg and Ido Erev (2002), 'Feedback-Based Decisions and their Limited Correspondence to Description-Based Decisions', draft paper, Columbia University.

Benaïm, Michel and Morris W. Hirsch (1996), 'Asymptotic Pseudo-Trajectories, Chain-Recurrent Flows, and Stochastic Approximation', *Journal of Dynamics and Differential Equations*, **8**, 141–74.

Blackburn, J.M. (1936), 'Acquisition of Skill: An Analysis of Learning Curves', IHRB Report No. 73.

Bolton, Gary E. and Axel Ockenfels (2000), 'ERC – a Theory of Equity, Reciprocity, and Competition', *American Economic Review*, **90**, 166–93.

Börgers, Tilman (1996), 'On the Relevance of Learning and Evolution to Economic Theory', *The Economic Journal*, **106**, 1374–85.

Börgers, Tilman and Rajiv Sarin (1997), 'Learning through Reinforcement and Replicator Dynamics', *Journal of Economic Theory*, **77**, 1–14.

Börgers, Tilman and Rajiv Sarin (2000), 'Naïve Reinforcement Learning with Endogenous Aspirations', *International Economic Review*, **41**, 921–50.

Bossuyt, Patrick M. and Edward E. Roskam (1987), 'Testing Probabilistic Choice Models', *Communication and Cognition*, **20**, 5–16.

Bracht, Juergen (2001), 'Estimation of Learning Models on Experimental Game Data', Discussion Paper No. 243, Center for Rationality and Interactive Decision Theory, The Hebrew University of Jerusalem.

Brenner, Thomas (1998), 'Can Evolutionary Algorithms Describe Learning Processes?', *Journal of Evolutionary Economics*, **8**, 271–83.

Brenner, Thomas (1999), *Modelling Learning in Economics*, Cheltenham, UK and Northampton, MA, USA: Edward Elgar.

Brier, Glenn W. (1950), 'Verification of Forecasts Expressed in Terms of Probability', *Monthly Weather Review*, **78**, 1–3.

Brown, James N. and Robert W. Rosenthal (1990), 'Testing the Minimax Hypothesis: A Re-examination of O'Neill's Game Experiment', *Econometrica*, **58**, 1065–81.

Bush, Robert R. and Frederick Mosteller (1951), 'A Mathematical Model for Simple Learning', *Psychological Review*, **58**, 313–23.

Bush, Robert R. and Frederick Mosteller (1953), 'A Stochastic Model with Applications to Learning', *Annals of Mathematical Statistics*, **24**, 559–85.

Bush, Robert R. and Frederick Mosteller (1955), *Stochastic Models for Learning*, New York: John Wiley and Sons.

Camerer, Colin (1995), 'Individual Decision Making', in John H. Kagel and Alvin E. Roth (eds), *The Handbook of Experimental Economics*, Princeton, NJ: Princeton University Press, 587–703.

Camerer, Colin F. and Teck-Hua Ho (1999), 'Experience-Weighted Attraction Learning in Normal Form Games', *Econometrica*, **67**, 827–74.

Camerer, Colin F. and Martin Weber (1992), 'Recent Developments in Modelling Preferences: Uncertainty and Ambiguity', *Journal of Risk and Uncertainty*, **5**, 325–70.

Camerer, Colin, Teck-Hua Ho and X. Wang (1999), 'Individual Differences in EWA Learning with Partial Payoff Information', Working Paper No. 99-010, University of Pennsylvania.

Carlsson, Hans and Eric van Damme (1993), 'Global Games and Equilibrium Selection', *Econometrica*, **61**, 989–1018.

Chen, Yan (2000), 'An Experimental Study of Serial and Average Cost Pricing Mechanisms', draft paper, Department of Economics, University of Michigan.

Chen, Yan and Yuri Khoroshilov (2001), 'Learning Under Limited Information', draft paper, Department of Economics, University of Michigan, January.

Conlisk, John (1993), 'Adaptive Tactics in Games – Further Solutions to the Crawford Puzzle', *Journal of Economic Behavior and Organization*, **22**, 51–68.

Conlisk, John (1996), 'Why Bounded Rationality?', *Journal of Economic Literature*, **34**, 669–700.

Cookson, Richard (2000), 'Framing Effects in Public Goods Experiments', *Experimental Economics*, **3**, 55–79.

Cournot, Augustin (1838/1991), *Recherches sur les Principes Mathematiques de la Theorie des Richesses*, Düsseldorf: Verlag Wirtschaft und Finanzen, original publication Paris: Hachette.

Crawford, Vincent P. (1991), 'An "Evolutionary" Interpretation of Van Huyck, Battalio, and Beil's Experimental Results on Coordination', *Games and Economic Behavior*, **3**, 25–59.

Crawford, Vincent P. (1995), 'Adaptive Dynamics in Coordination Games', *Econometrica*, **63**, 103–43.

Crawford, Vincent P. (1997), 'Theory and Experiment in the Analysis of Strategic Interaction', in David M. Kreps and Kenneth F. Wallis (eds), *Advances in Economics and Econometrics: Theory and Applications*, Seventh World Congress, vol. 1, Econometric Society Monographs, no. 26, 206–42.

Cross, John G. (1973), 'A Stochastic Learning Model of Economic Behavior', *Quarterly Journal of Economics*, **87**, 239–66.

Crossman, Edward R.F.W. (1959), 'A Theory of Acquisition of Speed-Skill', *Ergonomics*, **2** (1), 153–66.

Dekel, Eddie and Faruk Gul (1997), 'Rationality and Knowledge in Game Theory', chapter 5 in David M. Kreps and Kenneth F. Wallis (eds), *Advances in Economics and Econometrics: Theory and Applications*, Seventh World Congress, vol. 1, Econometric Society Monographs, no. 26, 87–172.

Dember, William N. and Harry Fowler (1958), 'Spontaneous Alternation Behavior', *Psychological Bulletin*, **55**, 412–58.

Dufwenberg, Martin and Georg Kirchsteiger (1998), 'A Theory of Sequential Reciprocity', Tilburg Center for Economic Research Discussion Paper no. 9837, April.

Ellsberg, Daniel (1961), 'Risk, Ambiguity, and the Savage Axioms', *Quarterly Journal of Economics*, **75**, 643–69.

Erev, Ido and Greg Barron (2001), 'On Adaptation, Maximization, and Reinforcement Learning Among Cognitive Strategies', draft paper, Columbia University.

Erev, Ido and Ernan Haruvy (2000), 'On the Potential Value and Current Limitations of Data Driven Learning Models', Mimeo, April.

Erev, Ido and Alvin E. Roth (1996), 'On the Need for Low Rationality, Cognitive Game Theory: Reinforcement Learning in Experimental Games with Unique Mixed Strategy Equilibria', working paper, University of Pittsburgh.

Erev, Ido and Alvin E. Roth (1998), 'Predicting How People Play Games: Reinforcement Learning in Experimental Games with Unique, Mixed Strategy Equilibria', *American Economic Review*, **88** (4), 848–81.

Erev, Ido, Yoella Bereby-Meyer and Alvin E. Roth (1999), 'The Effect of Adding a Constant to All Payoffs: Experimental Investigation, and Implications for Reinforcement Learning Models', *Journal of Economic Behavior and Organization*, **39**, 111–28.

Estes, William K. (1950), 'Toward a Statistical Theory of Learning', *Psychological Review*, **57**, 94–107.

Estes, William K. (1954), 'Individual Behavior in Uncertain Situations: An Interpretation in Terms of Statistical Association Theory', in Robert M. Thrall, Clyde H. Coombs and Robert L. Davis (eds), *Decision Processes*, New York: John Wiley & Sons, 127–37.

Falk, Armin and Urs Fischbacher (2000), 'A Theory of Reciprocity', Institute for Empirical Research in Economics, Working Paper No. 6.

Fehr, Ernst and Klaus M. Schmidt (1999), 'A Theory of Fairness, Competition, and Cooperation', *Quarterly Journal of Economics*, **114**, 817–68.

Feltovich, Nick (2000), 'Reinforcement-Based vs. Belief-Based Learning Models in Experimental Asymmetric-Information Games', *Econometrica*, **68**, 605–41.

Flood, Merrill M. (1954), 'On Game-Learning Theory and Some Decision-Making Experiments', in Robert M. Thrall, Clyde H. Coombs and Robert L. Davis (eds), *Decision Processes*, New York: John Wiley & Sons, 139–58.

Friedman, Daniel (1983), 'Effective Scoring Rules for Probabilistic Forecasts', *Management Science*, **29**, 447–54.

Friedman, Eric J. and Scott Shenker (1996), 'Synchronous and Asynchronous Learning by Responsive Learning Automata', draft paper, Rutgers University.

Friedman, Eric J. and Scott Shenker (1998), 'Learning and Implementation on the Internet', Mimeo, Rutgers University, August.

Friedman, Eric, Mikhael Shor, Scott Shenker and Barry Sopher (2000), 'An Experiment on Learning with Limited Information: Nonconvergence, Experimentation Cascades, and the Advantage of Being Slow', draft paper, Rutgers University, December.

Fudenberg, Drew and David M. Kreps (1993), 'Learning Mixed Equilibria', *Games and Economic Behavior*, **5**, 320–67.

Gandin, Lev S. and Allan H. Murphy (1992), 'Equitable Skill Scores for Categorical Forecasts', *Monthly Weather Review*, **120**, 361–70.

Gilboa, Itzhak and David Schmeidler (1995), 'Case-Based Decision Theory', *Quarterly Journal of Economics*, **110**, 605–39.

Gilboa, Itzhak and David Schmeidler (1996), 'Case-Based Optimization', *Games and Economic Behavior*, **16**, 1–26.

Gilboa, Itzhak and David Schmeidler (1997), 'Act Similarity in Case-Based Decision Theory', *Economic Theory*, **9**, 47–61.

Granger, Clive W.J. and Hashem M. Pesaran (2000), 'Economic and Statistical Measures of Forecast Accuracy', *Journal of Forecasting*, **19**, 537–60.

Green, Jerry R. and Nancy L. Stokey (1980), 'A Two-Person Game of Information Transmission', H.I.E.R. Discussion Paper No.751.

Güth, Werner, Rolf Schmittberger and Bernd Schwarze (1982), 'An Experimental Analysis of Ultimatum Bargaining', *Journal of Economic Behavior and Organization*, **3**, 367–88.

Guthrie, Edwin R. (1935), *The Psychology of Learning*, New York: Harper.

Hadi, A.S. (1992), 'Identifying Multiple Outliers in Multivariate Data', *Journal of the Royal Statistical Society*, Series **B 54**, 761–71.

Hadi, A.S. (1994), 'A Modification of a Method for the Detection of Outliers in Multivariate Samples', *Journal of the Royal Statistical Society*, Series **B 56**, 393–6.

Harley, Calvin B. (1981), 'Learning the Evolutionarily Stable Strategy', *Journal of Theoretical Biology*, **89**, 611–33.

Harsanyi, John C. (1967–68), 'Games with Incomplete Information Played by "Bayesian" Players', *Management Science*, **14**, Part 1: 159–82, Part II: 320–34 and Part III: 486–502.

Harsanyi, John C. (1973), 'Games with Randomly Disturbed Payoffs: A New Rationale for Mixed-Strategy Equilibrium Points', *International Journal of Game Theory*, **2**, 1–23.

Harsanyi, John C. and Reinhard Selten (1988), *A General Theory of Equilibrium Selection in Games*, Cambridge, MA: MIT Press.

Hey, John D. (1997), 'Experiments and the Economics of Individual Decision Making Under Risk and Uncertainty', chapter 6 in David M. Kreps and Kenneth F. Wallis (eds), *Advances in Economics and Econometrics: Theory and Applications*, Seventh World Congress, vol. 1, Econometric Society Monographs, no. 26, 173–205.

Hinton, G.E. and T.J. Sejnowski (1986), 'Learning and Relearning in Boltzmann Machines', in David E Rumelhart, James L. McClelland and the PDP Research Group (eds), *Parallel Distributed Processing. Volume I: Foundations*, Cambridge, MA: MIT Press, 282–317.

Ho, Teck-Hua and Keith Weigelt (1996), 'Task-Complexity, Equilibrium Selection, and Learning: An Experimental Study', *Management Science*, **42**, 659–79.

Hon-Snir, Shlomit, Dov Monderer and Aner Sela (1998), 'A Learning Approach to Auctions', *Journal of Economic Theory*, **82**, 65–88.

Hopkins, Ed (1999a), 'Learning, Matching and Aggregation', *Games and Economic Behavior*, **26**, 79–110.

Hopkins, Ed (1999b), 'A Note on Best Response Dynamics', *Games and Economic Behavior*, **29**, 138–50.

Hopkins, Ed (1999c), 'Two Competing Models of How People Learn in Games', working paper, Department of Economics, University of Edinburgh, October.

Huck, Steffen and Wieland Müller (2000), 'Perfect versus Imperfect Observability – an Experimental Test of Bagwell's Result', *Games and Economic Behavior*, **31**, 174–90.

Huck, Steffen, Hans-Theo Normann and Jörg Oechssler (1999), 'Learning in Cournot Oligopoly – an Experiment', *The Economic Journal*, **109**, C80–95.

Hull, Clark L. (1943), *Principles of Behavior: An Introduction to Behavior Theory*, New York: Appleton-Century-Crofts.

Kagel, John H., Chung Kim and Donald Moser (1996), 'Fairness in Ultimatum Games with Asymmetric Information and Asymmetric Payoffs', *Games and Economic Behavior*, **13**, 100–110.

Kajii, Atsushi and Stephen Morris (1997), 'The Robustness of Equilibria to Incomplete Information', *Econometrica*, **65**, 1283–309.

Kalai, Ehud and Ehud Lehrer (1995), 'Subjective Games and Equilibria', *Games and Economic Behavior*, **8**, 123–63.

Kandori, Michihiro, George J. Mailath and Rafael Rob (1993), 'Learning, Mutation, and Long Run Equilibria in Games', *Econometrica*, **61**, 29–56.

Karandikar, Rajeeva, Dilip Mookherjee, Debraj Ray and Fernando Vega-Redondo (1998), 'Evolving Aspirations and Cooperation', *Journal of Economic Theory*, **80**, 292–331.

Kelley, H.H., J.W. Thibaut, R. Radloff and D. Mundy (1962), 'The Development of Cooperation in the 'Minimal Social Situation', *Psychological Monographs*, **76**, whole no. 19.

Kimble, G.A. (1961), *Hilgard and Marquis', Conditioning and Learning*, 2nd edition, Englewood Cliffs, NJ: Prentice Hall.

Knight, Frank H. (1921), *Risk, Uncertainty and Profit*, Boston and New York: Houghton Mifflin.

Lakshmivarahan, S. and Kumpati S. Narendra (1981), 'Learning Algorithms for Two-Person Zero-Sum Stochastic Games with Incomplete Information', *Mathematics of Operations Research*, **6**, 379–86.

Lakshmivarahan, S. and Kumpati S. Narendra (1982), 'Learning Algorithms for Two-Person Zero-Sum Stochastic Games with Incomplete Information: A Unified Approach', *Siam Journal of Control and Optimization*, **20**, 541–52.

Lehrer, Ehud (1988), 'Repeated Games with Stationary Bounded Recall Strategies', *Journal of Economic Theory*, **46**, 130–44.

Levenson, Edgar (1998), 'Awareness, Insight and Learning', *Contemporary Psychoanalysis*, **34**, 239–49.

Levine, David K. (1998), 'Modeling Altruism and Spitefulness in Experiments', *Review of Economic Dynamics*, **1**, 593–622.

Lewin, K., Tamara Dembo, L. Festinger and Pauline Sears (1944), 'Level of Aspiration', in J. McV. Hunt (ed.), *Personality and the Behavior Disorders*, New York: Ronald Press, 333–78.

Mailath, George J. (1998), 'Do People Play Nash Equilibrium? Lessons From Evolutionary Game Theory', *Journal of Economic Literature*, **36**, 1347–74.

Matsushima, Hitoshi (1998a), 'Learning About Stochastic Payoff Structures', Faculty of Economics, University of Tokyo, Discussion Paper no. CIRJE-F-7.

Matsushima, Hitoshi (1998b), 'Towards a Theory of Subjective Games', Faculty of Economics, University of Tokyo, Discussion Paper no. CIRJE-F-9.

McKelvey, Richard D. and Thomas R. Palfrey (1995), 'Quantal Response Equilibria for Normal Form Games', *Games and Economic Behavior*, **10**, 6–38.

McKelvey, Richard D. and Thomas R. Palfrey (1998), 'Quantal Response Equilibria for Extensive Form Games', *Experimental Economics*, **1**, 9–41.

Mehta, Judith, Chris Starmer and Robert Sugden (1994), *American Economic Review*, **84**, 658–73.

Merlo, Antonio and Andrew Schotter (1999), 'A Surprise-Quiz View of Learning in Economic Experiments', *Games and Economic Behavior*, **28**, 25–54.

Merton, Robert K. (1957), *Social Theory and Social Structure*, Glencoe Illinois: Free Press.

Milgrom, Paul and John Roberts (1990), 'Rationalizability, Learning, and Equilibrium in Games with Strategic Complementarities', *Econometrica*, **58** (6), 1255–77.

Milgrom, Paul and John Roberts (1991), 'Adaptive and Sophisticated Learning in Normal Form Games', *Games and Economic Behavior*, **3**, 82–100.

Mitropoulos, Atanasios (1996), 'The Impact of Private Information on Allocation in Markets with External Effects and Private Monopolies', Dissertation for Diplom, Wirtschafts- und Sozialwissenschaftliche Fakultät, Universität Dortmund.

Mitropoulos, Atanasios (2000), 'Learning Under Minimal Information: An Experiment on Mutual Fate Control', Working Paper No. 10/2000, Faculty of Economics and Management, Otto-von-Guericke-Universität Magdeburg.

Mitropoulos, Atanasios (2001a), 'Learning Under Minimal Information: An Experiment on Mutual Fate Control', *Journal of Economic Psychology*, **22**, 523–57.

Mitropoulos, Atanasios (2001b), 'Little Information, Efficiency, and Learning – an Experimental Study', Working Paper No. 8/2001, Faculty of Economics and Management, Magdeburg.

Mitropoulos, Atanasios (2001c), 'On the Measurement of the Predictive Success of Learning Theories in Repeated Games', Working Paper No. 15/2001, Faculty of Economics and Management, Otto-von-Guericke-Universität Magdeburg.

Mitropoulos, Atanasios (forthcoming), 'On the Value of Structural Information in a 2x2 Repeated Game', *Economics Letters*, **78**, 27–32.

Monderer, Dov and Dov Samet (1989), 'Approximating Common Knowledge with Common Beliefs', *Games and Economic Behavior*, **1**, 170–90.

Mookherjee, Dilip and Barry Sopher (1994), 'Learning Behavior in an Experimental Matching Pennies Game', *Games and Economic Behavior*, **7**, 62–91.

More, Thomas (1518/1901/1993), *Utopia*, 1901. Ideal Commonwealths, New York, P.F. Collier & Son, The Colonial Press. Released July 1993 by the Internet Wiretap on http://www.d-holliday.com/tmore/utopia.htm.

Morris, Stephen, Rafael Rob and Hyun Song Shin (1995), 'p-Dominance and Belief Formation', *Econometrica*, **63**, 145–57.

Murphy, Allan H. (1972a), 'Scalar and Vector Partitions of the Probability Score: Part I. Two-State Situation', *Journal of Applied Meteorology*, **11**, 273–82.

Murphy, Allan H. (1972b), 'Scalar and Vector Partitions of the Probability Score: Part II. N-State Situation', *Journal of Applied Meteorology*, **11**, 1183–92.

Murphy, Allan H. (1973), 'A New Vector Partition of the Probability Score', *Journal of Applied Meteorology*, **12**, 595–690.

Murphy, Allan H. (1996), 'General Decompositions of MSE-Based Skill-Scores: Measures of Some Basic Aspects of Forecast Quality', *Monthly Weather Review*, **124**, 2353–69.

Murphy, Allan H. (1998), 'The Early History of Probability Forecasts: Some Extensions and Clarifications', *Weather and Forecasting*, **13**, 5–15.

Murphy, Allan H. and Daniel S. Wilks (1998), 'A Case Study of the Use of Statistical Models in Forecast Verification: Precipitation Probability Forecasts', *Weather and Forecasting*, **13**, 795–810.

Murphy, Allan H. and Robert L. Winkler (1987), 'A General Framework for Forecast Verification', *Monthly Weather Review*, **115**, 1330–38.

Nagel, Rosemarie C. and Nicolaas J. Vriend (1999), 'An Experimental Study of Adaptive Behavior in an Oligopolistic Market Game', *Journal of Evolutionary Economics*, **9**, 27–66.

Napel, Stefan (2000), 'Aspiration Adaptation in the Ultimatum Minigame', working paper, University of Karlsruhe, October.

Nash, John F. (1950), 'Non-Cooperative Games', Doctoral Dissertation, Department of Mathematics, Princeton University, May.

Nauck, Detlef, Frank Klawonn and Rudolf Kruse (1996), *Neuronale Netze und Fuzzy-Systeme: Grundlagen des Konnektionismus, neuronaler Fuzzy-Systeme und der Kopplung mit wissensbasierten Methoden*, 2nd edition, Braunschweig, Germany: Vieweg Verlag.

Nowak, Martin and Karl Sigmund (1993), 'A Strategy of Win–Stay, Lose–Shift that Outperforms Tit-for-Tat in the Prisoner's Dilemma Game', *Nature*, **364**, 56–8.

O'Neill, Barry (1987), 'Nonmetric Test of the Minimax Theory of Two-person Zerosum games', *Proceedings of the National Academy of Sciences*, **84**, 2106–9.

O'Neill, Barry (1991), 'Comments on Brown and Rosenthal's Reexamination [Testing the Minimax Hypothesis, A Reexamination of O'Neill's Game Experiment]', *Econometrica*, **59**, 503–7.

Ochs, Jack (1995), 'Games with Unique, Mixed Strategy Equilibria: An Experimental Study', *Games and Economic Behavior*, **10**, 202–17.

Otronen, Merja (1993), 'Size-related male movement and its effect on spatial and temporal male distribution at female oviposition sites in the fly Dryomyza analis', *Animal Behaviour*, **46**, 731–40.

Pascual, Lorenzo, Juan Romo and Esther Ruiz (2001), 'Effects of Parameter Estimation on Prediction Densities: A Bootstrap Approach', *International Journal of Forecasting*, **17**, 83–103.

Pavlov, Ivan Petrovic (1954), *Sämtliche Werke*, Berlin: Akademie Verlag.

Peirce, C.S. (1884), 'The Numerical Measure of the Success of Predictions', *Science*, **4**, 453–4.

Posch, Martin (1997), 'Cycling in a Stochastic Learning Algorithm for Normal Form Games', *Journal of Evolutionary Economics*, **7**, 193–207.

Prasnikar, Vesna and Alvin E. Roth (1992), 'Considerations of Fairness and Strategy: Experimental Data from Sequential Games', *Quarterly Journal of Economics*, **107**, 865–88.

Rabin, Matthew (1993), 'Incorporating Fairness into Game Theory and Economics', *American Economic Review*, **82**, 1281–302.

Rabinowitz, L., Harold H. Kelley and R.M. Rosenblatt (1966), 'Effects of Different Types of Interdependence and Response Conditions in the Minimal Social Situation', *Journal of Experimental Social Psychology*, **2**, 169–97.

Rapoport, Amnon and Richard B. Boebel (1992), 'Mixed Strategies in Strictly Competitive Games: A Further Test of the Minimax Hypothesis', *Games and Economic Behavior*, **4**, 261–83.

Robson, Arthur J. and Fernando Vega-Redondo (1996), 'Efficient Equilibrium Selection in Evolutionary Games with Random Matching', *Journal of Economic Theory*, **70**, 65–92.

Rosenthal, Robert W. (1981), 'Games of Perfect Information, Predatory Pricing and the Chain-Store Paradox', *Journal of Economic Theory*, **25**, 92–100.

Roth, Alvin E. and Ido Erev (1995), 'Learning in Extensive-Form Games: Experimental Data and Simple Dynamic Models in the Intermediate Term', *Games and Economic Behavior*, **8**, 164–212.

Rubinstein, Ariel (1989), 'The Electronic Mail Game: Strategic Behavior Under Almost Common Knowledge', *American Economic Review*, **79**, 385–91.

Rubinstein, Ariel (2001), 'A Theorist's View of Experiments', *European Economic Review*, **45**, 615–28.

Rustichini, Aldo (1999), 'Optimal Properties of Stimulus–Response Learning Models', *Games and Economic Behavior*, **29**, 244–73.

Salmon, Tim (1999a), 'An Evaluation of Econometric Models of Adaptive Learning', Mimeo, Division of Humanities and Social Sciences, California Institute of Technology, August.

Salmon, Tim (1999b), 'Evidence for "Learning to Learn", Behavior in Normal Form Games', Mimeo, Division of Humanities and Social Sciences, California Institute of Technology, September.

Sanders, F. (1963), 'On Subjective Probability Forecasting', *Journal of Applied Meteorology*, **2**, 191–201.

Sarin, Rajiv (2000), 'Decision Rules with Bounded Memory', *Journal of Economic Theory*, **90**, 151–60.

Sarin, Rajiv and Farshid Vahid (1999), 'Payoff Assessments without Probabilities: A Simple Dynamic Model of Choice', *Games and Economic Behavior*, **28**, 294–309.

Sarin, Rajiv and Farshid Vahid (2001), 'Predicting How People Play Games: A Simple Dynamic Model of Choice', *Games and Economic Behavior*, **34**, 104–22.

Savage, Leonard J. (1971), 'Elicitation of Personal Probabilities and Expectations', *Journal of the American Statistical Association*, **66** (336), Theory and Methods Section, 783–801.

Schelling, Thomas C. (1960), *The Strategy of Conflict*, Cambridge, MA: Harvard University Press.

Schlag, Karl H. (1998), 'Why Imitate, and If So, How? A Boundedly Rational Approach to Multi-Armed Bandits', *Journal of Economic Theory*, **78**, 130–56.

Schmalensee, Richard (1975), 'Alternative Models of Bandit Selection', *Journal of Economic Theory*, **10**, 333–42.

Schuster, K. Peter and Karl Sigmund (1981), 'Coyness, Philandering and Stable Strategies', *Animal Behavior*, **29**, 186–92.

Selten, Reinhard (1975), 'Re-examination of the Perfectness Concept for Equilibrium in Extensive Games', *International Journal of Game Theory*, **4**, 22–5.

Selten, Reinhard (1991), 'Properties of a Measure of Predictive Success', *Mathematical Social Sciences*, **21**, 153–67.

Selten, Reinhard (1998), 'Axiomatic Characterization of the Quadratic Scoring Rule', *Experimental Economics*, **1**, 43–62.

Selten, Reinhard and Joachim Buchta (1999), 'Experimental Sealed Bid First Price Auctions with Directly Observed Bid Functions', in D. Budescu, I. Erev and R. Zwick (eds), *Games and Human Behavior: Essays in Honour of Amnon Rapoport*, Mahwak, NJ: Lawrenz Erlbaum Ass.

Selten, Reinhard and Rolf Stoecker (1986), 'End Behavior in Sequences of Finite Prisoner's Dilemma Supergames', *Journal of Economic Behavior and Organization*, **7**, 47–70.

Shachat, Jason and Mark Walker (2000), 'Unobserved Heterogeneity and Equilibrium: An Experimental Study of Bayesian and Adaptive Learning in Normal Form Games', Mimeo, 30 May.

Shenker, Scott (1995), 'Making Greed Work in Networks: A Game-Theoretic Analysis of Switch Service Disciplines', *IEEE/ACM Transactions on Networking*, **3**, 819–31.

Shimp, Charles P. (1966), 'Probabilistically Reinforced Choice Behavior in Pigeons', *Journal of the Experimental Analysis of Behavior*, **9**, 443–55.

Sidowski, J.B. (1957), 'Reward and Punishment in the Minimal Social Situation', *Journal of Experimental Psychology*, **54**, 318–26.

Sidowski, J.B., L.B. Wyckoff and L. Tabory (1956), 'The Influence of Reinforcement and Punishment in a Minimal Social Situation', *Journal of Abnormal and Social Psychology*, **52**, 115–19.

Simon, Herbert A. (1956), 'A Comparison of Game Theory and Learning Theory', *Psychometrika*, **21**, 267–72.

Skinner, Burrhus F. (1938), *The Behavior of Organisms*, New York: Appleton-Century-Crofts.

Slembeck, Tilman (1998), 'A Behavioral Approach to Learning in Economics', draft paper University of St Gallen, September.

Slembeck, Tilman (1999), 'Low Information Games – Experimental Evidence on Learning in Ultimatum Bargaining', Discussion Paper No. 9903, Department of Economics, University of St Gallen, March.

Slonim, Robert L. (1999), 'Learning Rules of Thumb or Learning More Rational Rules', *Journal of Economic Behavior and Organization*, **38**, 217–36.

Smith, Vernon (1990), 'Experimental Economics: Behavioral Lessons for Microeconomic Theory and Policy', Nancy L. Schwartz Memorial Lecture, Northwestern University.

Sonsino, Doron (1997), 'Learning to Learn, Pattern Recognition, and Nash Equilibrium', *Games and Economic Behavior*, **18**, 286–331.

Spence, Kenneth W. (1951), 'Theoretical Interpretations of Learning', in S.S. Stevens (ed.), *Handbook of Experimental Psychology*, New York: John Wiley and Sons.

Staddon, John E.R. and J.M. Horner (1989), 'Stochastic Choice Models: A Comparison Between Bush–Mosteller and a Source-Independent Reward-Following Model', *Journal of the Experimental Analysis of Behavior*, **52**, 57–64.

Stahl, Dale O. (1999), 'Population Rule Learning in Symmetric Normal-Form Games: The Model and Estimation Algorithm', Mimeo, April.

Stahl, Dale O. (2000), 'Rule-Learning in Symmetric Normal-Form Games. Theory and Evidence', *Games and Economic Behavior*, **32**, 105–38.

Stahl, Dale O. (2001), 'Population Rule Learning in Symmetric Normal-Form Games: The Model and Estimation Algorithm', *Journal of Economic Behavior and Organization*, **44**, 1–17.

Sulganik, Eyal and Itzhak Zilcha (1996), 'The Value of Information in the Presence of Futures Markets', *Journal of Futures Markets*, **16**, 227–40.

Suppes, Patrick and Richard C. Atkinson (1960), *Marcov Learning Models for Multiperson Interaction*, Stanford, CA: Stanford University Press.

Tang, Fang-Fang (1998), 'A Comparative Study on Learning and Stability in Normal Form Games: Some Experimental and Simulational Results', working paper, Department of Economics, National University of Singapore.

Thibaut, John W. and Harold H. Kelley (1959), *The Social Psychology of Groups*, New York: John Wiley and Sons.

Thorndike, Edward L. (1898), 'Animal Intelligence: An Experimental Study of the Associative Processes in Animals', *Psychological Monographs*, **2** (8).

Thorndike, Edward L. (1932), *The Fundamentals of Learning*, New York: Teachers College, Columbia University.

Van Huyck, John B. (1997), 'Emergent Conventions in Evolutionary Games', draft 'http://erl.tamu.edu/JVH_gtee/cc2.pdf', December, prepared for Charles R. Plott and Vernon L. Smith (eds), *Handbook of Experimental Economics Results*, Amsterdam: North-Holland Elsevier.

Van Huyck, John B., Raymond C. Battalio and Richard O. Beil (1990), 'Tacit Coordination Games, Strategic Uncertainty, and Coordination Failure', *American Economic Review*, **80**, 234–48.

Van Huyck, John B., Raymond C. Battalio and Richard O. Beil (1991), 'Strategic Uncertainty, Equilibrium Selection, and Coordination Failure in Average Opinion Games', *Quarterly Journal of Economics*, **106**, 885–910.

Van Huyck, John B., Raymond C. Battalio and Frederick W. Rankin (2001), 'Selection Dynamics and Adaptive Behavior without Much Information', draft paper 'http://erl.tamu.edu/JVH_gtee/OS6.PDF', Texas A&M University, October.

von Neumann, John and Oskar Morgenstern (1944), *Theory of Games and Economic Behavior*, Princeton, NJ: Princeton University Press.

Vulkan, Nir (2000), 'An Economist's Perspective on Probability Matching', *Journal of Economic Surveys*, **14**, 101–18.

Walker, James T. (1996), *The Psychology of Learning*, Upper Saddle River, NJ: Prentice Hall.

Winter, Sidney G. (1982), 'Binary Choice and the Supply of Memory', *Journal of Economic Behavior and Organization*, **3**, 277–321.

Yang, Chun-Lei, Joachim Weimann and Atanasios Mitropoulos (2001), 'Game Structure and Bargaining Power in Sequential Mini-Games: An Experiment', Working Paper No. 4/2001, Faculty of Economics and Management, Otto-von-Guericke-Universität Magdeburg.

Yates, J. Frank (1982), 'External Correspondence: Decompositions of the Mean Probability Score', *Organizational Behavior and Human Resources*, **30**, 132–56.

Index